D1433971

EDWARD IV
&
ELIZABETH
WOODVILLE

EDWARD IV
&
ELIZABETH WOODVILLE

A TRUE ROMANCE

AMY LICENCE

AMBERLEY

For Tom, Rufus and Robin

First published 2016

Amberley Publishing
The Hill, Stroud
Gloucestershire, GL5 4EP

www.amberley-books.com

Copyright © Amy Licence, 2016

The right of Amy Licence to be identified as
the Author of this work has been asserted in
accordance with the Copyrights, Designs and
Patents Act 1988.

ISBN 978 1 4456 3678 8 (hardback)
ISBN 978 1 4456 3694 8 (ebook)

British Library Cataloguing in Publication Data.
A catalogue record for this book is available
from the British Library.

Typesetting and Origination by Amberley
Publishing
Printed in the UK.

CONTENTS

Of all the kings that ever here did reign,
Edward named Fourth, as first in praise I name;
Not for his fair outside, nor well-lined brain,
Although less gifts imp feathers oft on fame;
Nor that he could, young-wise, wise-valiant, frame
His sire's revenge, joined with a kingdom's gain;
And, gained by Mars, could yet mad Mars so tame,
That balance weighed what sword did late obtain;
Nor that he made the Flower-de-luce so 'fraid,
Though strongly hedged of bloody lion's paws,
That witty Lewis to him a tribute paid;
Nor this, nor that, nor any such small cause;
But only for this worthy knight durst prove
To lose his crown, rather than fail his love.

Astrophil and Stella, Philip Sidney, 1580s

INTRODUCTION

Edward IV is a king who has been damned with faint praise. He has largely escaped the school syllabus, the popular documentary, the tourist pilgrimage. It is difficult to find his face on the china mugs and bookmarks that fill the shelves in properties owned by English Heritage or the National Trust. Many people cannot place Edward's reign in time, or tie it to a specific historical event; instead his name elicits puzzled questions and his achievements have been largely forgotten. He has attracted little attention in comparison with the historical behemoths of his great-great-grandfather, the Calais-conquering Edward III, or his grandson, the intermittently uxorious Henry VIII.

It is no surprise that the lens of history tends to illuminate the more colourful characters or that acts of chance can propel certain long-dead individuals into the public consciousness. We only need look at the way the discovery of Richard III's bones in 2012 sparked a renewed interest in his life and reign, culminating in the televised reburial which attracted viewers from around the world. Yet prior to the Leicester excavations, Richard's face was already instantly recognisable. What is more remarkable is the place Richard occupies in popular culture for his two-year reign, beside the twenty-two years in which his now unremembered brother was King of England. Edward was no less colourful, no less dynamic or engaging, no less controversial. Edward too usurped a throne and murdered a king in the Tower of London. More than this: he came back from exile and conquered England, twice. His victories at the battles of Mortimer's Cross, Towton, Barnet and Tewkesbury demonstrate a military genius on a par with the achievements of Crécy or Agincourt.

Yet for some reason Edward did not inspire those who created 'history'. Not in the sense of historiography, or the processes of recording, in the centuries that followed his death. He has been overlooked by the cultural 'greats' who formed the reputation of his brother: Shakespeare did not name a play after him, David Garrick did not play him, Hogarth did not paint him. Such plays, performances and paintings are the stepping stones by which kings become icons. Edward has become the ghost of a king: a historical filler before Richard III assumed the throne, a bit-player in Shakespeare's trilogy about Henry VI, the father of the Princes in the Tower, the husband of the White Queen. Edward has become one of our many 'missing kings' on whom the spotlight has failed to shine. This is as inexplicable as it is inexcusable.

Yet Edward's contemporaries thought well of him. He was a popular king for many reasons, both on personal and political levels, as well as for his feats of military prowess and his deeply cultured and magnificent court. In the 1470s, Edward's once sworn enemy John Fortescue wrote that Edward 'hath done more for us than ever did king of England, or might have done before him. The harms that hath fallen in getting of his realm be now by him turned into the good and profit of us all. We shall now more enjoy our goods, and live under justice, which we have not done of long time, God knoweth.' However, Edward's reputation suffered in later centuries. Four hundred years after Fortescue, the Victorian historian Bishop William Stubbs commented that 'Edward IV was not perhaps quite so bad a man or so bad a king as his enemies have represented' but condemned him as 'vicious beyond anything that England had seen since the days of John.' To him, Edward was a man 'guilty of an unparalleled list of judicial and extra-judicial cruelties which those of the next reign (Richard III) supplemented but do not surpass.' Somewhere between the paragon of peace and the vicious villain lies the real Edward. Or rather it might be a number of real Edwards, as in life he was just as inconsistent, evolving and variable as any multifaceted human being whose persona straddles both public and private realms.

There is much material for the historian to explore when it

comes to Edward's reign, much more than his secret marriage and his military prowess. His court witnessed a cultural flowering in comparison with the austerity and turmoil of that under Henry VI. Edward's was a consciously modelled Arthurian court: that of a charismatic leader flanked by loyal knights, which introduced 'a new paradigm of militant chivalric rule.'[1] And as Thomas Malory's *Le Morte d'Arthur* reflected, those loyalties were torn asunder by rivalry, ambition and treason. As a function of this magnificence, Edward understood the importance of appearances, consciously crafting his own performance under the Burgundian influence in what can be seen as an act of early Renaissance self-fashioning. Yet as well as looking forward, this theatricality looked backwards to the troubled golden persona of Richard II, from whose Mortimer heirs Edward's claim derived. Unlike Richard though, Edward survived attacks upon his kingship, threats to his life and imposed exile. His reign also witnessed cultural changes with the proliferation of educational and conduct manuals inspired by Italian humanist concepts, creating a royal household devoted to reverence and service, a court whose lines were redrawn to become a well-regulated body that could paradoxically embrace both thrift and majesty. Yet this new court was determined by conduct as much as birth. Edward might be imposing, but he was also warm and accessible; newcomers were made welcome and men of culture and ability could be advanced, as well as the old nobility. As might be anticipated, this created problems. Yet the answer to those problems was Edward himself, in his dynamic rule by personality; a larger than life, lusty and powerful man – something of a medieval superhero – winning astonishing victories against the odds, with wisdom and charisma.

At Edward's side was Elizabeth Woodville, an unlikely queen, whom he had chosen in spite of tradition, in spite of advice, perhaps even in spite of himself. Her beauty was legendary, but on almost every other level she was an unacceptable choice for an English queen. She was a widow, a mother, five years the king's elder, born and married into Lancastrian families, the daughter of a mere knight and she came with a large retinue of relatives. Her father was a man whom Edward had, until recently, held in contempt. However, it is less remarkable that Edward married her than that he actually admitted it four months later. He might have denied the ceremony, invalidated it retrospectively or bought her silence, as rumour suggests he had done with previous lovers. But Elizabeth was different. She may have begun her reign as unsuitable and unpopular, but she was in fact the perfect embodiment of the beautiful, submissive, fertile queen – an ideal portrayed in manuscripts and illustrations of the era. Edward broke with centuries of tradition when he saw her worth and overlooked her shortcomings.

Yet personal worth is a subjective quality. Elizabeth has been characterised by historians as haughty and grasping, as cold and greedy, but these are the gender-biased labels that women of privilege attracted, just as Elizabeth's contemporaries attributed her good fortune to the use of witchcraft. When applied to the men of the day, the adjectives 'haughty' and 'grasping' become 'noble' and 'ambitious,' or even 'focused' and 'determined': essential qualities for any medieval aristocrat. However, unlike her rival, Queen Margaret of Anjou, Elizabeth never attempted to become a player in the arena of male politics. She was not a proto-feminist by any definition. Instead she played the gender role allotted to her to the full. And she suffered for it. If there have been more obvious victims of fifteenth-century patriarchy, such as Joan of Arc, Margery Kempe or Eleanor Cobham, Elizabeth has been one of the many other women who have been defamed by the self-appointed male scribes of that society and those that repeated their stance without question. When Elizabeth's position forced her to cut her losses in an unprecedented act of medieval realpolitik, Tudor historians veered between describing her in a state of suicidal collapse, and labelling her as a typical example of women's inconsistency, pride and susceptibility to flattery. Perhaps it is anachronistic to hope that the chroniclers of the sixteenth century try to see things from Elizabeth's perspective, when contemporary physicians still believed that women were underdeveloped, physically imperfect versions of men. Just as Elizabeth could not step outside the mores of her time, the same constraints have bound those evaluating her life. Only recently have attempts been made to deconstruct the cultural goggles of interpretation in the interest of fairness. Yet this in itself may only be a question of serendipitous timing, being typical of the late twentieth-century zeitgeist.

It is not easy to reconstruct the lives of those who were born over five centuries ago. Each historian who attempts it makes another inroad through the uncertainties of the past, until the way is littered by overlapping routes and much of the same ground is being retrodden. Yet, to the right and left lie undiscovered countries, representative of the reams of documents, letters and other sources that have been lost or destroyed. When we attempt to fashion some sort of narrative, some character and identity for these distant people, it must be in the knowledge that is an artificial and flawed process; only a mere portion of their lives is represented in the surviving material and that is often glimpsed through the eyes of onlookers. This does not mean it should not attempted. It should be repeatedly retried, in the hope of striking a new chord, making a new connection or looking at old material afresh, which might link these multiple narratives into a more coherent whole. It should be undertaken with a sense of responsibility, with an open mind and the continual reminder to decode the biases of previous authors and explore a range of possible interpretations, rather than settling for the easiest or most obvious. The analysis of historical figures by this process perpetuates their cultural afterlife, an ongoing reassessment that will move their stories forward and a sense of renewal despite the centuries. It is only to be hoped that each biography touches upon a few truths that may contribute to a wider jigsaw of a long-dead individual, and that were they somehow able to read this one, Edward and Elizabeth might recognise in it a glimmer of themselves.

Amy Licence, Canterbury, November 2015

PREFACE

France, 1431

It was the last day of May, almost the start of summer. In the old marketplace at Rouen, men were building a pyre, piling up dry wood at the base of a stake that stood before the Church of Saint-Sauveur. The square was small and intimate, overlooked by tall, mismatched buildings: the wooden and plaster frontages of homes, shops and businesses with their rows of windows, from which the locals could watch the activity outside. A crowd had already gathered by the time the English soldiers arrived, carrying axes and swords, followed by a young woman, her head bare and her hands bound. She fixed her eyes ahead, at the scene set for her own death.

There is no surviving contemporary portrait of Jeanette of Domremy, the Maid of Orléans, also known as la Pucelle, Jehanne d'Arc, Jeanne d'Arc or Joan of Arc. One contemporary sketch of her survives at the side of a manuscript, beside an entry made by a clerk to the Parlement of Paris, Clément de Fauquemberghe, which described the defeat of the English at Orléans. Even this is a fairly generic picture of a young girl in profile, holding a sword, with the long flowing hair of her virgin state swept back off her face and down her back. Her nose is strong, her lips pursed. Yet de Fauquemberghe never saw the maid in the flesh. It was drawn from imagination, from her reputation in the popular mind.

Joan's appearance had proved to be her undoing. Eyewitnesses described how she had cropped her hair in a blunt style, just above her ears, in the male fashion of the day, far from the rippling locks de Fauquemberghe endowed her with. She was reputedly short and stocky, softly spoken and, as she told her examiners, aged around nineteen. Her squire, Jean d'Aulon, described her as beautiful and shapely[1] but she frequently adopted the clothing of a common soldier: the shirt, braies, doublet, hose, tabard and overcoat that allowed her to travel with the French army and avoid undue attention. She had some justification for this, as the accounts of her trial detail her efforts to fight off a number of unwanted sexual advances and preserve the virginity she had vowed to keep. Her habit of cross-dressing quickly drew censure. The regent of France, John of Lancaster, Duke of Bedford, described her as 'a woman disordered and defamed, being in man's clothes and of dissolute conduct.'[2] And this was the key to Joan's downfall: she had transgressed the boundaries of her birth and gender. She had dared to take on a masculine role, to lead and inspire, to participate in a masculine field, to set an example to military leaders, to advise a king. She had gone against the medieval order of nature. Worse still, she had done so with success.

Joan was a simple, devout country girl – the daughter of a farmer. Her early years had been spent in the fields, far from the city, the court or the battlefield. As a child she had begun to hear voices and see visions of the saints, who urged her to lead the army of France to defeat the English and drive them out of the country. Disguised as a man, she had travelled through the enemy's territory to meet the Dauphin and, later, to act as an encouragement and symbol at the Siege of Orléans. After having been inspirational in the French campaign in 1429 and 1430, Joan had been captured by the Burgundians, and was kept as a prisoner by John de Luxembourg at Beaurevoir Castle, before he had sold her to the English for 10,000 livres. Put on trial in Rouen for sorcery, her death sentence had originally been commuted to life imprisonment. However, while in prison she had reputedly resorted to wearing male clothing again, perhaps, according to her bailiff, on account of no other clothing being made available to her, or in response to an unnamed English lord's attempt to rape her. She had already been sexually assaulted by Aimond de Macy, a Burgundian knight who had visited her in her previous captivity under the Luxembourg family. Her change of clothing was enough to instigate a second, secular trial under Bedford's authority. This time she was condemned to death as a lapsed heretic. Her male attire was cited as evidence that she had broken her promises to repent.

Bedford's connection with Joan was an intimate one. Having heard of her exploits from a distance and paid a considerable sum to acquire her, he had brought her to his castle at Rouen. There, his duchess, Anne of Burgundy, had been placed in charge of investigating Joan's claims of virginity, overseeing a panel of matrons to conduct a physical examination of her young body in an attempt to establish whether her hymen remained intact. This was not uncommon practice in attempting to establish character and innocence, but the additional violation re-enforces the many assaults Joan suffered upon her person and her gender, reminding the modern reader just how vulnerable women were once they contravened male laws of obedience. According to the deposition of the notary Guillaume Colles, 'the Duke of Bedford was in a secret place where he saw Joan examined,'[3] which has led some to make the sinister inference that Bedford personally observed this event, or even that he visited Joan in prison via a secret passage from his lodgings. There is little doubt that the violation of 'fallen' women occurred with frequency, but no other direct evidence exists to support this claim. Extensive archaeological excavations at Rouen Cathedral have failed to uncover indications of any such secret tunnels, although it must be remembered that lack of evidence is not evidence enough. Chronicler Mathieu includes the detail that she was kept in an iron cage, and that her legs were chained, having spoken in person to the locksmith from whom the cage was commissioned. There was clearly great animosity between Joan and Bedford, and the fifteenth century is full of examples of when male-female antagonism resulted in assertions of power that were sexual as well as legal or political. During her trial Joan complained of several attempts to rape her. She represented the spirit of the French campaign to oust England from Normandy – a dangerous and unpredictable wildcard who had previously challenged the duke's position, addressing him in a letter as 'you ... who call yourself regent'.[4] So far as we know, Bedford treated Joan honourably, insofar as condemning her to burn can be considered honourable.

Before the crowd in Rouen marketplace, Joan spoke for about half an hour, asking those present to pray for her and forgiving them for their sins. By the end of her moving speech, even a number of her enemy Englishmen had been reduced to tears. Bedford himself would have been present, along with Louis of Luxembourg, Rouen's Archbishop, brother of the John who had held Joan at Beaurevoir. The sermon was delivered, then Joan's sentence was read to the assembled crowd. She was taken to the wood pile and secured to the stake. Before the pyre was lit, she made a last request, begging for a cross. A nearby soldier responded, giving her a humble little cross of wood on the end of a stick. She kissed it and tucked it into her clothing. By contrast, the magnificent silver cross was also brought out from the Church of Saint-Saveur, and held before her, as the first flames began to lick around the bottom of her feet.

In her last minutes, Joan's lips moved fervently in prayer, asking for forgiveness for her executioners and stating that the voices she had heard were real. She asked for holy water, called upon the name of Jesus, and was finally overcome by the smoke. After screaming out one final time, her head dropped on her breast and the Maid of Orléans breathed her last. It was probably the inhalation of smoke that killed her. At any rate, the English were taking no chances. According to the account of an anonymous witness,[5] Joan's naked body was displayed to the crowd, in order to stamp out rumours that she was either a man or a devil, then the fire was built up again, and she was burned a second, even perhaps a third time, until her bones and organs had finally been destroyed. Rumours of the survival of her heart and the sudden flight of pure white dove into the sky derive straight from medieval traditions of hagiography. Her ashes were gathered and dropped into the Seine. Bedford announced the news of her death to Europe.

Thus ended the life of Joan of Arc, although her legend had only just been born. Her death in the marketplace at Rouen charged the location with a terrible significance for the future English governors of Normandy, including the future house of York. Many of those who witnessed her final moments would still be alive eleven years later, when a baby boy was born at Rouen. He was named Edouarde, or Edward, and would one day become King of England. Joan's story is one of the transgression of boundaries, the dangers of female ability and power and their exercise in a man's world, of international politics, the fickleness of fortune and the transience of power. It raises the themes of sorcery, justice, femininity, gender relations and conflict, which would define the lives of Edward IV and his wife Elizabeth, who was both the great-niece of John de Luxembourg and the daughter of Bedford's widow.

ELIZABETH
1435–1459

'The most beautiful woman in the island of Britain.'

I

Four years after the burning of Joan of Arc, the English and French were converging on Arras. The city had been founded by the Gauls on a chalk plateau near the River Scarpe, around a hundred miles to the north of Paris in the Artois region. By the early Middle Ages it had become a centre of the wool trade and banking, attracting merchants to its narrow winding streets that snaked their way up to the gothic Cathedral of St Vaast. Inside those cool stone walls monks dipped their brushes into coloured pigments to depict the lives of saints and troubadors, while outside the local weavers gained such a reputation for their creations that across Europe tapestries were known by the generic term of an 'arras'. Visitors and residents alike flocked to the city's two colourful squares – hives of activity – where the markets were overlooked by tall town houses. These squares now resounded with the echo of horse hooves. People opened their shutters and paused their conversations to watch as a train of elegantly dressed knights rode boldly through the July sunshine.

In 1435 it was hoped that this famous city, this neutral territory, would provide the location for a lasting peace. War had raged between England and France for a century, spanning the reigns of four English kings and six of France, through the battlefields of Crécy, Poitiers and Agincourt, despite marriage alliances, treaties and promises of peace. Finally, negotiations were being planned for a lasting truce and a marriage between a daughter of Charles VII and the thirteen-year-old Henry VI of England. Around two hundred of Henry's knights crossed the Channel and were lodged in the city in the hope of redefining their relationship with the French. However, on 28 July the English were surprised by the arrival of the Burgundians, whose antagonistic presence they had not anticipated. The Duchess of Burgundy, a granddaughter of John of Gaunt, rode into the city in an ornamented litter, wearing cloth of gold and precious gems.[1] The Burgundian element introduced a different dynamic: an historically fickle balance of friendship with the English to complicate the existing Anglo-French mistrust. And, just as feared, Philip the Good realised he was better served by deserting the Lancastrians and allying with the new Valois dynasty.

Despite the tension, the meeting at Arras was a splendid occasion, with wealth, chivalry and power on display. On 11 August a combat was hosted in the great marketplace, where a Spanish champion in a vermilion mantle rode against one from Burgundy, followed by a day of fighting on foot, feasting on an 'abundance and variety of dishes' and Mass, with the attendees 'richly dressed in the most splendid of habiliments'.[2] Jewels and gold collars sparkled in the sun, while embroidery, colour and rich fabrics caught the eye. The fashion of the 1430s favoured horned headdresses, or henins, for women, and high-belted dresses lined with fur; men wore long houppelande coats with full sleeves, coloured hose and chaperon hats. The Arras streets that summer would have been a blend of the most gorgeous and expensive fashions that England, France and Burgundy had to offer, each trying to outdo their rival in a display of power and taste.

The entertainment may have proved a success, but the peace negotiations went less smoothly. The English were not prepared to renounce the French throne, especially as just seven months before Henry VI had been crowned king in Rouen Cathedral, along from the square where Joan of Arc had burned. His claim derived from the inheritance from his mother, Catherine of Valois, and the conquest of his father, Henry V, whom Catherine's father, Charles VI, had named as his heir. This proved to be the sticking point. As the French would not negotiate until the English had capitulated, an early stalemate seemed to threaten their good intentions. The French then offered to grant Normandy to England in lieu of the whole country and to arrange a marriage for Henry VI, but this was rejected. On 6 September the English left Arras, adamant that discussion was pointless as no agreement could be reached. The talks had proved a failure. Another eighteen years would pass before peace would be concluded. Yet one of the most significant players, the English Regent of France, had not set foot in Arras.

Back in Rouen, John, Duke of Bedford, was dying. When he expired on 15 September, in his own manor house of Joyeux Repos, only a week had passed since the collapse of the Arras talks. Gregory's Chronicle states that he breathed his last between two and three in the morning.[3] Contemporaries suggested that his death had been hastened by the bad news from Arras, where his absence had been felt, with the Dauphin Louis adding that 'when he was alive [Bedford] would have disquieted the proudest of us all'. Looking back from the sixteenth century, chronicler Hall believed that after Bedford's death 'that bright sonne, that commonly shone in France faire and beautifully upon the English men, began to be claudie and daily to wax darker'.[4] There is some truth in the assertion that Anglo-French relations declined after his death: the following year the English would have to evacuate Paris, in 1447 Rouen was permanently lost to the French and in 1453 Henry VI made huge concessions of land in order to marry the daughter of the Duke of Anjou.

Bedford's career as Governor of Normandy had encompassed a great victory at Verneuil, the zenith of English power in France and a humiliating defeat at the siege of Orléans. Yet his legacy had been mixed: culturally, he had been responsible for building a famous library of illuminated manuscripts, but the imposition of high taxes and the burning of Joan of Arc had made him deeply unpopular in the city. Now his death left another nineteen-year-old woman vulnerable. This time it was not Bedford's enemy whose life came to an end, but a phase in the life of his wife, which was about to take a very different direction. Ironically, it was in dying that Bedford made the most significant contribution to the love story of Edward IV and Elizabeth Woodville, and to the future of the English monarchy.

Bedford's young widow was Jacquetta, or Jacoba as she appears in some official documentation. Her name was a female deritivive of Jacob, or James, with Jacquet often being used as a French form of Jacob. She was the daughter of Peter of Luxembourg, the Count of St Pol, who had been a prominent figure at the Arras assembly, part of the great medieval dynasty that stretched back into the tenth century. Peter was the brother of the John of Luxembourg who had sold Joan of Arc to Bedford, and of Louis, Archbishop of Rouen, who had overseen her death in front of the Church of Sainte-Sauveur. Louis was also chancellor to Bedford for the final decade of his life and had pushed for his second marriage to take place; in fact, he was so trusted by Bedford that the duke named him as an executor of his will. The Luxembourg family had myths woven into their heritage; they claimed that their founding ancestor, Siegfried, had married a water goddess by the name of Melusina, who had been born half human and half 'fey' or fairy. Despite Melusina's stipulation for privacy one day a week, her husband observed her bathing and saw that the lower half of her had transformed into that of a serpent; his presence caused her and her bath to sink into the earth, never to be seen again. The legend was already well established by the time of Jacquetta's arrival, but the closest contemporary version of the story had been written by Jean d'Arras in his *Roman de Mélusine* of 1392–4. Later in life, Jacquetta owned a manuscript copy of the Melusine legend, but whether this was simply for the enjoyment of a popular story or because she put any store in it is not known.

As the eldest son, Peter of Luxembourg inherited his father's titles, and in 1405 he married Margaret de Baux, from the Baux region of Provence. She bore him nine children, of whom Jacquetta was one of the eldest, arriving in 1415 or 1416. She was fourteen when her uncle John brought the captive Joan of Arc back to his castle at Beaurevoir, near Cambrai; she may even have been present four months later, when John had sold the maid to the French for 10,000 livres.[5] In the autumn of 1432, when Jacquetta was seventeen, her uncle Louis had begun negotiations for her to become Bedford's wife.

The duke had been married once before, and by some accounts had been very fond of his wife. However, Duchess Anne had died 'of a lingering disorder' or of the plague at the age of twenty-eight, while visiting Paris in November 1432, and had been buried at the Chapel of the Celestines. She may have contracted her final illness when undertaking a mission of mercy, visiting the poor at the Hôtel Dieu. According to the French chronicler Monstrelet, the duke was 'sorely afflicted at her death', but he adds rather coldly that this was as a result of his fears that the alliance with Burgundy would be weakened. Six months later, on 22 April, John married Jacquetta at Thérouanne, half way between Calais and Arras. Monstrelet tells us that the wedding was conducted by Louis in the Bishop's Palace, where they feasted afterwards, and that the duke was so delighted with the match, 'the damsel [being] handsome, well made and lively', that he presented to the church two 'magnificent bells of great value' which he had sent for from England. It reads like a cliché beloved of bawdy poets like Chaucer: a lively, attractive young woman married to an older man, but unlike his May and Januarie, there is little to suggest that this match was not a success. On their way back to Rouen, the newly-weds stayed in Bedford's palace in the Hôtel de Bourbon in Paris, with a great hall and a chapel described by Henri Sauval as the most large and sumptuous of their kind in the city, not to mention Bedford's library, which had been brought wholesale from the nearby Louvre Palace.

Through this marriage, Jacquetta had become the first lady of Paris, but she was also a young and inexperienced wife. She had to adjust to the rule of her husband in both public and private domains, oversee the running of his household, represent him on formal occasions and please him in the bedroom. She had been raised in anticipation of making a prestigious match, but the early months of her new life must have been a period of learning. Her situation had some parallels with that outlined in a text of 1393 called *The Good Wife's Guide*, sometimes entitled after its anonymous author, the Ménagier de Paris, which had been composed by an older husband with the intention of instructing his new teenage bride. The text contains a range of recipes, about which Jacquetta's position meant she would not have had to worry herself, but there are also the details of a May wedding feast, providing enough for twenty bowls, which gives an indication of the kind of delicacies the duke and duchess may have enjoyed at their nuptials: fricassee of capons topped with pomegranate and red sugared almonds; a haunch of kid; goslings and chickens with orange and verjuice sauce; pigs; small rabbits; and crayfish jelly with venison frumenty for dessert, followed by conical wafers stuffed with cheese, iced cakes and the spiced wine hippocras.[6] The Ménagier gave his wife detailed instructions about where to purchase her supplies, but Jacquetta would not have had to concern herself with such mundane tasks. Weeks after the wedding, commissions were given out at Westminster for the provisioning of the duke's household in response to its expansion upon his marriage. A William Erby was charged to provide wood, tables, straw, benches, rushes 'and other necessaries' for John's hall and chamber; Robert Trewyck was responsible for supplying the house with hay, oats, peas, beans and similar items, while William Mayhewe brought wheat, wood and straw for the bakery, John Swayn brought poultry and Robert Porter brought meat and fish.[7]

Another section of the Ménagier's book deals with the behaviour expected of a young wife, in this case, the Parisian's fifteen-year-old bride, whose comparative innocence and willingness to learn prompted the author to write 'a simple general introduction to teach' her what to expect as a wife, both socially and sexually. Although the Ménagier's bride was of a lower class than Jacquetta, both young woman had to negotiate their way through a marriage to an older man. The book describes that 'to win the love of your husband and to give you in this world that peace which should be in marriage,'[8] all a man's commandments, 'whether they be made in earnest or in jest … should be of great import to you, since he that shall be your husband has bidden you to do them … act according to the pleasure of your husband … rather than according to your own, for his pleasure should come before yours.' As a wife, 'watch that you do not in any manner that which he has forbidden' and 'answer not back your husband … nor his words, nor contradict what he saieth,' but be 'humble and obedient' to him, as outlined in the scriptures. Such was the world in which Jacquetta was married, with its expectations of fidelity and obedience, where a duchess should be both demure and regal. Yet it was also a world which elevated the ideal of courtly love and conferred a degree of power upon certain women as a result of men's devotion to them. Christine de Pizan, who married at the age of fifteen, wrote of her older husband's gentleness and consideration. Both Jacquetta and her daughter were to learn this aspect of the contemporary gender dynamic.

Soon after her marriage, Jacquetta accompanied her husband across the Channel to the country that would be her future home. It was probably her first visit to England: embarking at Calais and sailing towards the white cliffs of Dover, travelling through Kent's rolling hills towards the majesty of Canterbury Cathedral, and on to Faversham, Sittingbourne, Rochester, Eltham and Blackheath, where the green fields petered out into the city of London. England in 1433 was ruled by Bedford's nephew, the twelve-year-old Henry VI, son of Henry V and Catherine of Valois, daughter of the King of France. During the boy's minority his court was overseen by Bedford's other brother, the Lord Protector, Humphrey, Duke of Gloucester, and Henry's tutor Richard Beauchamp, Earl of Warwick. Bedford had been summoned to attend the ninth parliament of Henry's reign, which was due to sit that July, so he and his new wife made a ceremonial entrance into London on 23 June, the eve of St John the Baptist's Day, being 'worthily received' by the mayor and aldermen.[9] Bedford had good reason to attend: he needed to counter rumours that he had mismanaged funds in France, which he did successfully, as on the day Parliament opened he was granted a number of manors in Somerset, Dorset and Wiltshire, as well as the earldom of Kendale with an annual income of £60.[10] The king also granted his uncle the use of Penshurst Place in West Kent, a fourteenth-century manor house built for a previous Mayor of London, within riding distance of the capital, to which Bedford set about making his own additions. It was a beautiful location for Jacquetta, overlooking the green Kentish downs, surrounded by gardens and featuring large, elegant rooms. Parliament sat until the middle of December, after which the duke and duchess celebrated Christmas and remained in England until Bedford was appointed Lieutenant of Calais on 12 July. Then, the duke departed for the final time.

After two and a half years of marriage to Jacquetta, Bedford's health failed and he took to his bed at the manor of Joyeux Repos in the north-east quarter of Rouen, the last area to be included in the medieval walls. It had once been the manor of Chantereine, a pleasure palace built by the dukes of Normandy, but had been developed by Bedford as a retirement home. At the age of forty-six he was not very old by contemporary standards, and it is not unreasonable to suggest that, with luck, he may have anticipated living another twenty years and fathering children with Jacquetta, even though his first marriage had been childless. The duke would have been able to afford nurses to tend him through his illness, along with his regular physician, Dr Philiberto Fernein, but it may have fallen to Jacquetta to oversee them, or to prepare some of the remedies for invalids, soups, bouillon and tisanes outlined by the Ménagier. Bedford made his will on 10 September, leaving all the ornaments and vestments of his chapel to the cathedral where he would be laid to rest, along with a gold cup made by his goldsmith and a silver cross. To Jacquetta he left 'all his lands, all his tenements ... whether in France or England, during her life', except for Harapute, which went to an illegitimate son of his named Richard. His widow was to enjoy these properties and the title of duchess until her death, whereupon they would revert to the English crown. Bedford's chancellor, Louis of Luxembourg, and the master of his household, Sir John Fastolf, were named among the will's many executors when it was proved at Lambeth House on 7 October.

II

Bedford's widowed duchess was wealthy, young and beautiful. Parliament was aware that Jacquetta might prove prey to admirers, just as the king's mother Catherine of Valois had upon the death of Henry V. Then they had ruled that the widowed queen must not remarry without royal permission, and now they followed that same precedent. On 6 February 1436, Henry granted Jacquetta her dower payment on the condition that she did not remarry without first gaining his consent, and asked Bedford's knight, Sir Richard Woodville, to escort her back to England. Woodville was then aged around thirty, having been born at the family property of The Mote in Maidstone, Kent, in 1405 or soon after. The connection with Bedford's household had been established by his father, also named Richard, who had been the duke's steward until his death, so his son would have already been familiar with Bedford's household and the duke's second wife. He would have been chosen for the task for this very reason, in the belief that his familiarity would be a comfort to the widow and that he could be trusted. In terms of competency for his commission, Woodville was an admirable choice, but when it came to the personal aspect of his charge, the king's trust was misplaced. At some point on the journey from Rouen to London, Jacquetta either succumbed to Richard's amorous attentions or she initiated a relationship, directly or indirectly, as the result of an existing or a new attraction between the two. At some point in 1436, or early in 1437, they were married in secret.

But the secret could not remain one for long. Returning to Henry VI's court, the Woodvilles were forced to admit what they had done, throw themselves upon the king's mercy and ask for forgiveness 'for causes as [Jacquetta] trusteth to God agreeable to him'. She confessed that she 'toke but late ago to Husband youre trew liegeman of your Roialme of England, Richard Wydeville, knight not having thereto youre Roiall licencse and assent,' and she admitted that 'for which the offense, they have suffred right grate stretness, as well in their persones as in their goddess' and asked Henry to impose upon them 'a reasonable fine, and thereupon to grant your gracious letters of pardon'.[11]

It may be that they married because Jacquetta was pregnant, or that she conceived soon after and her condition prompted their confession. Henry was angry at their defiance but he accepted their request; he could hardly do otherwise as the match was, by then, a fait accompli. On 23 March 1437, the Woodvilles were ordered to pay a fine of £1,000, which they raised by selling some of Jacquetta's properties in the West Country to Cardinal Beaufort, the king's half-uncle; their pardon followed seven months later, on 24 October, 'for intermarrying without the king's consent'.[12] It was around this time that Jacquetta gave birth to her first child, a daughter named Elizabeth, who is likely to have arrived at Woodville's home of Grafton Manor in Northamptonshire. That July, Richard had been awarded the office of Chief Rider of the Forest of Saucy, not far from the house, further suggesting their occupation. Excavations conducted in 1964–5 on earthworks in the area revealed a range of late thirteenth or early fourteenth-century buildings that appeared to be monastic in origin, including a small church with cloister but no aisle, a barn or hospital, kitchen and dovecot. These were converted to domestic use in the fifteenth century, and were owned by the de la Pole family, whose tenants the Woodvilles may have been until they bought the property for themselves in 1440. The site lies just to the west of the village of Grafton Regis, where the Church of St Mary the Virgin still stands, containing the tomb of Richard's grandfather, Sir John Woodville. Living at Grafton, Jacquetta bore two more children in rapid succession: Lewis in 1438 and Anne in 1439. Anne may have arrived during her father's absence, as that year Richard's role as Commander of Calais led to his involvement in the siege of Meaux, under the Duke of Somerset.

In the autumn of 1440, Richard visited London to take part in jousts and feats of arms at Smithfield, against the Burgundian Pedro Vasque de Saavedra, who intended to 'run a course with a sharp spear for his sovereign lady's sake'. Writing to John Paston, Robert Repps described Saavedra as a 'knyghte out of Spayne with a kerchief (scarf) of plesaunce enwrapped about his arm'.[13] Woodville met the challenger in the lists on 26 November, but Henry VI drew the proceedings to a halt after only the third stroke, reluctant to see any bloodshed. Only a week before, he had made a grant to Richard and Jacquetta of an annual £48 18s 7d arising from certain properties and forests, 'as part of the dower coming to her after the death of John, Duke of Bedford, her late husband, out of the King's heritage'. In spite of their hasty marriage, the couple's fortunes were finally restored.

In July 1441, Richard Woodville sailed from Portsmouth in the entourage of the Duke of York, who had been appointed as Lieutenant of France. Henry VI's biographer R. A. Griffiths states that Jacquetta accompanied her husband, which raises the interesting possibility that the duchess would have been in the company of York's wife, Cecily Neville, a similarly high ranking woman whose marriage to the king's heir put her at least on an equal footing with Jacquetta. York was heading for Rouen at the head of 5,000 men, and would remain there for the next four years, so the Woodvilles would be a natural choice of companions for him and his wife in the city that had once been their home.

Jacquetta may have taken her children with her to France, if she was there at all, or she may have left them at home in the care of a governess. Alternatively she might have remained in England, and it is perhaps conclusive that she did not bear another surviving child until 1444, suggesting a period of separation. Richard was certainly present during York's attempts to lift the siege of Pontoise from mid-July, and if she was with him Jacquetta may have remained as company with Cecily back in Rouen. It was shortly before York had left, or during his return to the city between the two Pointoise attacks, that Cecily fell pregnant with her son Edward.

If Jacquetta did, in fact, remain behind in England in 1441, she would have witnessed the unfolding of a terrible drama at the heart of the royal family – a story that raised the themes of witchcraft and the vulnerability of women that would have great resonance for the later life of the duchess. Events centred on Jacquetta's former sister-in-law, Eleanor Cobham, the second wife of the Duke of Gloucester, Bedford's younger brother. Having been married for over a decade and not borne a child, Eleanor enlisted the help of a witch named Margery Jourdemayne, who prescribed certain potions to aid her fertility, and astrologers to draw up the king's horoscope. There was little to cause offence in these actions alone, except that the astrological chart suggested that Henry would suffer a serious illness that summer. The implications of predicting or 'encompassing' the king's death were potentially treasonous, especially given that Gloucester and his children would be Henry's heirs until such time as he produced a child of his own. Reputedly, there was also a wax figurine made of the king, found in the possession of Eleanor's astrologer, suggesting the intent to harm through necromancy. Gloucester's relationship with Bedford had been strained and his enemies on the Privy Council now moved against him by discrediting Eleanor with accusations of witchcraft. When members of her household were arrested that June, Eleanor fled into sanctuary, but her astrologer's confession on 23 July sealed a fate that her husband was unable to protect her against: that October she was found guilty and forced to walk through the streets of London on three occasions, carrying a lighted taper. After that, her marriage was terminated and she was imprisoned for the rest of her life, outliving her husband, who died soon after being arrested for treason in 1447. Eleanor's story illustrates the fragility of power, especially for women at the top end of society, and the indirect ways their enemies could destroy them with slander. No doubt rumours of Eleanor's fate reached Grafton.

Little is known about the upbringing of Jacquetta's children; presumably it was typical of the ideals of health, education and nurture to be found in aristocratic nurseries of the time. Elizabeth and her younger siblings would have spent their early years in a predominantly female environment, learning to pray, read and write, hearing stories of religion and romance, being instructed in manners, playing games and taking exercise in the gardens and countryside around Grafton. The children would have benefitted from the advancement of their father's career, as he became knight banneret on 25 September 1442, and the fruits of Jacquetta's dowry meant they could enjoy a comfortable living. They were probably left behind in November 1444, when Jacquetta and Richard were chosen to join a large escort that would bring Henry VI's bride, Margaret of Anjou, north to England from her home in Lorraine. The duke and duchess may have been among the guests when Margaret was married in a small ceremony at Titchfield on 22 April, but they certainly played a ceremonial role at her Westminster coronation at the end of May: Jacquetta rode behind the queen in the decorated chariots that followed her from Blackheath across London Bridge, past pageant after pageant extolling the new queen as the bringer of peace. The following day, the duchess would have accompanied Margaret from the Tower to Westminster, through streets lined with Londoners, and also the next morning, 30 May, as part of her coronation train.

It has been suggested that the young Elizabeth Woodville was later given a position as a maid of honour in the household of Margaret of Anjou, as was often the case with the daughters of the medieval aristocracy. Given the family connections to the new queen, it would seem a fairly logical supposition, especially as Jacquetta had the futures of a number of children to consider, and, having turned fourteen in 1451, Elizabeth's age would have made her a suitable candidate. However, there is no evidence to suggest this actually did take place; in fact, it is possible that Tudor historians such as Thomas More and Edward Hall confused her with an Isabelle, Lady Grey, who does appear in the queen's records at an earlier date of 1445, charged with accompanying Margaret back from France. Although it is plausible that Elizabeth, known by the contemporarily interchangeable name of Isabelle, accompanied her parents on this journey at the age of eight, it is unlikely that she would have been referred to by her future married name, not becoming the wife of Sir John Grey for at least five years. This Isabelle may have been the same person as the Elizabeth Grey who received gifts of jewels in Margaret's accounts almost annually from 1445 through to 1453 – the wife of Sir Ralph Grey, a knight who was in 'daily attendance' upon the queen. Such duties and rewards suggest a woman of older years than Jacquetta's daughter. It cannot be ruled out completely that Elizabeth served Margaret of Anjou in some capacity, but no decisive evidence concluding this survives from the period.

Then there is the case of 'Elizabeth Wydeville's Diary', which reports to be a genuine daily account written by the girl while living with her parents at Grafton. It is quoted by T. R. Potter in his 1842 *History and Antiquities of Charnwood Forest*, from a manuscript 'locked up in Drummond Castle' in Lincolnshire, although such a work cannot currently be located, nor its existence verified. It may have actually been part of a work of fiction by London-based novelist and biographer Elizabeth Benger, called 'Elizabeth Woodville: an Autobiographic Sketch of the Fifteenth Century' which appeared in 1827 in *The Literary Souvenir*. Written in the style of the eighteenth century, and heavily influenced by hindsight which creates a vein of dramatic irony, the diary has been dismissed by many scholars as 'pure imagination'.[14] However, more recently, David Baldwin has been keen to defend certain aspects of the text as being historically authentic in detail, such as the timing and frequency of meals and the games and activities,[15] although this may well point to the accuracy of the author's research rather than the veracity of the text. When compared to similar letters of the period, the diary's expression of the days of the week and hours of the clock belongs more to the idioms of Benger's time than Elizabeth's, with some phrases becoming positively Austenesque. Additionally, the diary states that 10 May 1451 was a Thursday, but had Elizabeth been its author she would have known that the day was in fact a Monday; presumably she would also have known that in the consensus of her contemporaries, particularly the eyewitness of her coronation, that her hair was considered to be blonde, a 'faire yelow,' instead of black:

Thursday [Monday] morning, May 10, 1451

Rose at four o'clock, and helped Katherine to milk the cows: Rachael, the other dairy-maid, having scalded one of her hands in a very sad manner last night. Made a poultice for Rachael and gave Robin a penny to get her something comfortable from the apothecary's. Six o'clock – breakfasted. The buttock of beef rather too much boiled, and the ale a little the stalest. Memorandum to tell the cook about the first fault, and to mend the second myself ...

Seven o'clock – went out with the Lady Duchess, my mother, into the court-yard, fed five and thirty men and women; chid Roger very severely for expressing some dissatisfaction in attending us with the broken meat.

Eight o'clock – went into the paddock behind the house with my maiden Dorothy; caught Stump the little black pony myself, and rode a matter of six miles, without either saddle or bridle.

Ten o'clock – went to dinner. John Grey one of our visitants – a most comely youth – but what's that to me? A virtuous maiden should be entirely under the direction of her parents. John ate very little – stole a great many tender looks at me – said a woman never could be handsome in his opinion, who was not good-tempered. I hope my temper is not intolerable; nobody finds fault with it but Roger, and Roger is the most disorderly serving man in our family. John Grey likes white teeth – my teeth are of a pretty good colour, I think, and my hair is black as jet, though I say it – and John, if I mistake not, is of the same opinion.

Eleven o'clock – rose from table, the company all desirous of walking in the fields. John Grey would lift me over every stile, and twice he squeezed my hand with great vehemence. I cannot say I should have any aversion to John Grey: he plays prison-bars as well as any gentleman in the country, is remarkably dutiful to his parents and never misses church of a Sunday.

Three o'clock – poor farmer Robinson's house burnt down by an accidental fire. John Grey proposed a subscription among the company for the relief of the farmer and gave a matter of no less than five pounds himself to this benevolent intention. Mem (memorandum) Never saw him look so comely as at that moment.

Nine o'clock – the company almost all asleep. These late hours are very disagreeable. Said my prayers a second time, John Grey disturbing my thoughts too much the first. Fell asleep about ten and dreamt that John had come to demand me of my father.[16]

Whatever the truth of the reputed diary, it captures a bucolic domestic scene of a world on the verge of change. For a few years, all continued to be well with Elizabeth and her family. Richard Woodville's career continued to move from strength to strength: he was created Baron Rivers on 8 May 1448 and played a key role in the suppression of Jack Cade's rebellion two years later, for which he was rewarded by being admitted to the Order of the Garter. Jacquetta bore more children: ten more to add to her previous four, with John, Jacquetta and Lionel arriving in the mid-1440s, followed by Eleanor, Margaret and Martha, then Richard, Edward, Mary and Catherine. Remarkably, all these children survived to adulthood save for one, Elizabeth's closest sibling Lewis, who is mentioned in conflicting accounts as either having died as a small child or having been lost when he reached the age of twelve. In the same year that Jacquetta bore her fifth son, Richard, Queen Margaret delivered a child of her own, after eight years of marriage had led many to speculate whether there would be any royal heir at all. Her son, Edward, was born at Westminster on 6 December. His arrival would appear to confirm the Lancastrian line, but the circumstances of that year were far from stable. In fact, Prince Edward arrived amid a period of uncertainty and turmoil that cast the dynasty's entire future into doubt.

During the summer of 1453, the king had fallen ill. At the age of thirty, Henry VI had proved to be a pious and gentle character, usually in good health, with little indication of the strange decline that overtook him at his hunting lodge at Clarenden that August. He fell into a catatonic state, unable to feed himself, move or speak, or to recognise those around him. Modern medicine might diagnose a case of severe depression, prompted by the loss of the final French territories held by his father, or an inherited condition from his maternal grandfather, or perhaps the pressures of rule simply proved too much for a man temperamentally unsuited to his position. It was not a condition that was readily understood by the medieval mind, with its propensity to apply the labels of madness and witchcraft. After the physician's initial suggestions yielded no results, the king was moved to Windsor, where he remained motionless in bed while Margaret waited out the final months of her pregnancy. During his incapacity, the Duke of York was named as Lord Protector: first in 1454 and again, briefly, the following year.

By the time Henry had recovered, Jacquetta's eldest daughter had become a married woman. By all accounts, Elizabeth Woodville was a remarkable beauty, even called the 'most beautiful woman in the island of Britain', with her 'heavy lidded eyes like those of a dragon', high forehead and fair hair, some of which is conveyed in surviving contemporary portraits of around 1463 at Windsor and 1482 at Canterbury Cathedral, and in manuscript form in the book of the Skinner's Company and the Luton Guild Book. It is not quite true, as Charles Ross suggests, that Elizabeth had 'nothing to recommend her except her obvious physical attractions', as he admits she may not have been the right match for a king, but she was an eminently suitable wife for a member of the local gentry.[17] Her mother's royal connections and her father's burgeoning career made her a worthy catch, and by her mid-teens at least one man had already attempted to make her his wife.

Two letters survive that were written to Elizabeth when she was in her early teens, seeking her hand in marriage on behalf of the Yorkist Sir Hugh Johns, or Joneys. Johns certainly had some powerful allies who were not afraid to help him achieve a match of affection. Likely to have been written in the early 1450s, the first letter was penned by Richard, Duke of York, and makes clear that Johns had fallen in love with Elizabeth, 'for the grete wommanhode and gentillesse approved and knowen in your persone' and that she had 'his hert holy [wholly]'. Her feelings, though, were unknown: York admitted 'how it be of your disposicioun towardes him ... is yet to us unknown', but promised that if she 'fulfille our entent in this matier ... [to] be to him and you suche a lord as shal be to your brother grete wele and worship'. A second letter written by York's brother-in-law, Richard, Earl of Warwick, around the same time, added that a recent occasion when she had been in Johns' company had filled the knight with 'ful grete joy and ... grete chere' due to the 'greet love and affectioun that he hath unto your persone as wele for the grete sadness and wisome [wisdom] that he found and proved in you ... your grete and preised vertues and womanly demeaning'.

Yet Elizabeth did not marry Johns, for all the promises and entreaties of his powerful friends. He went on to wed a Maud Cradok, was made a Knight of the Holy Sepulchre in Jerusalem in 1441, lived in Swansea and died around 1485. Shortly after the writing of the letters, probably in the mid-1450s, Elizabeth was married to Sir John Grey of Groby Old Hall in Leicestershire. It may have already been arranged when the two letters were sent, and given that Groby was only fifty miles north of Grafton, the Greys were fairly local to the Woodvilles in terms of their social circle. John was the son of Edward, the 3rd Baron Grey of Ruthyn, and his mother, Elizabeth, was Baroness Ferrers of Groby, through which title her husband gained a seat in Parliament. The marriage may also have been suggested through a personal connection with Jacquetta's first husband: listed among the household for the Duke of Bedford in 1435, along with Richard Woodville, was a Sir John Grey, half-brother of the groom's father, a veteran of Agincourt, who died in 1439.[18]

As newly-weds, John and Elizabeth either lived with the groom's parents at Groby or at Astley in Warwickshire. The site of Groby Old Hall had been used as a defensive location since the days of the Normans. The remains of a castle mound, or motte, are all that survive of its original buildings. By the time John's parents lived there it was a mixture of mid-fifteenth-century red-brick buildings with black diapering, which were diagonal patterns in the brick work, creating the repeating shapes of diamonds. Some of the stonework incorporated in the great hall may have been reused from the original castle, but otherwise it remains a substantial manor house, with a tower which was added to considerably after John's occupancy. Twenty-five miles to the south-west, Astley Castle had come into the Grey family on the marriage of

John's grandfather, Reginald, and remains a pretty, pink-stoned crenelated building, which was recently sympathetically restored by the Landmark Trust. A licence was granted to the owners in 1266 to enclose the sandstone property, with later work being done in the fourteenth century. It had roofs of tile and lead, two storeys and attics, with moat, curtain walls and gatehouse. It seems quite likely that the young couple used this as their main home, while continuing to visit John's parents at Groby.

Fairly soon after the marriage, Elizabeth conceived her first child. It was fairly customary for a first-time mother to return to the home of her parents or in-laws in order to be supported through the weeks of lying-in, delivery and recovery, and Elizabeth appears to have stayed at Groby to give birth to Thomas in around 1455. The precise date of his birth is unclear, as it is based on a comment made in 1492 that he was then '37 and more,' meaning he had not yet turned thirty-eight, although retrospective attempts to date births in this era often prove inaccurate. He may have been born as early as 1452, if Elizabeth was married as soon as she reached the age of consent at fourteen and conceived on her wedding night or soon after. A second son, Richard, was born in the late 1450s.

While Elizabeth was involved in the business of bearing and raising children, the world beyond her bedchamber had become violent. The historic aggression between England and France had finally come to an end with the conclusion of the Hundred Years War, and in July 1456 Joan of Arc was granted a posthumous pardon, being declared innocent of heresy by Inquisitor-General Jean Brehal. Instead, the conflict had entered the English Parliament: relations had so deteriorated among the rival aristocratic families that an unexpected outbreak of violence marked the beginning of a national conflict, which was to define Elizabeth's life and those of her children.

2

EDWARD

1442–1459

'Your humble sons.'

I

In 1455, civil war broke out at the Hertfordshire market town of St Albans. It was an unlikely location, lying twenty-five miles to the north of the Palace of Westminster, where the aristocratic rivalries and disagreements which caused it had been building for years. It was the first battle of the period known today as the 'Cousins' War' or the 'Wars of the Roses', between the families of York and Lancaster, which have been characterised by the symbols of the white and red roses. The Duke of York's period of protectorship had allowed him to prove himself as a competent figure and increased his popularity in certain quarters. By this point he was forty-three and the father of a large family, in contrast to Henry's production of a single son. Technically, the protectorship had recognised that York was the most feasible male heir to the throne, while Prince Edward, born in October 1453, was still just a child.

Then there was York's longstanding enmity with Edmund Beaufort, Duke of Somerset. A personal dislike had been exaggerated by their competition for positions of authority in France and for finances from the English throne. Somerset was the grandson of John of Gaunt, Duke of Lancaster, from a line originally fathered out of wedlock, but later legitimised through marriage and an Act of Parliament. Somerset was also a close ally of Henry's wife, Queen Margaret of Anjou, whose own proposal to act as regent had been rejected in favour of York's. While Henry lay ill, York was determined to move against his enemies, whom he perceived to be the enemies of the state and king by virtue of their bad advice. He ordered that Somerset be arrested and sent to the Tower, in anticipation of putting him on trial for treason. Yet the trial never took place because, in late 1454, the king recovered. York resigned the protectorship and tactfully withdrew, while an angry Somerset was released, but the seeds of antagonism had been sown. When York and his allies were excluded from a Great Council meeting at Leicester and their loyalty was questioned, they felt forced to defend their position.

On 22 May 1455, an army headed by the duke, his brother-in-law the Earl of Salisbury and his wife's nephew Richard, Earl of Warwick, arrived in St Albans, where the king's army was waiting, headed by Henry himself and members of the Beaufort family. Although armed, the two sides anticipated that talking, or parley, might avoid the outbreak of violence. Several letters went back and forth, where York protested the 'subtile meanes ... made by oure Enemies' who never 'ceessed to studie, labour and compasse to bring' him and his allies into danger and were nursed 'undre the wynge of our Mageste Roiall.'[1] York demanded that Somerset be handed over to him, to undergo the trial he had previously escaped, but Henry was keen to protect his closest advisor. The talks failed. Around ten in the morning, the armies met for a brief but intense hour in the centre of town. The king himself was slightly wounded by an arrow grazing his neck and made an ignominious retreat to the nearby shop of a tanner, while the Lancastrian lords sought shelter in the abbey: Somerset was killed after hiding inside the Castle Inn in the centre of town. The Lancastrian John Grey may have fought on the side of his king, but if he did his presence went unrecorded. The bloodshed of St Albans genuinely shocked the aristocracy and changed the political climate in England.

York's family history was intimately connected with that of France, just as Jacquetta's was. Born in 1411, he was descended from Edward III by two lines, on which he rested his unique claim to the English throne. His mother, Anne Mortimer, was the great-granddaughter of Lionel of Antwerp, Edward's second son, but this inheritance passed through the female line and could be considered less strong. Anne had died in childbirth and York's father, Richard of Conisburgh, Earl of Cambridge, had been executed for his part in the Southampton plot of 1415, in which he had attempted to depose Henry VI's father in favour of an heir of the Mortimer line. Conisburgh was the son of Edmund of Langley, the fourth surviving son of Edward III. Fortunately Conisburgh had a brother, who redeemed the family name by being one of the only English lords to die at the Battle of Agincourt. His four-year-old nephew was permitted to inherit his title, becoming the 3rd Duke of York.

In around 1429, York made a prestigious marriage to another well-connected member of the extended royal family. His wife was Cecily Neville, the granddaughter of John of Gaunt, Edward III's third son from his liaison with Katherine Swynford. Although born out of wedlock, Cecily's mother Joan Beaufort was legitimised along with her brothers when Gaunt married Katherine in the final years of his life. They were able to inherit titles and land and were considered to be of full royal descent, but a clause passed after Gaunt's death barred them from ever inheriting the throne. This gave the York children a triple line of descent from the royal Plantagenets, and such an impediment to inheritance could easily be overturned by later rulings. Cecily was reputed to be a great beauty, the youngest of Joan's sixteen children, who proved to be as fertile as her mother. York's early years were spent in service to the throne, learning the duties of a knight, attending Henry VI's coronation in Rheims, before being appointed as Bedford's successor as Lieutenant of France in 1436. By the time he returned for a second term, in June 1441, Cecily had borne a daughter named Anne and a son, who was either stillborn or was lost soon after birth. Departing with them from Portsmouth was Sir Richard Woodville and, possibly, his Duchess Jacquetta.

Just ten years after Joan of Arc had been burned in Rouen's marketplace, the Yorks settled into the same castle where the Maid of Orléans had been held. Only the turreted donjon, or keep, now remains of what was a formidable building situated on Bouvreuil Hill, a former Roman amphitheatre to the north of the city, surrounded by a huge ditch and walls, which enclosed more towers, a gatehouse and inner courtyard. Cecily was established here with her retinue of ladies while York was engaged in military manoeuvres, repelling the French at Pontoise. The Hundred Years War had not yet reached its conclusion, and, just as Bedford had found, the job of governing the English-owned portion of France was a constant process of defence against the attempts of Charles VII and his sons to regain their former possessions.

Around this time, Cecily fell pregnant again, this time with her son Edward, or Edouarde, to follow the French spelling his parents used early in his life. Born on 28 April, probably in Rouen Castle, he would be referred to in the celebratory poem 'The Battle of Towton', written in the 1460s, as the 'rose of roan', or the rose of Rouen, and was probably called so from an earlier period in his life. Later, it would suit Edward's enemies to cast doubt upon his legitimacy, and the date of his arrival and his parentage were called into question. With York absent from Rouen from 14 July until 21 August, it would appear that Edward was conceived upon his father's return, allowing for a gestation of thirty-seven weeks. This would allow for him to be considered 'full-term' by modern standards and would fall within the bracket of a 'normal' birth. If he arrived a little early, and was perhaps a little on the small side, or if there were concerns about his survival, the midwife would have followed the usual practice of performing a ceremony of baptism immediately, without taking him out of the bedchamber. Edward did indeed grow into a tall, strong adult, but that does not preclude the possibility that he was weak, or thought to be weak, at birth. Considering that Cecily had lost her first son, she may have been mindful of the possibility of losing her second, and required such a baptism to take place. Edward appears to have received a small, quiet christening in comparison to his next sibling, Edmund, who received the rites in Rouen Cathedral itself. Perhaps Edmund was a larger, stronger baby. Elizabeth, Lady Say, and Thomas, Lord Scales, were appointed as Edward's godparents.

There is also the chance that Edward was conceived before York's departure, making for a forty-week pregnancy. In the twenty-first century, a pregnancy is allowed to run for two weeks over the typical forty week duration, to allow for miscalculations and late arrivals, but after this point the mother is strongly recommended to have labour induced. There is an increased risk of stillbirth or problems with the baby if this procedure does not go ahead. Little information survives about identifying and diagnosing pregnancy in the fifteenth century, which was largely reliant upon superstitious methods or unreliable tests made upon urine. It might be inferred from the outcome of Cecily's second pregnancy that she had already experienced one pregnancy which went overdue. Calculating due dates was not an exact science; if she and York had been consistently together during the weeks around the time of conception, Cecily may not have been aware that she was long overdue, especially if her second child had not been large. The circumstances of York's absence at Pontoise in 1441 highlight the unpredictable nature of pregnancy. The dates of his campaign allow for Cecily to have conceived a viable child either before his departure or after his return – they do not prove that York was not the father.

It is unlikely that a woman of Cecily's stature, raised to understand the importance of lineage and inheritance, would have compromised the paternity of her eldest surviving son, York's heir. She had witnessed the struggles of her own half-siblings against her own mother, to attempt to reclaim their birth right when her father's will ruled against them. Later rumours that Edward was fathered by a French archer named Blancbourne or Blaybourne were part of a political smear campaign designed by Edward's enemies to discredit him in the 1460s. In addition, York never questioned his son's paternity and Cecily was quite specific in her will, describing him as Edward's father: 'I Cecily, wife unto the right noble prince, Richard late Duke of York, father unto the most Christian Prince, my Lord and son, King Edward IV.' By the time Cecily composed this will, on her deathbed in 1495, Edward had already been in his grave for ten years. She was making her peace with God, making arrangements for her body to be laid to rest and preparing her soul for the afterlife – it is not an occasion on which she was likely to perpetuate a lie. Had Edward not been York's son, she simply need not have mentioned the fact. Just like witchcraft and immorality, accusations of adultery and illegitimacy were frequently the weapons of cowardice levelled at powerful women.

Little is known about Edward's early years. He was nursed by a Norman woman named Anne of Caux, whom he would remember with an annual pension of £20 in 1474. At least some, if not all of the responsibility for Anne's appointment would have fallen to Cecily, whose decision would have been based on the nurse's good character and healthy appearance, as it was thought these to be appropriate measures of the quality of her milk. Her character was thought to transmit itself to any child she suckled, so Cecily would no doubt have chosen carefully. Her appointment was vindicated in the coming years, with Anne feeding Cecily's subsequent children and returning with the family to England. Those subsequent children arrived quickly. Just four months after giving birth to Edward, Cecily fell pregnant again, and another son, Edmund, arrived in Rouen in May 1443. Within weeks she had conceived again, giving birth to Elizabeth in April 1444. Her second daughter was christened in Rouen Cathedral, just as Edmund had been, but her godmother was Jacquetta Woodville – another indicator that Jacquetta remained in France with Richard through this period. If the young Elizabeth was with them, she would have been aged four at the time of Edward's arrival, and by the time of his sister's christening she would have been six: old enough to have memories of these years in a way that Edward was not.

York was already thinking about his eldest son's future, given that he was a valuable marital commodity and the heir to a considerable lineage. With his royal connections, York sought a royal bride for Edward. A suitable candidate was suggested to him by the Duke of Suffolk, and York wrote to Charles VII of France proposing a match with one of his Valois daughters, the nieces of two French princesses who had previously become queens of England. Charles was the brother of Isabelle, second wife to Richard II, and to Catherine, the late mother of Henry VI himself. By seeking to match his son with one of the English king's cousins, York was making a statement about his position and the entitlements it brought. If Henry's only son should die young, Edward's children, with their royal French blood, would inherit his throne. This again suggests that there were no suspicions about Edward's paternity at the time, for the slightest taint of illegitimacy meant that Charles would not even have entertained the idea.

Initially, York hoped to match Edward with Charles's youngest daughter, Princess Madeline, or Magdalena, who had been born on 1 December 1443 at Tours. On 18 April 1445, York wrote to the king 'touching the matter of the marriage of one of my three honoured ladies, your daughters, and of Edouart of York, my eldest son' and was comforted and 'joyful' because Charles had given him cause to hope for an Anglo-French alliance and personal friendship. York proposed to send his ambassadors to Paris 'in order to treat, discuss and conclude the business of the said marriage', but Charles had reservations about the choice of bride. That June, he wrote that Madeline was of a 'very tender age' and offered her sister Joan instead. Having been born in 1435, Joan was then ten years old to Edward's three, but four other daughters borne to Charles between these two girls, including a pair of twins, had died young. It certainly would have been a lucrative alliance for York and secured Edward's future had it come about. But it did not, largely because York's future took a different direction. That September, after escorting Henry VI's bride, Margaret of Anjou, from Pontoise to Harfleur, York was summoned back to England by Henry VI after his five-year term of office as Lieutenant of France expired. The family landed at Dover in October, assuming this to be a temporary interlude before York's reappointment allowed them to return. York wrote again to Charles that December, apologising for the delay, but the following year he was replaced in office by the Duke of Somerset. There was to be no future role for him in France and plans for the potential marriage fizzled out. The reason for this is unclear, but it may have been that Charles had a change of heart, perhaps because after Henry VI's marriage that year, he anticipated English heirs which would have moved York and Edward further from the succession.

The next few years served to distance York even more. Instead of being reappointed in France, he was given the Lieutenancy of Ireland, possibly a move intended to marginalise him from the English court. The post came with a fee of 4,000 marks and an income of 2,000, but this barely covered the huge personal debts York had accrued in the service of the Crown: an undisputed £38,666 15s 4d.[2] His contemporaries saw his new position as akin to a period of exile, with the London Chronicle stating he was 'exsyled into Irlonde for hys rebellion', while Benet's Chronicle described him being 'banished' and one satirical poem echoed the notion that he was 'exciled from our soveraigne lords presens'.[3] York certainly felt that he was being excluded and delayed his departure until 1449, ultimately spending only a little over a year among the Irish, although that year was something of a bureaucratic success. More children joined the Yorks' nursery during these years, with Margaret arriving at the family home of Fotheringhay Castle in May 1446, although two sons, William and John, died young, before Cecily bore George at Dublin Castle in October 1449. Of her remaining three pregnancies, only one child, her son Richard, born three years after George, would survive infancy.

York's position was further complicated by his Mortimer inheritance. This went back to the reign of the childless Richard II, when Parliament had named York's maternal grandfather, Roger Mortimer, as the king's heir. As it happened, Roger had died before Richard, being killed at the age of twenty-four during a skirmish in Ireland. His son, Edmund, inherited the title Earl of March and the position of Plantagenet heir. However, he was not to keep it for long. The following year, Richard's cousin Henry Bolingbroke deposed the king, bypassing the eight-year-old Mortimer and being crowned as Henry IV. Edmund and his younger brother, Roger, were incarcerated in Windsor Castle, in something like a foreshadowing of the story of the Princes in the Tower. This pair of princes was more fortunate though, being raised as befitted their rank, with Edmund appointed to the regency council of the young Henry VI in the 1420s. Both brothers died young and childless: Roger in 1413 and Edmund of the plague in 1425. This meant the title Earl of March and the question of the Mortimer claim to the throne passed to the son of their sister Anne. In 1411, she had died after giving birth to Richard, future Duke of York, and in 1415 it was in defence of the Mortimer inheritance that Richard's father, Conisburgh, had risen in rebellion. York was acutely aware that his claim to the throne had been usurped by Henry IV. In 1450, the Mortimer name resurfaced in the mouths of rebels, as a more desirable ruling family than that of the Lancastrian line.

That summer, while York was in Ireland, a number of revolts broke out in the south of England, generally gathered under the title of Jack Cade's rebellion. The people's anger was similar to that felt by York: it was directed against the abuses and corruptions of the king's closest advisors and the expenditure of warfare against France, especially the loss of lands ceded by Henry upon his marriage. According to the London Chronicle and other contemporary accounts, their leader claimed alternately to be Jack Cade or John Mortimer, a reputed cousin of the Duke of York, who produced a manifesto titled *The Complaint of the Poor Commons of Kent*. In early June around 5,000 men gathered at Blackheath and the subsequent lists of pardon show they were not exclusively lower class, including two MPs, a knight and eighteen squires. Entering London, Cade declared himself mayor and reclaimed the city for the Mortimers. Two members of the king's household were put on trial and executed for treason before the rioting became more widespread, eventually proving to be the rebels' undoing when Londoners turned against them to defend their city. Cade's claims reached the ears of York in Ireland, potentially implicating him and proving to be of such concern that he returned to England that September, at the head of an army of between 3,000 and 5,000 men strong. His conciliatory letters to Henry may have reassured the king of his loyalty, but when York attended Parliament that November, he rode through the London streets with a drawn sword before him, a recognised symbol of royalty.

II

Edward was only eight years old during the summer of Cade's rebellion. The chances are that he was at the family home of Fotheringhay in Northamptonshire or already established in his own household at Ludlow. Along with Edmund, who was just a year younger than him, Edward's education was being undertaken at Ludlow Castle, a Marcher stronghold on the Welsh Borders; the castle sat on high ground surrounded by its market town. The details of it do not survive, but the ordinances he set down for the education of his own eldest son at Ludlow two decades later might suggest something of the daily regime he himself used to follow. Religion played a significant role, punctuating the day's timetable with prayers and services; the remainder of the boys' time would have been divided between academic learning supervised by tutors and moral education, deriving partly from the reading of literature and instructional manuals, although their cultural upbringing extended to meal times and all occasions when protocol, good manners and formality were observed. Given the location of his birth and nationality of his nurse, Edward may have been bilingual from an early age, combining French and English in his parents' home, and the library he owned as an adult indicated that he read for pleasure in both these languages. It would have also been essential that Edward was schooled in Latin, with formal documentation of the time appearing in any of the three languages. There was also time dedicated to sport and the chivalric training that would have been essential for aristocratic young men of the era: riding, hunting, jousting, hawking and feats of combat.

In 1452, fearful of the constant rumours spread against him, York attempted to strike at Somerset and remove his influence over King Henry. York had reason to be afraid, as the past two years had seen repeated attempts upon his life. In Kent, a man named Stephen Christmas was executed for saying that Henry should be replaced by Richard: 'talking a gayne the kyng, havynge maore favyr unto the Duke of Yorke thenne unto the kynge.' During the summer of 1451, York's former chamberlain, now Speaker of the House of Commons, Sir William Oldhall, planned to seize the king, and that September uprisings in Ilminster, Yeovil and in Norfolk were made in York's name. During Henry's eighteenth parliament, which sat that November, the MP for Bristol, Thomas Yonge, suggested that York be named as Henry's successor, and was sent to the Tower as a result. The family spent that Christmas together at Ludlow and it was from there that York wrote to Henry in an attempt to clear his name. Dated 9 January, his petition explained that he was aware the king had 'a distrust by sinister information of mine enemies, adversaries and evil-willers' and offered to swear his loyalty upon the sacraments before bishops. As Henry had already admitted, for 'a lang tyme the pepill hath yeven upon yow moche strange langage ... making menace unto oure persone be your saying, that you schuld fechid home with many thousandis, and that ye schulde take upon you that that ye nothir aught nor as we doutenat ye wole not attempte'.[4] Less than a month later, York raised troops from the local area, writing to the burgesses of Shrewsbury that his loyalty had been 'of none effect, through the envy, malice and untruth of the said Duke of Somerset, [who] laboureth continually about the King's highness for my undoing, and to corrupt my blood, and to disinherit me and my heirs'. On 23 February, Henry sent a delegation to find York and persuade him not to use force, but this failed. With around 8,000 men, York marched to London, arriving at Blackheath by the beginning of March. He found the city gates locked against him.

Henry and Richard met at Dartford. Exactly what York's real intentions were are not clear; the size of his force was intimidating, but he continued to profess his loyalty and the necessity of the removal of the king's evil councillors. Henry was clearly expecting trouble, as according to one contemporary his army could have been as much as three times as large as York's. However, York also had seven ships waiting in the Thames estuary, loaded with guns. These large shows of force were clearly a rehearsal for the real conflict of 1455, but on this occasion the king managed to dissolve the danger by tricking York into talks. Henry offered to place Somerset under arrest in the Tower while he listened to York's complaints, but when York entered the royal tent he found Somerset present. York was then disarmed and marched to London, where he was taken to his own home of Baynard's Castle and effectively kept under house arrest for two weeks. During this time he was conducted to St Paul's Cathedral and made to swear an oath that he would never again rebel against the king. This is where Edward enters the political arena.

At the start of March 1452, Edward was two months short of his tenth birthday. He had been at Ludlow with his parents that winter, as York planned his campaign, and probably remained there after seeing him depart. According to the London Chronicle, the Brut Chronicle and the Great Chronicle, York was released from custody because his son Edward, referred to for the first time as the Earl of March, was marching south from Ludlow with a retinue of Welsh retainers of 'likely men' to liberate his father. It may have been just a rumour, or even a threat or declaration of intent, but if the young Edward was prepared to lead a force to this end, it was a remarkable act of bravery for one so young. It cannot be easily dismissed, as it is consistent with his achievements on the field of battle at the age of eighteen, relative to his age. Nor would King Henry have been complacent about the possibility;

the nine-year-old boy may have been a dynamic and driven figurehead, but his retinue of Welsh lords could certainly have caused some damage and rallied other sympathisers to their cause. York was released and permitted to travel back to his family at Ludlow, perhaps intercepting Edward on the way. Parliament would rediscover their need of him when Henry fell ill the following summer.

Early in 1454, while York was acting as regent, he brought Edward to London with him. A newsletter written on 19 January by John Stodley, a London scrivener from the Society of Mercers, contained the news that 'the Duke of York wole be at Londone justly on Fryday next coming at night, as his owne men tellen for certain, and he wole come with his household meynee, clenly beseen and likely men. And th'erle of Marche cometh with hym, but he will have a nother feliship of gode men that shall be at Londone before hym.'⁵ Although Edward was not quite twelve, he had his own separate household accompanying him to the capital and had made the transition from the school room to affairs of state. It seems likely that York took him to Westminster, if not into actual meetings of the Privy Council, otherwise there would have been little point to the boy travelling with him at all. York might also have been intending to draw attention to the fact that he had a bright, capable son approaching the age of maturity, in contrast with the king's infant heir. The London that Edward experienced would have been centred round the court and Baynard's Castle close by Black Friars. At a minimum, Edward would have experienced the streets leading west from his home to Westminster – St Andrew's Hill, Fleet Street, Temple Bar and Charing Cross – and possibly also those stretching west to the Tower – Thames Street, passing St Mary Somerset, St Martins, All Hallows and St Magnus, Tower Street, Petty Wales and Tower Hill. The chances are that he saw a lot more of the city with his father, by road or river, before the king's health returned and the Yorks retreated to their estates once more.

Two letters survive from Edward's youth at Ludlow. They reflect the concerns of the two boys during their father's absence and indicate that they were already steeped in the circumstances and rhetoric of York's grievances. Although dictated to a secretary, they remain the only surviving letters by Edward or Edmund, so it is worth quoting at least the first fully, which can be dated to 26 March 1454 or 14 April 1455:

Right high and right mighty prince, our full redoubted lord and father,

We thank our blessed lord, not only of your honourable conduct and good speed in all your matters and business, of your gracious prevail against the intent and malice of your evil willers, but also of the knowledge that it pleased your nobleness to let us now late have of the same by relation of Sir Walter Devereux, Kt and John Milwater, Esq and John at Nokes, yeoman of your honourable chamber. Also we thank your noble and good fatherhood for our green gowns now late sent unto us to our great comfort, beseeching your good lordship to remember our porteux (religious book) and that we might have some fine bonnets sent unto us by the next sure messenger, for necessity so requireth. Over this, right noble lord and father, please it your highness to wit that we have charged your servant, William Smyth, bearer of these, for to declare unto your nobility certain things on our behalf, namely concerning and touching the odious rule and demeaning of Richard Croft and his brother. Wherefore we beseech your gracious lordship and full noble fatherhood to hear him in exposition of the same, and to his relation to give full faith and credence. Right high and right mighty prince, our full redoubted and right noble lord and father we beseech Almighty Jesus give you as good life and long, with as much continual perfect prosperity as your princely heart can best desire. Written at your castle of Ludlow on Saturday in Easter Week,

your humble sons,

E Marche

E Rutlonde[6]

The start of the second letter, dated to 3 June the same year, is formulaic enough, but ends with a personal touch:

Also we beseech your good lordship that it may please you to send us Harry Lovedeyne, groom of your kitchen, whose service is to us right agreeable, and we will send you John Boyce to wait on your good lordship.[7]

Edward would have been too young to fight at the Battle of St Albans in 1455, although at thirteen he was certainly able to understand its significance. Just months after the battle, the king fell ill again, and York stepped in as Lord Protector for a second time. Between November and the following February, Henry and Parliament accepted the need for York's support. During this time, York was able to reward his nephew the Earl of Warwick with the title of Captain of Calais, an appointment that was to prove vital for Edward later on. Given that Edward had accompanied York to London during his first Protectorate, it seems likely that, now just short of his fourteenth birthday, he may have also been with him during this period, when 'Lordes York and Warwick comen to Parliament in a good array, to the number of 300 men'.[8]

After this, the trail runs cold for a year or two. It is possible to trace the movements of Edward's father, who was staying at Salisbury House in Fleet Street that September, then visited Sandal, before returning to London in October and then heading north to sit in the parliament at Coventry, where according to Bale's Chronicle, York was physically attacked by Henry Beaufort, son of the dead Duke of Somerset. Edward might have been with his father for all or part of this, but equally he may have returned to Ludlow or visited other members of his family at Fotheringhay. Edward would also have been aware of the increasing tide of feeling in favour of his father's rule. York may have been blunt and tactless in his approach, as some historians have claimed, but as a viable alternative to the ineffectual Henry and his coterie of advisors, York was seen as a competent potential heir. Hardyng's Chronicle praises him as if his future reign was being anticipated, if not guaranteed:

> By whiche knowledge your discrete sapience
> All vyce evermore destroye maye and reprove,
> By virtuous love and blessedfull dilygence,
> And virtue love, that maye not ought greve
> How ye shall rule your subiects, while ye lyve,
> In lawe, and peace, and all tranquyllite
> Which been the floures of all regalyte ...
> O worthy prince! O duke of York I meane
> Discended downe of highest blodde royall ...

That maye this lande ought trouble or over ride
For twies it was so wonne with muche pride.[9]

In the light of this, York's eldest son can be forgiven for thinking that his family had a rightful claim to the throne, and that one day in the future he might be King of England.

In March 1458, the two sides made a show of reconciliation to placate the king. York, Warwick and Salisbury attended a 'Love Day' at St Paul's Cathedral, but Edward's presence was not mentioned in the letter describing events, written by William Botoner to the York family friend Sir John Fastolf: 'the Kyng came the last weke to Westminster, and the Duke of York came to London with hys owne housole (household) onlye to the nombre of cxl [140] hors, as it ys seyd.'[10] A poem written upon the occasion, surviving in the Cotton Vespasian B Manuscript, omits Edward from the proceedings: 'In Yorke, in Somerset, as I understonde, in Warrewicke, is love and charite, in Sarisbury eke, and in Northumbrelande, that every man may rejoise concord and unite.'[11] This does not mean definitively that Edward was not present or observing events, but simply that he may not have been a direct participant, or that he may have been among the 'lordes many oone' mentioned in a later stanza. A month away from his sixteenth birthday, Edward would have understood the tensions underpinning the event, given that more attempts had been made on his father's life in the run up to it. When Parliament was summoned to sit in Coventry in 1459, York, Warwick and Salisbury were excluded and concluded correctly that their loyalty was to be questioned. With the threat of treason and attainder imminent, they began to raise troops in their defence.

The next battle came in September 1459, when Salisbury was marching from his Yorkshire home of Middleham to join with York at Ludlow, and found his way blocked by the queen's army at Blore Heath. Having secured a victory despite commanding smaller forces, he then hurried to join his allies, who were preparing for the arrival of another army headed by the king himself. The seventeen-year-old Edward was present when they came together at Ludlow, with Warwick bringing reinforcements from Calais to swell the numbers. However, the question of treason hung in the air. York and his allies had been attainted as rebels, just as they had feared, but just to the south of Ludlow itself Henry's personal banner was visible to York's troops, which shattered their morale. According to Stowe's Chronicle, York claimed the king was dead and ordered masses to be said for his soul, in an attempt to trick his men into fighting, but if this was true it was the action of a desperate man. York dug in at Ludford Bridge, in a defensive ditch by a crossing over the River Teme, and erected a barricade of carts upon which he placed cannon. The rumour of treason soon spread around the camp despite York's best efforts. In addition, his force was smaller than that of the king, 'over-weak', according to the London Chronicle. Then, overnight, the men from Calais defected to Henry and York realised that to engage his army would result in disaster.

During the hours of darkness, Edward must have been part of the frantic discussions to decide their next course of action: whether to submit, stand their ground or flee. It is possible that Duchess Cecily and her younger children were resident in Ludlow Castle, less than half a mile away. Two chronicles place York's family there: Hearne's Fragment, later written by a servant of Edward, claimed that the duchess, 'residing there, had her wardrobe rifled and her furniture spoiled', while Abbot Whethamsted wrote that the 'noble duches of York [was] unmanly and cruelly' treated. There is no evidence to support the romantic legend that Cecily stood with her children at the market cross in Ludlow to face the oncoming troops, nor is there much likelihood that she suffered the physical assault or rape that some historians have suggested, as the subsequent reprisals for this action would have been unavoidable. There is a chance that Cecily and her other children were not in Ludlow at all, or were already travelling to a place of safety when York decided he had no choice but to flee the country. He and Edmund headed for Ireland, while Edward accompanied Warwick and Salisbury to the south coast, where their loyal friend Sir John Dynham offered his ships to help them escape to Calais. Edward later rewarded John's mother Joan and her servants for their assistance, with a royal wardship and £80 'by way of regard and in recompense for their true services, labour and diligence at the last departure of the king that now is, from his realm towards his town of Calais and for his safe conveyance to the said town'.

It must have been an ignominious departure, stealing away

in the middle of the night while their loyal men slept, but they understood the alternative was almost certainly a traitor's death and the enforced penury of their families. It was probably practical questions that drove Edward to ally with Warwick instead of York. As Earl of March, and his father's eldest son, the family inheritance was safer if they were apart. If the event of the king capturing one of them, the other would still be able to return and defend their title. On the night of 12 October 1459, Edward, Earl of March, became a fugitive.

3

THE MAKING OF A KING
1459–1461

'Whose fame the earth shall spread.'

I

As the sun rose behind the Welsh hills, the soldiers lying behind the
barricades said their prayers and looked about for their leaders.
It did not take long for word to spread through the camp that
the Yorkist leaders had fled, conceding defeat even before arms
had been raised. There may have been no explanation offered, or
none required, given the presence of the king among the enemy
and the obvious disparity between the armies; some may have felt
indignant or abandoned, while others slunk away in relief. York's
abandoned troops were pardoned and returned home in peace,
and on 30 November Henry offered to extend that pardon to all
those who submitted to him within eight days. Parliament met at
Coventry as planned and passed Acts of Attainder against York
and both his elder sons, as well as Warwick, Salisbury and his
countess.

In the interests of her children, Cecily travelled to Coventry,
as John Bocking wrote to John Paston on 7 December that 'the
Duchesse of York come yester-even late, as the bringer hereof shall

more plainly declare yow'.[1] Cecily was brought into the council chamber to witness her husband's disgrace and hear the lords swear a new oath of allegiance to Henry, Margaret and Prince Edward. Under the circumstances, it was the only thing to be done, even by those lords who remained privately loyal to York, such as his cousin Viscount Bourchier, Cecily's brother Edward Neville, Lord Abergavenny and Sir William Herbert of Raglan, who would later be swift to rejoin the Yorkist cause. Perhaps Cecily reminded the king of their mutual descent from John of Gaunt, as Lancastrian cousins by birth, despite her marriage and husband's rebellion. It was a wise move, asserting the loyalty to Henry that York had continually stressed and preventing the same fate befalling her as had been visited upon the Countess of Salisbury. On 20 December, Henry granted her an income of 1,000 marks 'for the relief of her and her infants who had not offended against the king'.

Cecily and her younger children were then sent into the custody of her sister Anne, the wife of the Lancastrian Duke of Buckingham, where she was kept 'fulle strayte and many a grete rebuke', although this rather conflicts with the fact that she was permitted to travel around the county.[2] York's lands reverted to the crown and a large percentage was given to Owen Tudor, the king's stepfather, while Ludlow was plundered by soldiers 'wetshod in wine', looting properties and defouling women.[3] York Castle and other family properties were also broken into and despoiled. The Davies Chronicle states that the king's advisers swooped in to gather 'riches immeasurable' from the 'rightful heirs', but this only served to turn the tide against the Lancastrians, as 'the hearts of the people were turned away from them that had the governance of the land, and their blessings were turned to cursings'. The unbridled nature of the Lancastrian army was to prove its own undoing in the coming year, even on the occasions when it achieved great military successes.

Across the Channel, Edward remained in Calais, listening for news of England or of his father and brother in Ireland. The town had been in English hands since the Battle of Crécy in 1346, when Edward III famously laid siege to the city and reduced the burghers to their knees. It covered an area of around twenty miles and in 1400 around 12,000 people were living inside its formidable walls. Dominated by Calais Castle, which no longer stands, it was a medieval town of typical churches, tall townhouses, marketplaces

and squares, its gabled roofs glimpsed in a manuscript illustration
from Jean de Waurin's *Chroniques d'Angleterre*. As the three earls
planned their next moves, these months must have been something
of an education for Edward, learning from such seasoned veterans.
Salisbury was then almost sixty, and had extensive military
and political experience, having been appointed Warden of the
Welsh Marches by Henry V in 1420, as well as a Justice of the
Peace. He had served in France with York and sat on Henry VI's
Royal Council in the 1430s, before becoming embroiled in the
Neville–Percy feud that had initially led his family to side with
York against the Lancastrian Percys. His eldest son, Warwick,
was then just over thirty and already emerging as a dynamic and
formidable force in English politics, having served with his father
in the north and possibly taken part in the 1448–9 war against
the Scots. Margaret of Anjou considered him such a serious threat
that she cut off his supplies, attempted to have him arrested and
may have been behind at least one assassination attempt which
the earl only narrowly escaped. Warwick was not prepared to
bow to Lancastrian authority and conducted his own piratical
escapades in the Channel, preying on German and Castilian ships
while building his own diplomatic connections with France and
Burgundy. In addition, there was Edward's uncle William Neville,
who gained the title of Lord Fauconberg through marriage. He
had served in Scotland and France through the 1430s and 40s,
becoming a field commander and Knight of the Garter, and been
captured in France and ransomed after four years, emerging with
debts owed to him by the Crown. His allegiance had shifted from
Henry to his brother-in-law during the period of the duke's first
Protectorate in 1455. Between them, the three must have formed an
impressive set of teachers, advising and guiding the young Edward,
who could only have learned from their combined experience and
wisdom. Also at Calais, they were joined by Francesco Coppini,
Bishop of Terni, and papal legate to England, who had been sent
by Pius II to recruit Henry to support his crusade. His assessment
of the English king was that he was 'a man more timorous than a
woman ... who left everything in his wife's hands' and his support
lent further credence to the Yorkist cause.

As attainted traitors, the three earls were not expecting to be left
in peace to enjoy their exile. Plans were afoot across the Channel

to bring them to justice and these were to bring Edward into direct conflict with his future father-in-law. Despite offering his friends a safe haven in Calais, the Earl of Warwick had no legal claim to the town, having been deprived of its captaincy in 1458. To make matters worse, the position had then been granted to Henry Beaufort, son of the dead Duke of Somerset. Young Beaufort had survived the Battle of St Albans after suffering terrible wounds, and had rapidly become one of Queen Margaret's closest allies; he would become one of the most implacable Yorkist opponents over the next few years. He was not content to let Warwick resume control of Calais and had mounted a raid to recapture the town, but had hitherto only managed to take one of the outlying forts at Guisnes. Undeterred, Beaufort ordered the construction of a new fleet, to be built at the Thanet port of Sandwich. Overseeing the work was none other than the Lancastrian Richard Woodville.

On 15 January 1460, John Dynham sailed from Calais in a surprise attack upon Sandwich. Situated close to Kent's East coast, where the River Stour flows in from the meeting point of the English Channel and the North Sea, Sandwich had long been one of the crucial Cinque Ports and a major centre for shipbuilding. Today the harbour has silted up and the town lies almost two miles from the shoreline at Sandwich Bay, but then it was a bustling marine centre. When Dynham arrived, early in the morning, the Woodvilles were still in bed. The fleet was destroyed and Sir Richard, Jacquetta and their eldest son Anthony were captured and taken back to Calais. A letter written by William Worcester, now among the Paston collection, estimated the time of the raid to be between three and four in the morning, but the letter incorrectly states that Woodville had retaken Calais. In fact, the opposite was true: Richard and his family were treated as prisoners, although Jacquetta was swiftly released following the custom of the honourable treatment of women. That same night, father and son were roundly abused with insults that dwelt largely on question of rank: 'my Lord of Salisbury berated [Woodville], calling him a knave's son, that he should be so rude as to call him and these other Lords traitors, for they should be found the king's true liegemen, when he should be found a traitor etc. And my Lord of Warwick berated him and said that his father was only an esquire … and since then he himself had been made by marriage

... and that it was not his place to have such language of Lords of the King's blood. And my Lord of March berated him in such like wise.'⁴ They were held in Calais for the next six months. Less than four years would pass before Edward would defy convention and marry the daughter of this 'knave's son'. No doubt the story of her parents' capture reached Elizabeth in the countryside at Astley.

Before that though, Edward had an extraordinary coup to achieve. As the earls planned their return, they drew on the rhetoric of the Jack Cade rebellion ten years before, published in *Articles of the Commons of Kent*. None of the criticisms of Henry VI's rule had been resolved in the meantime and there was considerable opposition to the influence of Queen Margaret and her councillors, especially in London and the south. In Norfolk, a Friar Brackley went so far as to consider the Yorkists to be saviours of the country.⁵ That March, Warwick travelled to Waterford in Ireland to meet York and discuss their next move. Next, the Yorkists circulated a manifesto before leaving Calais, featuring the names of York, Edward, Warwick and Salisbury, and citing the failures of the government, losses in France, abuses in the legal system and the bad advice and greed of the king's favourites, who had planned their Attainder in order to benefit from their lands. Their criticisms bore the lengthy title of *These be the Points and Causes of the Gathering and Assembling of us, the King's True Liegemen of Kent, the which we trust to remedy, with help of him, the King, our Sovereign Lord, and all the Commons of England*. In it, they directly questioned the nature of kingship and its exercise of power: 'They say that our sovereign Lord is above law and that the law was made but to his pleasure and that he may make and break it as often as him list ... the contrary is true.' Henry's false friends also informed him that 'the commons ... would bring in the Duke of York to be their king, so by these false men's leasings [rumours] they made him to hate and to destroy his very friends'. The rebels claimed they would be found the king's true men, and the true guilty ones would be found 'by a just and a true inquiry by the law'.

Early in June, Lord Fauconberg made another humiliating attack upon Sandwich, destroying the fleet Beaufort had been rebuilding since January. This gave the Yorkists a foothold into England, and by the end of the month Edward, Warwick and Salisbury had joined him there with around 2,000 men. Word of their arrival was spreading and their loyal followers in Kent were flocking to join them. The rebels marched west unimpeded from Sandwich to Canterbury, where they found a warm welcome. Those appointed by the Lancastrian regime to resist them soon allowed them entry to the city and pinned upon the gates was a ballad of welcome, recorded in the Davies Chronicle and perhaps penned by a local cleric, implicated by its use of Biblical quotations and Latin phrases:

> Richard Duke of York, Job thy servant insigne,
> Edward Earl of March, whose fame the earth shall spread,
> Richard Earl of Salisbury named Prudence,
> With that noble knight and flower of manhood
> Richard, Earl of Warwick, shield of our defence,
> And little Fauconberg, a knight of great reverence.

Another poem of the time had a similar message, expanding on the initial couplet and heralding Edward as a saviour and stressing his legitimacy:

> E for Edward, whose fame the earth shall spread
> Because of his wisdom named prudence
> Shall save all England by his manliness
> Wherefore we owe to do him reverence.
>
> M for March, true in every trial
> Drawn by discretion that is worthy and wise
> Conceived in wedlock and coming of royal blood
> Joined unto virtue, excluding all vices.

On 2 July, the Yorkists approached London. After negotiations with a dozen of the city's elders, they were admitted into the capital; they sent their troops to the Smoothfield, or Smithfield, and gave thanks at St Paul's for their success. At some point, Edward secured the freedom of his mother and younger siblings, who joined him in the capital, staying in a Southwark mansion owned by the Duke of Bedford's one-time retainer, Sir John Fastolf. Those loyal Lancastrians who remained in London retreated to the Tower, including Edward's own godfather Thomas, Lord

Scales. News came that the king was gathering an army near Northampton, so Edward secured a loan of £1,000 from the city to equip himself, Warwick and Fauconberg before heading north. Salisbury remained behind and laid siege to the Tower. In response, Lord Scales turned the fortress's deadly weapons upon the city, including a primitive kind of flame thrower emitting 'wildfire', thought to be a type of napalm, which 'burned and hurt men and women and children in the streets',[6] only becoming worse when doused with water. This brutal move, designed as a deterring show of force, only turned the mood of the city against the Lancastrians. With 'much harm' being 'done daily' by Scales, the citizens dragged cannons into position and blasted a hole in the Tower's curtain wall, while others blockaded the fortress from the east and by water, so that it was starved of provisions for five days. On 19 July, Scales conceded defeat and attempted to escape, but he was recognised by a group of boatmen and lynched. His body was dumped in the churchyard of St Mary Overy; Edward would later give his godfather an honourable funeral.

Today, the grounds of Delapré Abbey are peaceful enough, with its gardens and wooded park open to the public. However, on 10 July 1460 it was the location where the Yorkist army met that of King Henry, to the south of Northampton. Reputedly, the action was witnessed from the Eleanor cross, so probably took place somewhere near the site of the present golf course, within sight of the order of Clunaic nuns. Only around half an hour of fighting took place before the Lancastrian Sir John Grey of Ruthin changed sides and his men laid down their weapons. A number of the king's men, including Edward's uncle the Duke of Buckingham, were killed in a failed attempt to prevent the enemy reaching Henry, who was waiting in his tent. His great seal, the symbol of the power of government essential to the passing of any laws, was entrusted to Warwick's brother, George Neville.

The nuns tended the wounded and the three hundred dead were buried in their graveyard,[7] which is now the walled garden. A contemporary poem, 'The Battle of Northampton', uses heraldic devices to describe the events in the extended metaphor of the hunt, with all its connotations of nobility. Warwick, the 'bere', and Edward, the 'bereward', defeat the 'dog' John Talbot and Buckingham, the 'buk'. Edward's valour and abilities were particularly noted: 'the bereward asked no questioun why, but on the dogges he set full rounde.' The poem presents the Yorkists' main motive as the country's salvation – their invasion being necessary due to 'the falsehood in every place' and the 'people crying for mercy'. Even King Henry is made to admit that his false advisors 'wrought agayne all kynde they labored to bring me in distresse'.[8] In reality, Henry had little choice but to accept the situation, and the triumphant Yorkists marched him to London, still professing their loyalty, just as they had after St Albans. Their declared intention was to assist him in the business of ruling the country, divorcing him from his evil councillors. Having the king in their possession meant they could be seen to be ruling in his name, instead of in their own interests, so on 30 July a parliament was summoned for the autumn. The Northampton poem also called for the return of the loyal York 'whom treson ne falshod never dyd shame but ever obedient to his sovereign'.[9] Yet over in Ireland, York had other ideas.

Hearing of his son's victory, York knew it was safe to return to England. By 2 October, he had reached Gloucester, but travelled slowly, gathering supporters in Ludlow and Hereford, and did not ride into London until over a week later. With a force of between 500 and 800 men, the duke headed for Westminster, with trumpets sounding in the streets and a regal sword borne before him: 'with his swerde born uppe right by for him thorowe the halle and parliament chamber'.[10] Parliament had been sitting for three days and his arrival was expected, although the action he took came as something of a surprise to all. Edward, Warwick and Salisbury were present when York strode into the king's chamber, and, laying hands upon the throne, 'there under the cloth of estate stondyng he gave them knowliche that he purposed nat to ley doaune his swerde' but to challenge his right 'and so toke his loggyng in the qwenys chamber'.[11] The room was shocked. It was a bold and decisive move, but until that point the Yorkists had only ever upheld their loyalty and desire to assist the king in the business of rule. Being heir was one thing, replacing the king was quite another. Warwick and Edward attempted to placate the duke, but the general response was hostile: 'few of the Lords countenanced him' and 'every state … began to whisper against him'. According to the chronicle of Jean de Waurin, Edmund, newly returned from

Ireland with his father, said to Warwick, 'Dear cousin, do not be angry, for you know that it (the crown) belongs to my father and he shall have it,' to which Edward replied diplomatically, 'Brother, offend nobody, for all shall be well.'[12] Where these lines of direct speech came from is unclear, but one thing was certain: York's declaration of intent proved to be a game-changer.

It took several weeks for the negotiations to reach their conclusion, to steer a path that would preserve Henry's regality and placate York's ambition. Edward may well have acted as the go-between, encouraging his father to be patient and settle for an alternative solution. Finally, Parliament consented to formalise the duke's position as Henry's heir, and although York may have been disappointed not to have been offered the crown, he consented to their terms. On 1 November, they processed to St Paul's to mark the occasion, with Henry wearing his crown, York walking with him and Edward carrying the royal train. By the Act of Accord, York was named Lord Protector during the king's lifetime, Prince of Wales, Duke of Cornwall and Earl of Chester, and awarded an annual income of £10,000. It also became a treasonable offense to imagine or 'encompass' York's death. As the act was passed, 'the right high and mighty Prynce Richard Plantagenet, Duke of York', swore an oath that he would 'never doo, consent, procure or stir ... anything that may be to the abriggement of the natural lyfe of Kyng Henry the Sixth or to the hurt of his reign or dignity royal'. Other loyal Yorkists were appointed to key positions, Salisbury became the King's Chamberlain, his son George Neville, Bishop of Exeter, was made Lord Chancellor, Viscount Bourchier became Lord Treasurer and Warwick was given a number of lands and wardships in Wales and Hereford. As York's immediate heirs, and now also in line to the throne, Edward and Edmund made similar promises and were awarded incomes of 3,500 marks and 1,500 marks respectively. As their father was a decade older than Henry, the likelihood of him ever succeeding to the throne may have appeared slim, but for Edward it was a definite reality. York was, in effect, a king without a title; a king by rights, but not yet in name; a king in waiting. Yet one implacable enemy would never agree to these terms.

The Act of Accord effectively disinherited Henry's son, Prince Edward of Westminster. Having been born in 1453, after eight years of marriage, he was almost seven years old at the time that his father signed away his inheritance, in hiding in the north with his mother. Despite the various rumours that suggested he was not the king's son, Henry acknowledged the boy and treated him as his own; it is more a measure of the duress he came under from York and Parliament in the winter of 1460 than any doubts over his own paternity that made him sign the Act. Margaret of Anjou was not prepared to see her son's inheritance set aside and her supporters among the English lords, headed by Henry Beaufort and York's reprobate son-in-law Exeter, could not accept York's supremacy, so they began to gather troops around Hull. On 9 December, York, Salisbury and Edmund, Earl of Rutland, set out for the north, leaving Warwick to hold London. Having proven himself, Edward was now trusted as an independent military figure, and was sent into the Welsh Marches to confront the challenge posed there by the king's half-brother, Jasper Tudor.

Towards the end of December, York and his company reached Sandal Castle in Yorkshire, where they spent the Christmas period. Ten miles away, in Pontefract Castle, the Lancastrian army was waiting for them. An initial skirmish between Beaufort's men and York's outriders may have led to an agreement to refrain from combat over the coming season, which usually lasted until 6 January. On 30 December, York and a party of his men left the castle, believing themselves to be safe. It may have been a foraging party to replenish supplies, or they may have been deceived by the concealment of the queen's large army or an ambush effected by dressing some troops up in women's costume. The incident was reported to the Duke of Milan as an error on York's part:

> And it came to pass that, although they were three times stronger, yet from lack of discipline, because they allowed a large part of the force to go pillaging and searching for victuals, their adversaries, who are desperate, attacked the duke and his followers. Ultimately they routed them, slaying the duke and his younger son, the Earl of Rutland, Warwick's father and many others.[13]

The circumstances are unclear but the outcome was absolute. During the fighting, York was killed, reputedly just 400 yards from the Castle gates. Also among the dead were the seventeen-year-old Edmund, perhaps cut down in flight, as some sources suggest; Salisbury's son Thomas, who was the same age, was also killed. Salisbury himself was captured and later executed at Pontefract Castle. The severed heads of all four men were placed upon Micklegate Bar in York, with the duke's dressed in a paper crown to mock his royal claims. Another Milanese ambassador, this time to the French court, reported Henry's response to the battle and suggested the probable motive for the attack: 'When the king heard this he was much moved, although the Duke of York seems rather to have been slain out of hatred for having claimed the kingdom than anything else.'[14]

The terrible news probably reached Edward around New Year, while he was at Shrewsbury. It meant that the terms of the Act of Accord had been broken and the heir had been unlawfully slain. Worse than that, their actions had been treasonous, treacherous and broke the codes of chivalric conduct. Edward was now the head of the family and, in his eyes, the rightful King of England.

II

Early on a cold February morning,[15] Edward drew his troops together to meet the approaching Lancastrian army, bitter at the loss of his father and brother, determined to exact revenge and to urge his own right to the throne. He was almost nineteen, tall, at six foot three and a half inches, and had learned from some of the best. In addition, he had something of a genius for military campaigns, leadership and inspiring his men. He had intended to confront Queen Margaret, who was marching south, but news that a large army led by Jasper Tudor was heading towards him had stopped him in his tracks. Having awaited the enemy in his Mortimer property of Wigmore Castle, he marched his men four miles to the south and lined them up at a crossroads near a crossing of the River Lugg, an area known as Mortimer's Cross.

What happened next demonstrates Edward's abilities as a leader and his quick-thinking in turning the tide in his favour. In the east, in the direction of the village of Kingsland, a meteorological phenomenon was created by the reflection of the sun through ice crystal clouds or fog. Known as a parhelion, or sun dog, this created the impression of three suns in the sky at around ten o'clock on the morning of 2 February 1461, an unusual and striking sight that would have been interpreted as an omen or sign. Such strange occurrences, like storms and comets, could instil fear into the mind of the common soldier, and Edward was quick to recognise and harness this. The Davies Chronicle quotes Edward as adopting this as a sign of the approval of the Holy Trinity, saying, 'Be of good comfort and fear not. This is a good sign, for these three suns stand in token of the Father, the Son and the Holy Ghost, and therefore let us have a good heart, and in the name of Almighty God go against our enemies.' Other authors have suggested he punned upon the notion of the sun and of the three surviving sons of York: himself and his younger brothers, George and Richard. Shakespeare's version of the event stresses the sense of unity placed on this moment, and Edward later adopted the symbol of the sunne in splendour, with its sense of divine approval, for his reign:

> Three glorious suns, each one a perfect sun;
> Not separated with the racking clouds,
> But sever'd in a pale clear-shining sky.
> See, see! They join, embrace and seem to kiss,
> As if they vow'd some league inviolable:
> Now are they but one lamp, one light, one sun.
> In this the heaven figures some event.

The sun was of particular importance to Edward, in an era when heraldic devices featured on badges, banners and homes. From the age of fifteen he had owned a copy of Roger Bacon's translation of *Secretum Secretorum*,[16] an Arabic treatise covering topics of magic, astrology, alchemy, medicine, statescraft and similar topics. This text associated the health of the country with the power of the king, who was himself connected with the heat and life of the sun. Thus, the appearance of the sun at this critical time threw Edward's abilities into relief beside the weak direction and ill health of Henry VI. Edward was soon to order the minting of new pennies in his name to feature the Yorkist white rose, a cross and the rising sun.

Edward's stirring words to his men proved decisive. At Mortimer's Cross, he won a great victory over the combined forces of Owen

Tudor, the king's stepfather; his son Jasper, Earl of Pembroke; and James Butler, Earl of Wiltshire. Owen was captured and taken to Hereford, where he was led to the marketplace and beheaded, despite believing until the last that his life would be spared. As Gregory's Chronicle relates, his final words were 'that hede shalle ly on the stocke that was wonte to ly on Quene Kateryns lappe' and his head was set upon the market cross where a madwoman combed his hair, washed the blood off his face and set more than a hundred candles to burn around him. Warwick was still in London with Henry when reports reached him of Edward's victory and Margaret's impending return to the capital. He readied himself at once to intercept her, leaving with a significant Yorkist force drawn from the southern counties. A. C. Gigli wrote to an associate in Brussels that

> the King and my Lord of Warwick left here on the 12th, with a large concourse (grande populo) from Kent and the surrounding districts, as well as from this place, with them, and the Dukes of Norfolk and Suffolk, the Treasurer, my Lord of Bonavilla, and councillors and many other noblemen, to encounter their opponents, who were said to be thirty miles from here.[17]

Just two weeks later, Warwick's army met with the forces of the queen at St Albans. Having also lost his father at Wakefield, the earl was keen to exact retribution on Beaufort and other of the queen's advisors, writing to the Pope early in January that 'with the help of God and the King, who is excellently disposed, all will end well'.[18] He also had to prevent Margaret's army from reaching London, without the support of Edward and his Welsh troops. Thus the strategically placed town was subjected to a second battle, which proved to be a decisive victory for the Lancastrians. The mood had changed since 1455, when the first bloodshed was met with a sort of numb shock, a reconciliation and pardons in Parliament. Six years later, the armies were larger and those involved had more scores to settle. The codes of chivalry, so important in defining the nature of the earlier conflicts, had been overturned by acts considered to be cowardly and treasonous. This was to be no half-hour skirmish. Warwick had brought a number of savage instruments of war into the town, including caltrops, which were spiked metals balls half-buried in the ground, to catch horses' hooves or men's feet, and pavisses, large shields that sat on the ground and allowed an arrow to be shot through a narrow slit. He led the central third of his army, flanked by his brother John Neville, Marquis of Montagu, and John de Mowbray, Duke of Norfolk. It may have been their enemy's superior numbers or Warwick's position that meant he was unable to move his troops freely. On 17 February, around 10,000 or 12,000 Lancastrians isolated Warwick's archers in the driving rain and snow and inflicted huge casualties. The town was then subjected to ravishment by the royal army, whom the eyewitness Abbot Whethamsted likened to rabid animals.

Warwick had been in charge of Henry VI, who had been positioned in the Yorkist camp about a mile out of the town. The Milanese ambassador describes how he was found sitting under a tree 'where he laughed and sang' and welcomed his liberators. Two men set to guard him were sentenced to death, in a decision attributed to Queen Margaret, who is reputed to have asked her eight-year-old son, Edward, what their fate should be. The truth of this may never be known; it may be as much a colourful anecdote to discredit the queen by her enemies as the equally scurrilous rumours spread about the Yorkists at the time. The key players emerged unscathed from St Albans, but the battle did claim one significant loss. Elizabeth Woodville may well have been with her mother, among the royal party who were staying in the Abbey,[19] or she may have been awaiting news at Astley. Either way, the news was bad. Within hours or days, Elizabeth learned that her husband, John Grey, had been killed during or as a result of the fighting; had she been in St Albans she may even have seen his body, or been at his side as the injured were brought into the abbey. She was now a widow with the future of two sons to consider. It is likely that at this point, or soon after, she went with her mother to Grafton.

Warwick's defeat left the road to London open. Now with one victory apiece, the decisive question was which side would take the city and, by extension, the country. However, London itself had an opinion on this, as reports had already reached the capital about the behaviour of Margaret's armies: of the looting, rape and pillaging in the town of Beverley on 12 January and other similar acts as they moved south. The Croyland Chronicle described how this unleashed a swathe of general anarchy. When the army ran amok, 'paupers and beggars flocked forth ... in infinite numbers ... and universally devoted themselves to spoil and rapine, without regard of place or person'. The Brut Chronicle has that 'the city of London dreaded being robbed and despoiled' and a letter from the papal legate Francesco Coppini, who had sided with the Yorkists, described the atmosphere there:

> The people are incensed and in the worst possible humour against those who do not desire peace. There are two reasons for this: firstly, the countless acts of cruelty related of [the queen's] party, whereas [the Yorkists] with him and ourself with them are really disposed to an honest and honourable peace, salutary for both parties.

In Norfolk, Clement Paston echoed this fear on 23 January, praising the readiness of those who followed their lords and helped defend the country against 'the pepill in the northe (who) robbe and styll ... and gyffe a way mens goods'.[20] Another letter in the Milan Archives,[21] written two days after the St Albans battle, states that the city gates were kept closed, under a 'good guard', so that the people did not suffer from 'harm or lack of governance'. Tut they were still very wary, however, as 'the shops keep closed, and nothing is done either by the tradespeople or by the merchants, and men do not stand in the streets or go far away from home'.

In an extraordinary move, the city sent a delegation of aristocratic ladies north to meet Margaret – Elizabeth's mother, Jacquetta; the widowed Lady Scales; and Edward's aunt, the widowed Duchess of Buckingham – to persuade the queen to restrain her troops. Margaret agreed, but added that 'at the same time they did not mean that they would not punish the evildoers'. Jacquetta may have been chosen because Richard Woodville was then leading part of the Lancastrian army and had also at this time persuaded his friend Sir Henry Lovelace, Warwick's Steward, to betray his lord and support Henry VI.[22] London awaited news. The city magistrates issued a proclamation that all citizens should 'keep fast' to their houses and 'live at peace' to allow the Lancastrians to return, but the queen turned her main army away and headed for Dunstable. Giving the appearance of retreat, she then dispatched two bands of soldiers to attempt to break through the city gate at Aldgate.[23] It was an unexpected move that changed the direction of the conflict. Reports that Edward and Warwick were heading towards the capital with a large army sent the people into turmoil. As the *Brut* relates, the pair responded cleverly, by sending 'word to the mayor and city' that they would protect London from the marauding enemy. The citizens were 'glad of their coming, hoping to be relieved by them' and after Edward arrived on 27 February, he conferred with the lords and estates, who 'concluded forasmuch as King Henry was gone northward, that he had forfeited his crown and ought to be deposed'.

Following the death of his father and the breach of the Act of Accord, Edward was going to settle for nothing less than the throne. All pretence of serving Henry was now abandoned. Now that the Yorkists had lost control of him, they could no longer claim to be fighting in his name, nor could they summon troops to fight in the king's name, unless they created an alternative king of their own. The Croyland Chronicle described Edward's popularity and suitability as a leader, being 'received with unbounded joy by the clergy and all the people, and especially by the citizens of London; and amid all the acclamations of all he was made King of England ... for he was then of vigorous age, and well fitted to endure the conflicts of battle, while, at the same time, he was fully equal to the management of the affairs of the state'.

On 1 March, Warwick's brother George Neville, Archbishop of Exeter since 1458, addressed a group assembled at St John's Field at Clerkenwell, explaining Edward's claim to the throne and listing the ways in which Henry had broken his promises. The crowd were then asked if Henry should remain king and the response was a predictable and resounding denial. Edward was proclaimed king instead. The London Chronicle adds that 'it was demanded of the people whether Henry was worthy to reign as king any longer or not. Whereunto the people cried hugely and said Nay, nay. And after it was asked of them whether they would have the Earl of March for their king, and they cried with one voice, Yea yea.' Gregory has a different comment, equally positive, which states that all the city 'thonkyd God and sayde that he that had London forsake wold no more to them take' and 'lette us walke in a new wyne yerde and lette us make us a gay garden in the monythe of Marche with this fayre white rose and herbe, the Earl of Marche'. Celebratory poems, such as 'The Battle of Towton', also used the image of the rose of Rouen and helped established the iconography of the Yorkist regime:

Now is the rose of Rone [Rouen] growen to a gret honoure,
Therfore syng we everychone, 'I-blessid be that floure!'
I warne you everychone, for you shuld understonde,
There sprange a rose in rone [Rouen] and sprad into englonde ...

The northen party made hem strong with spere and with sheld;
On palmesonday affter the none the met us in the feld.
With-in an owre the were right fayne to fle and als to yeld
xvii thousand the rose kyld in the feld.
Blessid be the tyme that euer god spred that floure.

Gregory's Chronicle also contained the verse,

The Rose came to London, full royally riding
Two archbishops of England they crowned the Rose King
Almighty Lord! Save the Rose, and give him his blessing,
And all the realm of England joy for his corowning,
That we may bless the time that ever God spread that flower.

Edward remained at Baynard's Castle, where messengers brought him the news, whom he received cordially, thanking them and God. Two days later proclamations were read in London, summoning the people to assemble at St Paul's. Edward solemnly processed there in the company of other Yorkist lords to hear a Te Deum sung in the cathedral before riding to Westminster Palace. Wearing royal robes, he took the sceptre in his hand and the cap of estate on his head, before sitting down in the king's marble chair. On 4 March, he swore the royal oath, marking the start of his reign, although his coronation and anointing would not follow until that June. Two days later he issued proclamations to the sheriffs of thirty-three counties, asking that they accept him as king and promising that any Lancastrians that submitted to his authority within ten days would have 'grace and pardon of his life and goods'. A small number of Lancastrians were named, including those who had deserted at Ludford Bridge and fought at Wakefield, as being exempt from this pardon, and a price of £100 was put on their heads. It was a far better stage-managed coup than York had attempted the previous October, amid very different circumstances, yet Edward could not have done it without the existence of the Act of Accord. Warwick and his brother clearly played a key role, but the earl should not necessarily be judged with the hindsight that later generations used to award him the epithet of 'Kingmaker.' He had recently suffered the defeat of St Albans while Edward was the victor of Northampton and Mortimer's Cross, and the driving force behind these events. Edward certainly needed Warwick's support, but he was the one with the royal claim, confirmed by the Act of Accord, and it was his military genius and charisma which won the battles that brought him the throne. However, his throne was not yet secure: there was one more decisive battle to win. England had room for only one king.

29 March 1461, Palm Sunday, has been described, with considerable justification, as the 'most brutal day in English History'.²⁴ Edward's army assembled between the villages of Saxton and Towton, in the midst of a terrible snow storm, with the sleet driving in their faces as they scanned the fields and nearby river. The Yorkists were low on supplies and the day before had suffered a demoralising attack by a group of rogue Lancastrians who ambushed them at Ferrybridge, which deprived them of the lead of Lord Clifford and around 500 men. Warwick escaped with an arrow wound to the leg. However, the army was still a sizeable force, with estimates of its numbers suggesting 35,000,²⁵ and perhaps 10,000 more on the new king's side. Over half England's peerage turned out to support Henry. Among the ranks opposing Edward, Fauconberg and Warwick, were Sir Richard Woodville and his son Anthony, with Jacquetta and Elizabeth waiting anxiously at Grafton for news. According to the Croyland Chronicle, they engaged in 'a most severe conflict, and fighting hand to hand with sword and spear, there was no small slaughter on either side'. The London Chronicler called it a 'sore and long and unkindly fight' which pitted 'the son against the father, the brother against brother, the nephew against nephew', while Hearne's Fragment sets much of the action in the dark, amid the driving snow. The Yorkists had the south position with Queen Margaret's forces to the north; Edward had the advantage of the weather, with the wind behind his arrows, while those of the Lancastrians fell short

of their targets. Waurin pities the poorly equipped men: 'It was so cold from the snow and hailed so much that the armed men and horses were a pitiful sight and what made it worst for them, they were badly supplied.' In the middle of the afternoon, John Mowbray, Duke of Norfolk, arrived with fresh troops to swell the Yorkist army, and this no doubt proved decisive, in terms of morale as well as in numbers. An evocative account of the battle is given in a letter written by George Neville to Coppini, who was then in Flanders:

> That day there was a great conflict, which began with the rising of the sun, and lasted until the tenth hour of the night, so great was the pertinacity and boldness of the men, who never heeded the possibility of a miserable death. Of the enemy who fled, great numbers were drowned in the river near the town of Tadcaster, eight miles from York, because they themselves had broken the bridge to cut our passage that way [and] a great part of the rest who got away [were] slain and so many dead bodies were seen as to cover an area six miles long by three broad … Of the behaviour of the king [Edward IV] … in fighting manfully, in guiding, encouraging and re-forming [his] forces, I would rather your lordship hear it from others than from me.[26]

Croyland states that the Lancastrians were cut down in flight 'like so many sheep for the slaughter … [making] immense havoc among them for a distance of ten miles'. The Lancastrians fled west to the nearby River Cock, where many were drowned in the freezing waters; those who survived were pursued for miles and cut down. Croyland heard from those who helped bury the bodies afterwards that '38,000 warriors fell on that day, besides those who were drowned in the river'. Gregory claimed it was 35,000, Hearne placed the number slightly lower at 33,000 and modern estimates tend towards Neville's more cautious 28,000. Richard and Anthony Woodville survived the day – although Anthony was initially reported dead – and were among those Lancastrians captured in the aftermath. They were surprising survivors, as Edward had given the order that lords be killed rather than spared, and the vicious rout that followed the collapse of the king's army spared few men. Gregory's Chronicle claims that forty-two knights were captured and put to death after the battle. Henry VI, Margaret and their son, Edward, recognised the scale of their defeat and fled into Scotland, along with Beaufort and a small coterie of supporters.

Edward did not return to London at once. William Paston wrote to his brother John on 4 April that 'Oure soverayn lord hath wonne the feld and uppon the Munday next after Palme Sunday he was resseyved into York', where he spent Easter. William Paston suggests he was given a warm welcome, 'with great solemnity and processions' and while there he ensured that the heads of his father, brother, Salisbury and Sailsbury's son Thomas were removed from Micklegate Bar. According to Gregory, Edward 'tarried in the North a great while and made enquiries of the rebellions against his father' and 'made alle the contray to ben sworne unto hym and his lawys'. Herne tells us he went on to Durham, then Newcastle, and was at the family home of Middleham on 6 May, 'setting all things in good order in the north'. The Lancastrian cause was decimated and its duchy lands absorbed into the crown's estate. On 14 May, the Woodville men were attainted as traitors and had their lands confiscated.

III

The situation was just as unpromising for Elizabeth. Not only had she lost her husband at St Albans, but in retrospect he was judged guilty of treason for taking arms against Edward and his estates were forfeit to the crown, including a Leicestershire estate known as Bradgate Park, which was part of the manor of Groby. This meant that Elizabeth's sons could not inherit their father's lands, although there should still have been the inheritance of their grandparents to provide for their future. One of her early twentieth-century biographers, David MacGibbon, suggests that Bradgate was seized by Warwick, in a 'cruel confiscation' as a means of punishing the widow for having married Grey instead of his candidate, Sir Hugh Johns,[27] but this can only be a matter of speculation.

Elizabeth had hoped to rely upon the financial support of her husband's mother, Elizabeth Ferrers, Baroness Ferrers of Groby, but this was not to be. The baroness had been widowed in 1456, with her husband Edward dying soon after his son's marriage to Elizabeth. However, the first baron had made provision for his heirs by arranging for the income of three manors to be set aside as their income, totalling an annual 100 marks. This should automatically have gone to Elizabeth's sons upon their father's death, and in February 1461, when John lost his life at St Albans, she would have assumed they would be well looked after. However, at some point before May 1462, the baroness remarried a much younger man – one of King Edward's cousins named Sir John Bourchier, who was the son of the late Duke of York's sister Isabel. Bourchier assumed the title of baron, along with all its privileges, and there followed some disagreement as to whom this portion originally intended for old baron's heirs should be paid. It left Elizabeth in a difficult financial situation, dependent upon her parents with her sons' futures uncertain. It may have been during this period of concern that she first met the new Yorkist king. Twenty-first century readers must not allow their hindsight to colour this occasion: there is no way that Elizabeth could have known she would become Edward's wife. If she saw him at all, it was as the leader of a dynasty which had deprived her of her husband, her future and her inheritance.

In June, Edward spent two days at Stony Stratford, just five miles south of Grafton. It would appear that the Woodvilles took this opportunity to submit to him, or he summoned them to do so and they complied, as before he left, he instructed his chancellor that 'of our grace especial' he had 'pardoned and remitted and forgiven unto Richard Woodville, knight, Lord Rivers, all manner of offences and trespasses of him done against us'. This was dated to 12 June, and included the reinstated income of 300 marks that was due to Jacquetta as Bedford's widow, with the stipulation that 100 marks should be made available to her immediately. Only a month had passed since Edward declared the Woodville men traitors. What had changed his mind? Did he see Elizabeth at this point? The Woodvilles may not have judged this to be the right moment to raise her inheritance, as she was later forced to write to Lord Hastings to ask for assistance in the matter. The business of the moment for the Woodvilles was to submit to Edward's kingship and ensure good relations with the new regime. It is likely that the young king saw Elizabeth during his brief stay in the area, and admired her, perhaps even recognised her from any former acquaintance that the small court circle would have facilitated. His attraction to her may have encouraged him to forgive her male relatives, whom he had so roundly abused at Calais a year before. However, none of this can be stated with any degree of certainty. That autumn, as Warkworth relates, Richard was knighted as part of Edward's peacemaking appointments: 'The Lord Rivers Earl Rivers ... and other gentlemen and yeomen he made knights and squires, as they had deserved.'

Attempting to reconstruct something of Elizabeth's personal feelings during this time is fraught with difficulties. It is impossible to guess at the nature of her marriage to John Grey, or to suggest the extent of her grief. Fifteenth-century marriages could be cut short by illness, accident or warfare, and the notion of 'until death do us part' had far more relevance in a society when this event might only be short years away. Remarriage was common, partly for practical reasons, but this must be set alongside the frequent occurrences of matches of affection that did last decades, such as in the case of Elizabeth's parents. The question of whether or not Elizabeth had loved John Grey may be an anachronistic one; he had been a good match for her, had given her the status of a married woman and she had borne him two children. To lose the independence she'd had as a wife and return home to live under the roof of her parents was a backwards step in the eyes of society; in many ways a widow was infinitely less powerful than a wife, although the presence of her father and brothers meant she was not unprotected. Equally, it may have been that she had chosen Grey out of love, or had grown to love him, and was genuinely grieving his loss in 1461. She may have met Edward during this time and rejected any interest he expressed in her. She would certainly have been in mourning, and perhaps the young king respected this and kept his distance, although the memory of her beauty remained with him.

For Elizabeth, the immediate concerns were practical ones: providing for her sons and her future. Some widows entered religious establishments, but these were usually older women who were unlikely to marry again, who were childless or whose children were adults. Elizabeth knew she had to fight for her family. She was still young, attractive and had proved herself fertile. She would have been an excellent match for many suitors, especially those who might be harbouring Lancastrian sympathies given her mother's prior connections. MacGibbons states that Elizabeth 'doubtless received offers of marriage from not a few court gallants and country nobles and gentlemen'. He specifically names Jocelyn de Hardwycke of Bolsover, son of Sir John, nephew of 'the Stag of Hardwicke,' of Hardwick Hall in Derbyshire, who were cousins to John Grey's mother, Baroness Ferrers. MacGibbon draws on an 1845 essay by Henry Coore, which cites an old tradition that Elizabeth visited Hardwick Hall and agreed to marry Jocelyn, 'who had for a long time ardently admired her' although this was kept secret until the financial arrangements for her sons had been settled. [28] According to the very romantic-sounding legend recounted by Coore, Jocelyn and Elizabeth came across some 'gypsies' while hunting in Hardwick Park, one of whom related that 'a royal prince fair lady thou shalt wed but troubles dire shall fall upon thine head'.[29] As Elizabeth's later biographer David Baldwin rightly alerts us, this anecdote is highly suspicious, given the lack of source material when it comes to the connection, or indeed Jocelyn's existence, let alone the anachronistic appearance of the 'gypsies'.[30] It is claimed that Jocelyn never married, devoting 'his whole life to the service of his queen, whom he continued to adore as much as ever', although he later served Edward, sharing his exile in 1470–1, and was killed fighting for Henry Tudor at Bosworth in an attempt to rescue Elizabeth from Richard III. However, there is no knight named Hardwicke listed among the Yorkist retinue, suggesting that this story is a later elaboration.

It is more likely that Elizabeth remained in mourning, overseeing the education of her sons. Jacquetta had borne her last child in around 1458, so there were young children at Grafton for the Grey boys to play or share lessons with. Richard and Edward Woodville were born in around 1453 and 1454, with their two younger sisters Mary and Catherine arriving in 1456 and 1458. Given that the family fortunes had been so intimately connected with the house of Lancaster, the new regime opened a chapter of uncertainty in the Grafton household. The women probably recognised that they needed to wait for the dust to settle to see the extent of the changes, such as whether Jacquetta would continue to receive the income she was entitled to as Bedford's widow or whether the new king would be receptive to their petitions for aid.

Edward's coronation took place on 28 June 1461. He made his state entry into London two days before, riding along the south bank of the Thames to be met by the mayor and aldermen dressed in scarlet and 400 commoners in green. They accompanied him through the city to the Tower, where he carried out the ceremony of appointing new Knights of the Bath, including his younger brothers, George and Richard, as well as those who had fought beside him at Towton. Edward was anointed and crowned in Westminster Abbey on St Peter's Day, 'with great solemnity of bishops and other temporal lords. And upon the morn after, the King went crowned again in Westminster ... in the worship of God and St Peter.' Then, unusually, he was crowned for a second time in St Paul's, perhaps to allow for the presence of larger numbers of witnesses in a coronation for the commoners, 'at which time there was as great a multitude of people in Paul's as ever was seen afore in any days'.[31]

A series of coronation verses written in the form of an acrostic called 'Twelve Letters to Save England' proclaimed support for the new regime: 'For the wylle of Edward, kyng most ryall, that is the moste purpos that we labour for.' Edward's succession was also heralded with poetry in Bristol – 'Welcome Edwarde our son of high degree' – and the verses composed in the next year or so, called 'Edward Dei Gratia', stress his right to rule 'oute of the stock that longe lay dede' and that he had divine support, as 'God hathe chose thee to be his knight'. These and other poems emphasised Edward's descent from Edward III and the usurpation of his line by Henry Bolingbroke in 1399. 'A Political Retrospect' used the metaphor of an overgrown garden for the Lancastrian regime, with Edward finally vanquishing the languorous black clouds of the unstable Henry VI and restoring order and harmony to the country as the true heir:

> Wherfore, I lykken Engkland to a gardayne
> Which that hath been overgrowen many yere
> With wedys, which must be mowen down plain
> And than shal the pleasant swete herbes appere.

Wherfore all trewe englyssh people, pray in fear
for King Edward of Rouen, our comforter,
That he keep Justice and make wedes clear
Avoyding the black clouds of languor.

In the space of a few weeks, Edward had won what had initially seemed like an impossible victory, against heavy odds. Less than a year earlier, he had been in exile in Calais, an attainted traitor who had fled the battlefield in ignominious darkness. Undoubtedly, Edward's own considerable abilities lay behind his meteoric rise to power, but it had been a collaborative effort, building on York's long years of striving, the achievement of the Act of Accord and the support of Warwick and his Neville relatives. Yet it was Edward who had been crowned in Westminster Abbey, Edward whose signature would appear on new laws and appointments, Edward who had the final say. And he would not forget it.

4

TO FULFIL AN IDEAL
1461–1464

'Princely and knightly courage.'

I

It is difficult to underestimate the impact Edward's succession made in 1461. After years of uncertainty, characterised by losses in France, insurrection, an unstable king, unpopular favourites, warfare and political volatility, Edward's youth, ability and good looks confirmed the contemporary notion of what a king should be. More than that, he had won a string of military victories and played his hand well, seizing opportunities as they arose without making some of the tactical blunders his father had committed. Contemporary literature such as the *Secreta Secretorum* and *De Regimine Principum* expressed an ideal of majesty correlative with ideals of masculinity, thus in every way the king was the ideal man: a heroic and successful leader, just and fair, virtuous and devout. John Fortescue, writing to guide Henry VI's son, drew from the Book of Kings to state that 'the office of a King is to fight the battles of his people and to judge them rightfully'.[1] Of all these qualities, the most significant testing ground was warfare, with the poet Thomas Hoccleve writing that a king should be so 'manly of corage and herte' that he would rather die fighting than 'cowardly and shamefully flee'. In the 1450s, William Worcester added that the 'manly man' fought for himself and his fellowship and would not abandon his companions, although he had wisdom enough to know when to fight and when to retreat.[2] It would have been difficult for Edward's contemporaries not to be influenced by the comparison of his deeds on the battlefield with the image of Henry VI sitting under a tree and laughing to himself as his troops clashed with Warwick at St Albans. With a king's health being considered intimately connected to the 'health' of his nation, or 'commonweal', Edward's prowess promised to bring back a much needed peace and stability to England.

Firstly, Edward looked the part. His subjects were used to decoding the visual symbols of kingship: the jewels, fabrics, servants and palaces which accompanied the king, setting him apart from his fellow man, even elevating him to the status of a divinely appointed figure – something of a super being. It followed that the more showy the wealth and exaggerated the style, the more power an individual wielded. Put simply, money mattered, and the show of majesty was often enough to convince the relevant audience that they were witnessing true majesty. A significant factor of Henry VI's weakness had been his inability to play the part convincingly, in terms of his behaviour and appearance. He favoured plain and simple clothing over ermine and cloth of gold, and his preferred lifestyle was ascetic rather than luxurious – he would wear a rough hair shirt next to his skin on the occasions of feast days. Sir John Fortescue's treaty, *De Laudibus Legum Anglae* or *The Governance of England*, had exhorted Henry to dress the part, in 'rich clothes and rich furs ... rich stones and other jewels and ornaments ... rich hangings and other apparel for horses'. Henry was a model of piety, but not of kingship. Throughout his reign, Edward understood the need for finery, rewriting the sumptuary laws in 1463 and 1465 to control what each rank of society could wear, setting the trend in European fashion and remodelling his court along Burgundian lines. In 1466, he would award his wife annual wardrobe expenses of £1,200 and purchased a jewel worth £125 to celebrate the birth of his daughter.

Edward was also very handsome. All his surviving portraits date from after his death and although fashions in beauty change, none seem to do justice to the glowing descriptions that date from his early years. When his skeleton was measured in 1789, he was found to have stood six foot three and a half inches tall, considerably more than Henry VI at five foot nine or ten. The German visitor Gabriel Tetzel, who met Edward in 1466, called him 'a handsome upstanding man', while the Croyland Chronicler, who may or may not have had access to the court, said that 'when in the flower of his age' Edward was 'tall of stature ... [and] elegant of person, of unblemished character, valiant in arms, and a lineal descendant of the illustrious line of King Edward III'. Thomas More, who was five when Edward died, said he was 'of visage lovely, of body mighty, strong and clean made' and Polydore Vergil, who never saw Edward in person, moving to London in 1502, repeated the view that Edward was 'very tall of personage, exceeding the stature of almost all others, of comely visage, pleasant looks [and] broad breasted'. There is no doubt that Edward was incredibly handsome.

In addition, Edward appears to have been genuinely popular – above the expected platitudes of contemporary chroniclers and those writing in the reigns of his descendants. He was generous and forgiving, according to Vergil, provoking 'the people to love him with all kinds of liberality', and was friendly and familiar towards all, of high or low birth. He knew his place and what was due to him, but early accounts suggest he had something of 'the common touch'. A newsletter in the Milanese State Papers describes how Edward had become king, as a 'boon from above', with the author adding that 'words fail me to relate how well the commons love and adore him, as if he were their God'. The flip side of this appears to have been his appetite for women, and it seems quite likely that he had a number of affairs or casual encounters during the first years of his reign. As Gregory's Chronicle states, 'Men marvelled that our sovereign lord was so long without any wife,' and it was 'ever feared that he had not been chaste in his living'. Mancini added that Edward pursued the 'married and unmarried, the noble and lowly', and Vergil, writing retrospectively, stated that Edward would 'readily cast an eye upon young ladies'. Even Thomas More described the king's 'greedy appetite' for women. This was hardly a new vice for a king, nor for a young man of such good looks following a meteoric rise to power, but his early amours would later resurface to the cost of his dynasty.

Some had doubts about the new king on account of his youth and inexperience. The Bishop of Elphin feared that Edward was too much under the influence of his mother, Cecily, writing to Coppini that she held him 'at her pleasure', while Coppini was also urged by his doctor to write to congratulate Edward, 'not forgetting on any account, to write to the Duchess of York'. King Louis of France commented that England had 'but two rulers– M. de Warwick and another, whose name I have forgotten'. Most of these doubts came from outside the realm. Those who had witnessed Edward in action on the battlefield had little doubt about his leadership abilities and the frequent occurrence of his signature or initials upon government documents right from the start of his reign attests to his extensive personal involvement. Edward clearly practised a general policy of forgiveness and generosity, with some notorious Lancastrians escaping the process of attainder, which drew criticism of the king in some quarters. The Paston Letters include the observation that the common people 'grudge and say how that the King receiveth such of this country ... as have been his great enemies, and oppressors of the commons, and such as have assisted his highness, be not rewarded; and it is to be considered, or else it will hurt'.[3] Some were openly hostile, as was to be expected, with a London notary, John Clerk, refusing to go and see Edward's coronation, saying, 'Twat and turd for him: I would as readily see the hunting of a duck, as him!'[4] However, Edward was quick to respond to the reports of uprisings and discontent that arose in the winter of 1461/2.

After six decades of Lancastrian rule, many of Henry VI's supporters were, understandably, not prepared to give up on the line of Henry IV and Henry V, for the sake of this newly arrived young man, no matter how much he looked the part. Some of these loyalists had invested in the old dynasty through three or more generations of service, and the livelihoods of their families were tied to Lancastrian fortunes. Many had resisted York's claim to the throne and opposed the Act of Accord. Pockets of resistance sprang up in Hampshire in November, followed by the west in January and in the Midlands weeks later. On 12 February, a plot was uncovered led by John de Vere, 12th Earl of Oxford, which was particularly disappointing for Edward, as De Vere had served under York in Rouen during the 1440s, where his wife had borne his second son, John, just months after Edward's own arrival. Yet there could be no mercy for such obvious treachery. The earl and his eldest son, Aubrey, were executed along with Sir Thomas Tuddenham at Tower Hill at the end of February. Edward allowed his contemporary John to inherit his father's title although the new earl would continue to have fluctuating loyalties towards the Yorkist regime. Also in February, Edward established a commission of barons and judges to investigate and try cases of treason and rebellion. He knew the Lancastrian cause still had many supporters and the threat had by no means been vanquished.

Edward also understood the need for the king, especially a new king, to be a visible presence. Today, famous faces are immediately accessible on and made familiar by the internet, but before the arrival of the printing press in England or a reliable system for disseminating news, there was no substitute for the king's physical presence; otherwise he was expecting people in the far-flung corners of his realm to profess loyalty to an abstract ideal alone, in which case, one king was as good as any other. Henry VI had been on the throne for almost forty years, since he was an infant, so it was important that his replacement should appear in person before his people, and seen to be an instrument of peace and justice. In 1461, following his victory at Towton, Edward travelled in the Marches and south-west, before heading up to Newcastle and witnessing the execution of his father's old enemy James Butler on 1 May. Then the new king went south through traditional Lancastrian territories, staying overnight at Preston, Warrington, Manchester, Chester, Stafford, Eccleshall, Lichfield, Coventry, Warwick and Daventry.⁵ That summer following his coronation, Edward travelled through the south, from east to west, starting in Sandwich and Canterbury, reaching Lewes in West Sussex on 23 August, then on through Hampshire, Salisbury and Devizes, reaching Bristol on 4 September. Here, a pageant was performed for him at Temple Gate and Temple Cross, with St George slaying a dragon and William the Conqueror appearing while a king and queen watched from a castle. According to Chilcott's *Descriptive History of Bristol*, Edward ordered the execution of a Lancastrian knight, Charles Baldwin or Baldwin Fulford, and his two squires on his visit, standing in a window to watch them ride past on their way to their deaths. The scene was immortalised by the eighteenth-century Bristolian poet Thomas Chatterton:

Kynge EDWARDE sawe the ruddie streakes
Of lyghte eclypse the greie;
And herde the raven's crokynge throte
Proclayme the fated daie.

'Thou'rt ryght,' quod hee, 'for, by the Godde
That syttes enthron'd on hyghe!
CHARLES BAWDIN, and hys fellowes twain,
To-daie shall surelie die.

The knight speaks passionately in defence of Henry VI, describing Edward as 'exalting' himself, suggesting usurpation or overreaching, but he also refers to 'Richard's sonnes', which includes Edward's brothers George, Duke of Clarence, and Richard III, reminding us of this poem's historical perspective.

'Ne! hapless HENRIE! I rejoyce,
'I shalle ne see thye dethe;
'Moste willynglie ynne thye just cause
'Doe I resign my brethe.

'Oh, fickle people! rewyn'd londe!
'Thou wylt kenne peace ne moe;
'Whyle RICHARD'S sonnes exalt themselyes,
'Thye brookes wythe bloude wylle flowe.

'Saie, were ye tyr'd of godlie peace,
'And godlie HENRIE'S reigne,
'Thatt you dydd choppe youre easie daies
'For those of bloude and peyne?

Edward stayed in Bristol for a week, lodging with the mayor, forging important deals and connections with the city's trading quarter. From there, he travelled to Gloucester, Hereford and home to Ludlow on 18 September. He stayed there eight days, granting the town a new charter for 'the laudable and gratuitous services which our beloved and faithful subjects the burgesses of the town of Ludlow have rendered unto us',[6] and then returned to London, in time for the meeting of his first parliament. The following

January he was in Kent, then Cambridgeshire, Huntingdonshire and Lincolnshire in March. In Norfolk, Margaret Paston was relieved at the change of leader, writing that she hoped for 'a good rule and a sad in this country in haste, for I heard never say of so much robbery and manslaughter in this country as is now within a little time'.

Edward may have taken advice from his mother, but from the very start he was an active and involved king. His earliest appointments show that he was keen to restore law and order and be a visible leader of his council during the six months between the summoning of his first parliament and its meeting that November. A sprinkling of those rewarded during Edward's first months as king gives a good flavour of the way he rewarded loyal friends and family. There was some continuity: among the subsidies, manors, lordships, farms and incomes, many existing arrangements were confirmed in the Close Rolls in additional to new appointments and grants. That June a number of men, including Thomas Osborne, William Eustace, William Philip, Edward Skelton, Thomas Walton and Walter Bright were awarded 12*d* a day as the king's sergeants at arms, with a new livery gown made for them each year. The royal wardrobe was also instructed to cater for men such as James Damport and John Convers, who were made squires of the household, and John Brycheold, the king's plumber. An Edmund Glase was made clerk of the king's aviary, while Richard Willy received 6*d* a day as yeoman of the beds. John Wykes was appointed controller of the king's mines, drawing an annual revenue in silver and gold from Devon and Cornwall; the citizens of Winchester were instructed to pay an annual salary to a Thomas Walterot 'for good service' On 1 July, the county of Cornwall was ordered to pay John Dynham 600 marks, 'as he lent the king that sum in his need' during his flight in 1459. A William Hill became purveyor of all the masonry and stoneworks at Westminster and the Tower, and Richard Whetehill was appointed Controller of Calais. William Lee, a citizen of London, was granted the office of janitor of the Tower of London at 12*d* a year, and Thomas Stratton, whom Edward appointed to be clerk and overseer of his works, was to have 'during his good behaviour' certain liveries 'of raiment, furring and lining of tartron' or tarterin. This seems to have been standard for all Edward's court. William Cotton, keeper of the great wardrobe, and Edmund Blake, clerk of the king's works, had an allowance of nine yards of cloth and one piece of tartron for the summer and nine yards of long coloured cloth, eight rows of furring and thirty-two venters of miniver for their hoods.[7] Soon the corridors of Westminster were thronging with men dressed in the York colours of murrey and blue.

Loyal friends were rewarded in the first few years of Edward's reign. At the time of the coronation, Warwick was an earl, Great Chamberlain, Constable of Dover and the Cinque Ports, Master of the King's Falcons and had custody of various stewardships and lordships throughout the realm. That December he was made a Steward of England and the following year he became Lieutenant of the North and Warden of the West Marches, bringing him a lucrative salary. His brother John, soon to be marquis, received manors and lands and, in 1464, the earldom of Northumberland from the Neville's great rival family, the Percys. William Neville, Lord Fauconberg, soon to be earl, became an Admiral of England and received a number of lucrative lordships, as did his brother George, who would become Archbishop of York in 1465. In these first few years, a new Yorkist peerage was established, with Edward creating eight new barons and elevating others to earldoms, offering his own viable alternative to the old Lancastrian network of allegiance.

Edward's wider family were looked after too. As well as ennobling his younger brothers and providing for them and his unmarried sister, Margaret, Edward's mother Cecily was granted incomes from a number of towns, including Wyche in Worcester, the port of Kingston upon Hull and the city of York, to be paid to her annually on the anniversary of York's death at Wakefield. Margaret Talbot, neé Beauchamp, Countess of Shrewsbury and Warwick's wife's half-sister, was granted the wardship and marriage of Viscount Lisle's heir, while Richard Croft the younger, whose 'odious rule' at Ludlow had been a cause of complaint for a young Edward, was granted overseer of the manor of Woodstock and its gardens and meadows at 8*d* a day or 40*s* a year for life for his 'good service'. Some familiar names, famous to a twenty-first-century reader for their or their family's future roles in the dynasty, appear among these early appointments, picked out for the loyalty they had shown to the Yorkist cause. John Howard, Duke of

Norfolk, became Edward's carver, 'trusting in his loyalty' for £20 a year; Humphrey Stafford, Earl of Devon, was made Lord High Constable of England; and Ralph Hastings was given £50 a year for his 'good and unpaid service' for which he was now appointed an esquire of the body.[8]

Edward's first parliament met on 4 November. The speaker, Sir James Strangeways, praised the new king for his

> noble and worthy merits, princely and knightly courage, in ... great and victorious acts ... the beauty of person it has pleased Almighty God to send you, the wisdom that, by his grace, accompanies it, and the blessed and noble disposition and dedication of your said highness to the common weal and government of your said realm, and to God's church there.

It was an occasion to explain and justify the new regime, confirm the advancement of his supporters and punish the enemy. The London Chronicle tells us that 'many lords and barons were convicted and judged of treason [and] many notable manors and possessions were forfeited to the king', while 'many others that were of low degree [were] exalted to great honours and [given] such lords' lands as were overturned at the field'. Edward created George as Duke of Clarence and Richard as Duke of Gloucester, while John Dynham was knighted, John Neville became Marquis of Montagu, George Neville was confirmed as chancellor and Fauconberg was made Earl of Kent. It is also from this chronicle entry that the anecdote about Warwick derives, which has the earl holding court at his London house of L'Erber and keeping open house to such an extent that six oxen were consumed every day there at breakfast alone. The later historian Vergil described Edward at this time as inspiring 'the people generally to love him by all kinds of liberality, giving to the nobility most large gifts, and moreover, to gain universally the favour of all sorts, he used towards every man of high and low degree more than meet familiarity'.

First on Parliament's agenda were the recent events that put Edward in power, including the loss of his father: 'The pitouse and dolorouse Deth of that noble and famouse Prynce, and oure Ryght honourable Lord of worthy memorie, youre Fader the Duc of York, verey and rightful heire, and in Right King of the said reame.' This was the new regime's opportunity to record their version of history, to create a narrative as the victors of the struggles, to formalise their reasoning into fact. Its legal standard was the Act of Accord. Parliament stated that Edward had quite rightly acted upon the desire to avenge York and ascend the throne himself: 'It pleased your high Mageste, though all the sorowe and lamentacion ... to adjoyne youre moost noble persone of Knyghtly corage, according to the nature of youre high birth and the tender zeal and natural love that your seid Highness bare unto the defence ... of your seid Reaume and Subgetts and to the resistence of the malicious entent and purpose' of his enemies. Thus Edward had the claim of his royal descent, justified by the Act of the previous October, but he was also correct in taking England by the right of conquest. The terms of the Act had also compelled him to pursue York's killers, as their behaviour had been treasonable according to its terms. Divine approval was also cited: it had pleased God to grant Edward this victory 'to the grete and grounded joye and consolacion of youre seid Reame and Subgetts.' Next, the behaviour of Queen Margaret and her followers was further blackened: 'Destroying and spoiling [the land] ... neyther sparyng Godds chirch, the violation thereof, ne his ministers of the same, ravishing and defouling religious women, maidens, widows and men's wives; shedding in manner of tyranny innocent blode; entendynge to the fynall and extreme destruction and subversion or youre seid Reame.' During the time of Henry VI, according to this parliament, lawlessness had been common and Edward's role was to restore justice. Thus, Edward was justified again, in acting to restore order. He was thanked by Parliament on behalf of the commons, for his defence of London, for his wisdom, his noble merits, his princely and knightly courage, his great and victorious acts, his benign grace, his blessed disposition and the 'beaute of personage that it hath pleased Almyghty God to send You'.[9] Edward was now king in law as well as by descent and conquest.

In 1462, a specific threat arose in the north, as the Scots were preparing to invade in support of Henry VI and Margaret. The Lancastrians had been offered shelter by the young King James III and his mother, the regent Mary of Guelders, who was only four years younger than Margaret and understood what it was to be a foreigner protecting the rights of a child. Although there had been some skirmishes over the border castles, which continued to change hands that summer, a sizeable army was gathered, under the personal lead of the eleven-year-old James, who proceeded to besiege Norham Castle. Edward wanted to defeat the Lancastrian threat once and for all and make peace with the Scots, so he planned a major expedition north, drawing on Parliament and the clergy to fund him, and set out in July. However, Warwick and his brothers had already taken action, being established in the north. Edward only got as far as Northampton when he received word that they had successfully ended the siege and pursued the enemy back across the border. Margaret and Prince Edward fled abroad, separating from Henry, who was left behind in hiding in Scotland. Edward returned to the capital for a month or two, but by the end of September he was in York and remained there until New Year, watching the volatile situation closely. A truce would be agreed between England and the Scots in December 1463.

One of the key players in the north was Henry Beaufort, the young Duke of Somerset. In an extraordinary move, Edward now not only forgave Beaufort and overturned the Act of Attainder passed against him in November 1461, but drew him into his intimate court circle. From the start, the new king had actively provided for the widows and children of his enemies, with the old Duke of Somerset's widow, Margaret, having confirmed the £166 13s 4d she had been awarded annually for life by her husband, as well as £500 granted her by Henry VI. Beaufort had been sent by Queen Margaret on a mission to France to raise support for the Lancastrian cause, but returned home promptly on the death of the French king Charles VII. In his absence, his lands had been confiscated, the majority of which were given to the nine-year-old Richard, Duke of York. As late as autumn 1462, Beaufort was still fighting for the Lancastrians, leading their forces in Scotland and holding the fort of Bamburgh in Northumberland. By the end of the year, though, he had decided to make peace with Edward, surrendered his position and travelled to London. Edward granted him a pardon on 10 March and restored his titles and lands at the sitting of his second parliament, which met from 29 April 1463.

Just like Edward, Beaufort was a great-grandson of John of Gaunt and only five years older than the new king. The pair were natural companions, with Henry described by Chastellain as 'a great lord and one of the finest knights' in England. He had fought valiantly at the Battle of St Albans, where he may have witnessed his father's death, and been so badly wounded he was carried off in a cart. After this, he had briefly been placed in Warwick's custody, although he was back with his mother the following year. By 1463, Henry was considered the hope of the Lancastrian dynasty, and a royal match was proposed for him with his cousin Princess Joan of Scotland, whose mother had been a Beaufort. Quite what motivated him to align himself with the Yorkists is unclear, but it may have been in order to secure the release of his younger brother Edmund, who was then being held in Edward's custody. According to the chronicler Gregory, Edward and Henry became close: 'He lodged with the king in his own bed many nights and sometimes rode hunting behind the king ... the king loved him well.' It was not unusual for a king to have bedfellows of the same gender, for security and companionship. It was also a symbolic gesture: the ultimate way Edward could demonstrate his trust in his cousin was by allowing him to be present while Edward was at his most vulnerable. In summer 1463, Edward took Somerset with him when he rode north into Yorkshire, but the people there were less forgiving than their king. Beaufort was attacked by the common people at Northampton and they would have killed him if Edward had not saved him 'with fair speech and great difficulty'. He was sent to Chirk Castle for his safety, but either this incident or his isolation turned Beaufort back towards the Lancastrians. Inside the grey-stone bastion of the Mortimers, he began to plot his return, perhaps unnerved by the attack or seized by a sudden sense of guilt for betraying his own. Most modern historians are in agreement when they doubt that it was his intention all along to defect from Edward, but the truth of this cannot be stated categorically. Gregory's Chronicle has Beaufort sneaking away north around Christmas time that year, betraying the trust placed in him by his cousin.

The following April, John Neville, Earl of Montagu, was leading an army north to escort Scottish envoys to York, when he was ambushed by troops led by Beaufort. On 25 April, the young duke was outnumbered at the Battle of Hedgeley Moor and narrowly escaped with his life as his men scattered. The Lancastrian Sir Ralph Percy, long-standing enemy of the Nevilles, was killed in the fighting, and later that year Montagu was rewarded with the Percy title of Earl of Northumberland. On 15 May, Montagu surprised Beaufort at Hexham in Northumberland, bearing down upon the Lancastrians from high ground, so that they fled or floundered on the river bank. Montagu took a number of prisoners, perhaps around thirty leading Lancastrians, including Beaufort, and beheaded them in Hexham that evening. Somerset was buried in Hexham Abbey. This effectively decimated the dynasty's hopes in the north. Then, in 1465, Henry VI was captured. Warkworth tells us he was found in a religious house in Lancashire: 'He was betrayed, being at his dinner at Waddington Hall, and was carried to London on horseback, with his legs bound to the stirrups.' It seemed that Edward's regime was finally secure.

II

Yet Edward's court was to become more than just secure. It was to witness a cultural flourishing that not even his enemies would be able to quash, and an exuberance and vitality that could be seen to herald the arrival of the Renaissance in England. Edward's biographers have tended to focus more on his court during the second half of his reign, citing its considerable cultural achievements under the influence of his exile spent in Burgundy, and they are right to draw attention to the reorganisation of the royal household, the patronage of the printing press, the collection of illuminated manuscripts and the remarkable building programme that Edward established. Yet this has often been at the expense of exploring the cultural climate and achievements of his early years as king.

Any monarch needs time to establish their individual style; at the change of any regime there are threats to deal with, political and legal matters to resolve, a solid security required before culture can begin to flourish. Edward was certainly facing constant challenges from the Lancastrians, the Scots and French, which were not fully resolved until the Battle of Hexham in 1464. In addition, he was still very young in the early 1460s, but looking back upon those years, Privy Councillor Thomas Norton later reflected that the period 1464–5 was a golden age of patriotic idealism.[10] This was the result of Edward's character and his deliberate efforts to model himself upon the legendary King Arthur, a connection which was celebrated by one of the most famous poets of his reign.

After the long, difficult years under Henry VI, when the court was strung between the tensions of factional politics and the king's extreme piety, Edward's youthful chivalry presented something of a joyous contrast, a relief and change of direction. Edward was active and daring, where Henry was comparatively passive and timid; Edward was healthy and lusty, where Henry's reign had been caricaturised by periods of inertia and something of a prudish attitude towards matters of love. The new king was over two decades younger than Henry, young enough to be his son, and something of Edward's energy, his zest for life, now infused the corridors of Westminster. Henry's attitude towards his functional, ascetic clothing had set a sombre tone, whereas Edward went all out for colour and spectacle, although it was important to him that the proper rules of social entitlement were followed. Etiquette and manners, ritual and performance were an essential component of the chivalric order, with each man treated 'according to his degree' and even enemies like Henry Beaufort being treated with the dignity their rank required. Henry's restrained piety was now in direct contrast to Edward's vigorous masculinity, his prowess in battle and his imminent marriage and fatherhood. He had victories to celebrate, enemies to quash and, according to the chroniclers, women to woo: it was the stuff of legends, such as were found in the popular version of history told by Geoffrey of Monmouth. And at the centre of Monmouth's twelfth-century work, which had been taken to the heart of the English people, was the legendary King Arthur. Filled with his loyal Yorkists and Garter knights, Edward's early court established a new cultural mood, a new enthusiasm for life and its pleasures, and, as Arthur says in a later version of his story, told by Thomas Malory, his knights pleased him more 'than right great riches'.

The parallels between the English Knights of the Garter and Arthur's Knights of the Round Table were no accident. Malory's Arthurian oath taken at the round table, with its ideals of chivalric behaviour, was likely to have been based on that sworn by the Garter knights or combined with that of the Knights of the Bath.[11] The Order of the Garter was founded by the king's great-great-grandfather Edward III in 1348; representing the highest rank of chivalry, it is bestowed on St George's Day each year at Windsor Castle. The original knights were depicted in a manuscript of the Bruges Garter Book, made in London around 1430–40, which included Edward IV's other ancestor Roger Mortimer, from whom his York, Mortimer and March claims descended. Edward's later choice to found a chapel at Windsor dedicated to St George shows the importance of the order to him. Interestingly, when the order was founded there were 404 knights, but this had fallen to an all-time low of 193 in 1459, rising to 237 in 1465 after Edward's enthusiasm swelled the ranks.[12] Membership of this exclusive club was in Edward's gift, but was limited to twenty-five, including the king, as there were twenty-five knights pictured on the Winchester round table. Thus, members could only be appointed upon the deaths, disgrace or resignations of existing knights. It is in the context of this band of chivalric brothers that Edward's acceptance of Henry Beaufort in 1463 must be seen. Beaufort may have been a Lancastrian, but he was young, handsome and brave: an ideal companion for the new king. Edward's embodiment of the benevolent Arthur figure made him embrace his cousin and former enemy like a brother, taking him into his company and under his protection, like a chapter from the Arthurian tales. Beaufort's treachery only confirmed the literary trope of betrayal, reflecting Arthur's own experience of betrayal by his close friend Lancelot – initially portrayed as the ideal knight, the bravest and most true – or his son Mordred.

Edward's Garter knights were a mixed bag. He had inherited a number who had been appointed during the reign of Henry VI, although not all were Lancastrians: the Earl of Warwick, Lord Wenlock and William Neville, Lord Fauconberg, were among them. A number of Henry's knights had been killed in battle in 1459–61, so Edward was able to make a few new appointments of his own, choosing to honour his brother George, Duke of Clarence; John Tiptoft, Earl of Worcester; William Hastings, Baron Hastings; John Neville, Lord Montagu; William Herbert, Baron Herbert of Raglan; and Sir John Astley. With the exception of Clarence, most of these men were in their thirties, making a new, younger coterie than the old guard, such as Lord Wenlock, John Sutton, Baron Dudley, Henry Bourchier, Earl of Essex, and even Richard Woodville, who were two decades older.

In fact, Edward was doing more than simply following an Arthurian tradition. He was trying to be Arthur – to prove that he was, in fact, the second coming of the once and future king. Although Edward was not to father a legitimate son until 1470, there is also the compelling detail that his illegitimate child, probably fathered during these years, was given the name Arthur. From 1461 onwards, Edward ordered a number of genealogies to be drawn up tracing his descent back through the Mortimer line to Arthur and his heir Cadwallader, to delineate his English and Welsh roots. These were distributed among the nobility, who were tasked with spreading the word, equipped with the necessary evidence to squash dissenting Lancastrians. Edward's genealogists hailed him as 'Arthur returned from Avalon, the red dragon revived', a beast that was familiar to him from Monmouth's history, a copy of which was certainly owned by the York family, later finding its way into the possession of Richard, Duke of Gloucester. Professor Sydney Anglo has identified at least fifteen different documents drawn up at the time of Edward's reign to stress his link with Arthur and the superiority of the Yorkist claim.[13]

One of the surviving rolls, currently held in the Philadelphia Museum of Art, covers the period from 'Japhet the son of Noah lineally descending to Brutus the first king ... and from him to Edward the fourth king of that name', and even depicts the fall of Adam and Eve in the Garden of Eden. As his interpretation of the parhelion at Mortimer's Cross demonstrates, Edward was skilled in the use of images and symbols to further his cause. The Philadelphia Edward Roll uses the banners of St George, Constantine, Brutus, Saxon kings Ethelbert, Ethelred and Edmund the Martyr, King Arthur, as well as the king's more immediate family connections. Then there are the heraldic devices of Edward's sunburst and the Yorkist fetterlock and white rose, as well as the white lion of the earls of March and the white hart of Richard II, stressing that the king had named his Mortimer nephews as his heirs before being usurped by the Lancastrian line. Edward himself is portrayed as a knight on horseback, stressing his chivalric persona, underneath a range of symbols suggesting divine intervention. The roll also records his motto, 'comfort and joy', in stark contrast to Henry's '*modus et ordo*', or 'method and order'. Such genealogies were nothing new: they were part of an established dialogue between the warring factions of the fifteenth century, as a former Lancastrian roll had attempted to entirely exclude Edward III's second son, Lionel of Antwerp, from whom Edward VI drew his Mortimer claim. Other similar works featured images of Edward enthroned wearing the triple crown of England, France and Spain, or Edward and Elizabeth praying before God. This culture was echoed in one of the most significant literary works to come out of Edward's reign, Thomas Malory's *Le Morte d'Arthur.*

But who exactly was Thomas Malory, and was he in a position to be able to reflect Edward's personality and court in his poem? In fact, the composition of Malory's work, even the identity of the poet himself, has long been cause for speculation among scholars of literature and history. Malory himself places the completion of his work within the framework of Edward's reign, stating that it 'ended the ninth yere of the reygne of King Edward the Fourth', suggesting a date of 1469. His marginal comments and prayers imply that the work was written while Malory was in prison, central to contemporary events but temporarily distanced from them. It appears likely from the text that the author was inspired to use the fictional world of the Arthurian court to draw parallels with Edward's reign. However, *Le Morte d'Arthur* is not just a manual of chivalry; it addresses a shifting culture, a court in transition from the medieval to the modern, commenting on political issues and the natures of men.

Yet the identity of the poet has been called into question. A number of potential Thomas Malorys have been identified, raising the question of whether the author had knowledge of Edward's court to draw upon. Out of the potential candidates, a Sir Thomas Malory of Newbold Revel in Warwickshire, born between 1415 and 1418, appears the most likely. This Malory had a colourful career, frequently in and out of prison for a range of offences, including theft, kidnapping, extortion, rape and violence. Writing about *Le Morte d'Arthur* Richard Barber suggests that Malory's 'missing' years of 1462–8 were spent in some capacity at court; indeed, his name appears on the list of knights who attended Edward in 1462 on his planned trip north to Alnwick and Bamburgh, which resonates with Lancelot's deathbed line, 'Somme men say it was Anwyk and somme men say it was Bamborow.'

Barber poses the theory that Malory was employed in some 'low level' at court, but a 'little senior in standing to a Squire like John Paston'.[14] Not necessarily a member of Edward's court, but part of the 'throng of minor gentry' who attended it regularly in search of the king's favour, he was close enough to be able to comment upon the king and court. Malory was imprisoned between June 1468 and February 1470, during which period he appears to have composed his work, based upon Edward and his court. He died on 14 March 1471 and was buried in the Greyfriars Church near Newgate prison. At least two versions of his text survived, and were used by William Caxton to compile the version he printed in 1485.

While the concept of Camelot itself represents something of a Utopia, Malory identifies the historic city as having been Winchester, in Hampshire. However, when it came to recreating the city in poetic terms, which of his experiences of great castles and cities did Malory draw on when creating his literary images? Winchester had already been adopted as an Arthurian location during the reign of Edward III and Malory knew of the existence of the wooden round table there, perhaps falling in line with Hardyng's Chronicle, which indirectly locates Camelot in the city by stating that Uther Pendragon set up the table there. Malory mentions Winchester four times in the poem, but had he ever been to the city? At least one academic points out that it doesn't fit his descriptions. Winchester has the River Itchen, which rises in New Cheriton and flows for twenty-eight miles to Southampton; it isn't a long river, like the one described in *Le Morte d'Arthur*, which is capable of transporting large items to Camelot, such as the bier of Elaine, the Lady of Shalott, and the marble stone containing Balin's sword. Malory's river sounds more like one of the size and nature of the Thames. Winchester also lacks a St Stephen's Cathedral or Church.

It may be that Malory hadn't been to Winchester, or was fusing it with other places he knew well. John Rous, the author of a history of the Neville family, states that the city of Warwick was the original site of Arthur's court, with Warwick Castle itself as Camelot. This makes an interesting connection with Thomas Malory of Newbold Revel, a Warwickshire village just twenty miles to the north-east of the castle. Perhaps Malory had been to the castle, or at least seen it, and it provided him with inspiration when creating his own version of an idealised court. According to his biography, the poet served as a soldier under the Earl of Warwick and acted as a knight of the shire of the country from 1443, giving him ample opportunity to draw on his surroundings. Although Malory had been in and out of prison for various crimes, he had been pardoned by Edward in 1461. Ultimately though, his loyalties lay with Warwick, and it was his choice to side with the earl when he rebelled in 1468, for which he was arrested again.

So as Malory sat down to compose his work, picturing Arthur in his court at Camelot, he may have been imagining Winchester, or Warwick, or Westminster. Does it really matter? His audience would have been sophisticated enough to recognise that a process of poetic licence had taken place. There is a difference between attempting to locate Arthur's mythical city, which Malory certainly does, and drawing artistic inspiration from an existing court to craft a portrait. Also, Malory was imprisoned in London; perhaps he wanted to relocate Arthur's court for personal and political reasons, for the same motives that Shakespeare employed a range of 'foreign' locations to create a symbolic distance. What does seem significant, is that while Camelot may have been a moveable feast, Malory's King Arthur is likely to have been modelled upon Edward himself.

The theory of Edward-Arthur is a logical one, considering the king's own efforts to identify with the mythical king. Medievalist Beverley Kennedy goes further to associate the Arthurian triumvirate of Arthur, Lancelot and Gawain with the three York brothers, Edward, George and Richard. Similarly Edward's youthful choice of the beautiful Elizabeth, made for reasons of love alone, reflects Arthur's selection of Guinevere as a bride. Just as Arthur did, Edward began his reign with a period of 'judicial enquiry and restitution'[15] following the death of his father and his allies, as well as the continuing resistance of a number of Lancastrians. The confiscation and restoration of lands and titles took a considerable amount of Edward's attention in 1461–2, just as Malory described:

And many complayntes were made unto sir Arthur of grete wronges that were done syn the dethe of kyng Uther, of many londes that were bereved lords, knyghtes, ladyes and gentilmen; wherfor kyng

Arthur maade the londes to be yeven ageyne unto them that oughte them.

It was during the early part of Edward's reign that the identification of Edward with Arthur was established, as it was clearly widespread by 1471, when two different poets favourably compared the kings. Malory's portrayal of Edward's court is one of an idyll of chivalry and romance, with knights joined in fellowship and loyalty which turns to mistrust and betrayal. It illuminates the mood of Edward's early years, when he and Warwick were still close, and the deterioration into conflict that marred the later 1460s. Through the veil of popular storytelling, it comments upon the fissures that developed at court and the disintegration of the ideal group of brotherly knights. One of the first events to fracture the alliance of the knights would be the king's unexpected marriage.

Edward's court was certainly a dazzling place – a paragon of Arthurian elegance. Visiting England in 1466, Gabriel Tetzel was awed by the royal palaces, which were supplied 'in such costly measure ... that it is unbelievable that it could be provided' with furnishings of cloth of gold, velvet and damask, ermine and silk, making the English court the 'most splendid' in all Christendom. This was high praise indeed, considering that Tetzel had come straight from the Burgundian court, which was renowned for its culture and elegance. Even Croyland stated that it had 'no other appearance than such as fully befits a most mighty kingdom filled with riches'. The king came to be known for his fine clothing, with the richest furs and materials reserved for the elite, and for the elaborate protocol of the mid-1460s, which dictated that even high-ranking courtiers and relatives remain on their knees before their new queen. The anonymously written poem 'Urbanitatis', written to instruct young men at court in correct manners and decorum, is also likely to date from the early 1460s, with its advice to doff their cap before a lord, bow upon their right knee before the king and keep their chin up while speaking to him.[16] An emphasis was placed on music and the development of the chapel royal, with the 1465 reappointment of Henry Abingdon, Henry VI's overseer of the Children of the Chapel, at a salary of 40s, for the 'exhibition, instruction and governance of the Childer of our chapel'. However, perhaps the entertainment that most dominated

Edward's early court during times of peace was the Arthurian pastime of jousting. During the early 1460s, it became a regular court event for the first time since the days of Richard II.[17]

Froissart's Chronicles outline the key elements of the joust, including its connection with romantic love and its ritual and honourable nature, all of which appealed to Edward. At Windsor on 29 May 1466, Sir John Tiptoft, Earl of Worcester, drew up a list of rules at the king's request, 'to be observed or kept in all manner of jousts of peace royal, within this realm of England, reserving always to the queen, and to the ladies present, the attribution or gift of the prize, after the manner and form accustomed: to be attributed for their demerits according to the articles ensuing'. The Tiptoft rules state that prizes may be won by whoever breaks the most spears or bears a man down with a spear, but men might lose a prize if they strike a horse, or an opponent who had dropped their lance or whose back was turned. The 'most splendid tournament of the age' took place at Smithfield in June 1467, when Elizabeth's brother Anthony Woodville jousted against Antoine, Bastard of Burgundy, as part of the negotiations for the marriage of Edward's sister Margaret to Charles the Bold. Antoine, Charles's illegitimate half-brother, arrived in London on 30 May and was received by the king three days later.

The lists at Smithfield were 120 feet long and 10 feet wide, with galleries all around to accommodate the king, queen and many noblemen and women from England, Burgundy, France and Scotland, 'in their richest dresses'. On the day the tournament began, the two champions entered their pavilions and submitted to the rituals of being searched and questioned before fighting on foot with spears and both departing 'with equal honour'. On the next day, Antoine's horse was killed from under him as they fought with swords and Edward called the event to a halt, despite their protests. After that, they fought on foot again with pollaxes until the Burgundian's helmet was pierced and the king again intervened, instructing the marshal, John Howard, to separate them. Fighting in peace time was a knightly pursuit, but potentially a very dangerous one, and part of Edward's role was to draw the line when danger threatened.

The following Sunday, the Burgundian visitors were feasted in the Guildhall of the Mercers in the company of 'sixty or eighty' ladies of rank, none of lower in status than the daughter of a baron. Among the company was the Burgundian Olivier de la Marche – a chronicler, poet, diplomat and soldier, whose own court reforms inspired Edward to restructure his household – who commented that the meal was 'great and plentiful'. There was still another week of entertainments to go, which was intended to culminate in Antoine hosting a banquet for Queen Elizabeth and her ladies; some reported that the whole event 'was inspired by the queen and her ladies'.[18] During the event, however, the tournament was cut short when news arrived in England of the death of Philip the Good, Duke of Burgundy, on 15 June, necessitating Antoine's return home. Monstrelet relates the event, stressing that Edward intervened because it was 'for amusement' and therefore no man should lose his life.

Monstrelet also related the fashions of 1467, recording the influence of Burgundian style at court, where Edward and Elizabeth led the fashion. This process had already begun two years earlier, with the arrival of Elizabeth's uncle Jacques de Luxembourg in London and his train of 100 Burgundian knights, sporting the latest fashions. The stylish Jacques is depicted in a matching gown and hat of scarlet in the 1473 Statuts, Ordonnances at Armorial de l'Ordre de la Toison d'Or, with his sleeves slashed and his coat of arms above his head. Following this exotic style, women replaced the long trains on their gowns with thick borders of fur or velvet and adopted circular hoods tapering to the top, draped with handkerchiefs with corners hanging to the ground. The girdle was already a fashion but these became wider and were made of silk; shoes became more richly decorated and gold necklaces were newly popular. Men's doublets became shorter, with the sleeves slashed to show their white shirt beneath and the shoulders padded to make a wider silhouette. Their hair was worn long, almost covering their eyes, under tall cloth bonnets, and they too wore gold chains. Men's shoes could be pointed to almost a quarter of an ell in length, which was slightly over a quarter of a metre – the widespread use of which Edward had litigated against in his Sumptuary Laws of 1465. As Monstrelet commented, the 'little gentlemen' would attempt 'to ape the nobles and the rich' even though it was 'unbecoming' to their status. All understood the importance of magnificence and the impact of outward display. None more so than the king himself.

Edward certainly fulfilled the ideals of kingship described by Sir John Fortescue in *The Governance of England*, written in around 1470:

> It shall need that the kyng haue such tresour, as he mey make new bildynges whan he woll, ffor his pleasure and magnificence; and as he mey bie hym riche clothes, riche furres … riche stones … and other juels and ornamentes conuenyent to his estate roiall. And often tymes he woll bie riche hangynges and other apparel ffor his howses … ffor yff a king did not so, nor might do, he lyved then not like his estate, but rather in miserie and in more subgeccion than doth a priuate person.

'Magnificence' is a concept that is crucial to understanding Edward's reign – one that no king had really exploited since the grand show of regality mounted by Richard II, who posed for his portrait on a surround of gold. Edward understood that his power was bound up in his persona, his appearance, his presence and his physicality. He dressed the part and surrounded himself with servants and knights whose clothing echoed their role, with everything from workers' liveries to relatives' gowns of cloth of gold being supplied by the royal wardrobe. In 1465 he appointed the trusted Sir Thomas Vaughan as Treasurer of the Chamber and the issue rolls indicate the importance of the jewel house right from these early years.[19] Edward also retained the services of a barber in his household, to shave him once a week and wash his head, feet and hands. He also looked after his health, spending the large sum of £87 18s and 7½d in May 1464 on John Clerk, apothecary, 'for certain physic supplied for the said King's use, and administered to him under the advice of the said king's physicians'.[20] It is surprising that such an image-conscious king did not commission a portrait of himself in the style of Richard II, although he would not have wished to invite parallels with a king who had been deposed and reputedly murdered. However, it would have been in keeping for pictures of Edward to have been painted, had he obliged his artists by sitting still long enough. The survival of a number of later works, some of which appear to stem from the same original, suggest that such portraits may have been made and subsequently lost. Then again, a portrait was no substitute for the real thing, and Edward's initial priority was peace not prosperity, so he made efforts to ensure his face was widely seen.

This sense of conscious majesty, pomp and ceremony was not at all incompatible with Edward's piety. It was in fact a demonstration of Edward's faith in God and God's authority in him. A coexistence of Paganism and Christianity in the Arthurian legends allowed for a blend of mysticism and romance, particularly after Chretien de Troyes's introduction of the quest for the Holy Grail, and the thirteenth-century retelling of Arthur's story in a Christian context in the Vulgate Cycle. The notion of knights undertaking holy quests tallied neatly with the tail end of the Crusades, with the ageing Pope Pius II setting out to lead a crusade against the Turks in July 1464. Duke Philip of Burgundy was keen to be involved and extorted Louis XI and Edward IV to participate, or at least contribute finances or soldiers. Edward agreed in theory and mooted the idea of going on crusade, but was occupied with crushing the rebellion in the north and the repercussions of his secret marriage. When Edward raised taxes that year, it may have been his intention to give the extra money to pay for archers for the Pope, as in 1469 Warwick would accuse him of using this money for himself. As it happened, the death on 15 August of Pius II who was exhausted after crossing the mountains around Ancona, dissipated the final crusade.

In fact, it was Anthony Woodville, one of Edward's 'chief confidants and the brother of his dear consort', who became the most famous pilgrim of the reign. Nigel Saul likens him to Malory's Lancelot or Gawain in his choice of the life of the knight errant. His first adventure was against the Moors in Portugal in 1471, and he went to Santiago de Compostela in 1473, where the Cathedral of St James was a popular location for English and European pilgrims alike. Edward, though, may have seen Anthony's adventures as a means of escape, reputedly commenting that it was 'kowardyness', as whenever there was work to be done, he left the kingdom.[21] However, in 1475, Edward used his influence to request safe conduct for Anthony from the Duke of Milan to visit shrines in Rome, Naples and St Nicholas at Bari; Anthony also acquired a papal indulgence for his burial in the Chapel of the Pew, Westminster. Pilgrimages could be fraught with danger, however, and Anthony experienced one of the typical misfortunes of travellers at Torre de Bacano the following March, when he was robbed of his jewels and plate to the value of at least 1,000 marks.[22] Elizabeth at once dispatched a royal servant to Rome with letters of exchange to the value of 4,000 ducats. A few days later, three Germans who were dealers in ultramarine were arrested and put on the rack, leading to the recovery of the jewels. The following month, Anthony was more cautious when he met with Philip of Burgundy near Bern, who was preparing to engage in battle with the Swiss. After suggesting that he fight alongside them, Woodville changed his mind and returned home. The Battle of Morat was fought on 22 June and proved disastrous for Philip, who suffered considerable losses. The story might have ended quite differently for the pilgrim, but he arrived back safely in England to fight another day. The idea of a crusade may have been attractive to Edward, but with his various domestic concerns, it was his brother-in-law who actually went.

The tomb of Thomas Becket in Canterbury Cathedral appears to have been one of Edward's favourite places of pilgrimage. He may have remembered the city's warm reception when he and Warwick arrived at the head of a rebel army in the summer of 1460; he returned as king to grant Canterbury a charter making it an independent county, separate from the rest of Kent. Then, butchers were paid £2 6s 8d for twenty sheep, the same amount for two oxen, 13s 4d for four swans and 2s a pair for a number of capons, making for a generous royal feast. Having visited twice in the first two years of his reign, Edward returned in 1463, staying in the forest of Blean on the hills outside, overlooking the cathedral. The 'hale in the Blene' was made ready for him at great expense, with red wine and malmsey costing 12s and 6d and an unusual entry in the accounts describing how a shilling was paid 'for china bought and given to the king'.[23] This might have been an early example of a special item of porcelain, as Ming dynasty plates were being exported to Europe at this time, with 'china' being the name used for what were still very rare pieces. The Victoria and Albert Museum contains some fragments of early pottery from this period, with a white glaze and cobalt blue decorations of flowers, scrolls and leaves. The collection includes one particularly beautiful vase, based on the shape of a drinking flask, which was made in China between 1400 and 1430, as well as a stem wine cup dating from the time of Edward's wedding, so it is not inconceivable that items of similar quality were brought to Edward's court along the same trading routes that had brought the plague the previous century.

Edward began his considerable building programme in the early years of his reign. Work commenced on the York family home of Fotheringhay Castle in around 1463, creating new apartments and turrets, latrines and kitchens. The following year, the book of the king's works include details of a 'garden and spinney which the king has made to enclose the little park immediately SE of the castle by the river'. Little now survives of Fotheringhay beyond a mound and a lump of stones. At the same time, he spent £10,000 on improvements to Dover Castle,[24] with a withdrawing chamber, new windows and fireplaces added in 1464 to the newly designated queen's side of the castle. There was increased traffic through Dover after Edward's ruling in 1464 that all those travelling to Calais must pass through the port. These changes demonstrate a balance between the needs for defence and a new domestic architecture: the Dover regulations and improvements came about after Edward's own experiences of entering and holding Calais as a haven for exiles, coupled with the importance of expressing kingly power. It helps to delineate the two key aspects of Edward's early reign: national stability and appropriate magnificence. *Le Morte d'Arthur* celebrates both, but the world of England's Arthur was about to be shaken by his choice of Guinevere.

5

THE SECRET WIFE
1464

'Comfort and Joy.'

I

Traditionally, it happened on May Day, early in the morning. While the dew was still fresh on the grass, two women slipped away from the manor house, leaving its inhabitants still asleep in their beds. They were mother and daughter, both beautiful with an aristocratic air, the younger woman in her mid- to late twenties and the elder approaching fifty. They hurried on foot across the Woodville land, towards the edge of the estate near Shaw's Wood, part of the larger Whittlesbury Forest. There stood a small priory or hermitage, dedicated to St Mary and St Michael, no longer supplied with its own chaplain since it merged with the nearby Abbey of St James. By the mid-fifteenth century, its quiet walls were used for family devotions: on 1 May 1464, it was to witness one of the most important ceremonies of the Wars of the Roses. Waiting inside was a tall, athletic and distinguished young man in rich clothes, a priest and choir boy, and two gentlewomen, to act as witnesses. There, before this tiny group, Elizabeth Woodville was married without pomp or ceremony to the King of England.

Thus the legend goes. Most of the details of this account are taken from Fabyan's Chronicle, which states that Edward slept just five miles away at Stony Stratford the day before, where he had paused on his way north to hunt in the forest that joined the town with the Grafton estate. Fabyan describes that after the ceremony, the couple consummated their union, staying in bed for three or four hours, before Edward rode back to Stony Stratford as if he had been out hunting. There was also the thorny issue of Richard Woodville, whom the young king had so roundly abused at Calais: 'Within a day or two, he sent to Grafton to the Lord Rivers ... showing to him that he would come and lodge with him a certain season, where he was received with all honour, and so tarried there by the space of four days.' Fabyan adds that Woodville was still not privy to the secret, as Elizabeth was brought to Edward's bed nightly, 'in so secret manner that almost none but her mother was of counsel'.

All that can be said with certainty is that at some point before the end of September 1464, Elizabeth married Edward in secret. The date and circumstances of this event are still being hotly debated among historians, especially because the choices Edward made were later used to undermine and depose his entire dynasty. When Elizabeth and Edward first met is unclear. Legend has her waiting for him under an oak in Whittlesbury Forest, to petition him for help to resolve the land dispute with her mother-in-law. Perhaps he did come riding by, hear her pleas and fall in love. When she became aware of his intentions and agreed to become his wife, knowing his position, she cannot have known what lay ahead, but she must have agreed to collude behind his veil of secrecy. It was not a decision she would have taken lightly – to marry the king – and by agreeing to go through the private ceremony, she must have trusted him enough to ensure that he would honour his word and that the proceedings that day were perfectly legal and legitimate. There is a chance, however, that Edward had no intention of honouring the marriage; that going through the ceremony was the only means by which he was able to inveigle Elizabeth into his bed and that he later intended to deny the match. He may have done similar things before with other women, especially those who would have been considered unsuitable to become queen. At five years the king's senior, the widow of a Lancastrian knight, whose two children were proclaimations that she was not the traditional virgin, Elizabeth certainly was not suitable. Just four years earlier, Edward had berated her father in Calais for his humble origins and assumptions. However, this time the king fell in love.

What was it about this woman that so captivated Edward that he was prepared to take such a risk? Without doubt, she was very beautiful. A coronation portrait of Elizabeth appears in the *Illuminated Books of the Fraternity of Our Lady's Assumption of the Skinners' Company*, one of the oldest and most prominent of London's medieval guilds. The illustration depicts Elizabeth in her coronation robes, an event which took place on 26 May 1465. She is dressed in a long, royal-blue gown with a gold trim, fastened at the neck with what look like two gold, flower-like clasps. Under this, she wears a long, scarlet robe with a central panel of ermine extending over her hips. The same fur lines her cloak, identifiable as white painted with tiny black flecks. The copious fabric lies in folds at her feet, hiding them entirely. Elizabeth's eyes stare straight out at us. Her face is generic enough, but her golden hair hangs long, loose and flowing, as a symbol of virginity, even though this queen was a widow with two young sons. She stands on a small patch of grass from which her symbol, the carnation, or gillyflower, grows, with its red and white flowers filling the space to either side of her. This is all enclosed within a decorative border, framing the queen in red, blue and gold, outside which lie more decorations of flowers and leaves. The illustration feels crowded, without a space left undecorated. In short, this is a symbolic representation of the queen's status, an abstraction of ideals, a queen as an icon.

It is no coincidence that the same manuscript also includes an image of the coronation of the Virgin Mary, who happens to be dressed in a red gown bordered with ermine, covered by a royal-blue cloak, with the same flowing golden locks and, apparently, the same features as Elizabeth. This overlap of queen and saint, this dichotomy of virginity and motherhood, this identification of the most powerful woman in the land with the most popular pre-Reformation cult, goes a long way to helping define what queenship meant during the fifteenth century.

Another illustration of Elizabeth can be found in the *Luton Guild Book*, which depicts her among the founding members of the Fraternity of the Holy and Undivided Trinity and Blessed

Virgin Mary. Elizabeth and Edward kneel either side of Bishop Rotherham, before the Trinity, flanked by Cecily Neville and other ladies, who might be Warwick's daughters. Like Edward, she wears a long, lilac-coloured cloak, edged with ermine, but hers covers a golden, V-necked Burgundian gown, embroidered with blue flowers and gathered in a high green waist. Her hands are clasped in prayer and her eyes appear downcast and demure. Her features are regular and serene, her mouth small and eyebrows high – more so perhaps than the other ladies, who are not completely dissimilar. All have their hair scraped back under henins, of which Elizabeth and Cecily wear the largest of all, in a heavy black with transparent drapes. This image is painted in the style of the Netherlands, and although this does not exclude the artist from travelling to England, it may actually date from the sixteenth century.

In Lambeth Palace's copy of the *Dictes and Sayings of the Philosophers,* an illustration can be found of Elizabeth, standing alongside Edward and their eldest son, being presented with a copy of the book by its translator, Anthony Woodville. It was printed by Caxton in 1477 and 1489, in the grounds of Westminster Abbey, dating this image firmly within Elizabeth's lifetime, and the age of her son Edward appears to correlate with the first print run. The portraits are rather crude and stiff, and Elizabeth appears rather statue-like and iconic, seated slightly behind Edward to his left, holding the formal regalia of her queenship. Her hair is long, blonde and loose, her features small. She wears blue robes trimmed with ermine and an ermine collar, over which hangs a gold chain. It is not a particularly flattering image, but this is likely to be the result of its place in the early history of its medium.

Elizabeth appears in two stained-glass images that date from the end of Edward's reign. The first is at Little Malvern Priory, where she is depicted kneeling in prayer, again facing her husband, with women behind her. Her gown is blue with gold and ermine trim and her cloak is a deep red. Her hair is invisible under an elaborate henin decorated with a prominent jewel, and her features are again small and uniform. The image has been dated to 1480–2, as an example of the Malvern workshop under master glaziers Richard Twygge and Thomas Woodshawe, who also worked on the nave of Westminster Abbey.[1] Around the same time, Elizabeth was portrayed with her family in Canterbury Cathedral, in a window above the martyrdom chapel which was probably the work of Edward's own glazier, John Prudde, who worked at Westminster Palace and would have been familiar with the queen's appearance. Here, Elizabeth is crowned, her gold coronet dotted with pearls and sitting atop a similarly decorated headdress. Her dress in this instance is white and gold and her cloak is purple – a colour scheme echoed in Edward's clothing. A long, gold rosary and chain hang from her waist and her hands are empty, fingertips touching in prayer. While Edward is flanked by images of sunbursts and white roses, Elizabeth kneels before what appear to be red gillyflowers or carnations, which she chose as her device for its associations with the Virgin Mary.

When it comes to paintings of Elizabeth, one in particular is best known today. A painted panel in Queens' College Cambridge shows her in a black and gold gown with a squarish neckline and sloping shoulders. There are many copies of this image, but the college considers the original to have probably been painted during her lifetime, perhaps even from a live sitting. Her hair, which is pulled back under a small hat and partial veil, appears golden, and her skin is very pale, alleviated by a slight blush of colour in her cheeks. Her features here are the best defined of all the images of Elizabeth, with her large forehead, high, curved brows and hooded eyes. Her nose is not small, but it is defined and delicate, as are her red mouth and pert chin.

Elizabeth's first clear contact with Edward's court comes only a few months before the suggested date of her marriage, on 13 April. She appealed to William, Lord Hastings, probably in his role as overseer of the Yorkist Midlands, for his assistance in the dispute that had arisen with Baroness Ferrers. Hastings agreed to intervene so long as Elizabeth split the rents and profits of the Grey lands with him, and that a marriage should be arranged between one of Elizabeth's sons and any future daughter born to Hastings. He had recently married Katherine Neville, Warwick's sister, but did not father a daughter for another seven years. It is difficult to know how to interpret this interaction. Some have suggested that it indicates Elizabeth had no idea of her impending marriage, as she would surely have appealed directly to the king for assistance had she been aware of her influence over him. Yet given the fact that Edward was keen to keep the match secret, it may be that he instructed Hastings to deal with the matter, and that Hastings may or may not have been aware of the king's intentions. The arrangement he struck with Elizabeth was a fairly hard bargain, only granting her half of the land she believed to be her due; perhaps it was the draconian nature of this that encouraged her to capitulate in the face of Edward's romantic demands.

By all accounts, Edward could be very persuasive. After all, apart from being tall, strong and handsome, he was the king, with all the complicated allegiance and loyalty this demanded from his subjects, both male and female. When it came to personal relations though, an awkward dynamic arose as the result of this allegiance, splitting the private and the public. Just how far could a woman resist him, confident that her right to refuse did not impinge upon the duty she owed her king? The reputation and fortunes of her family might rest upon such a decision. It raises a range of questions about the autonomy of women's bodies and the degree to which they could exercise choice when it came to their sexuality. As a widow, Elizabeth had considerably more freedom that she would have done as an unmarried girl, but in this instance, the traditional role of her father as her protector has been subverted by the part played by her mother. Jacquetta's involvement, possibly without the knowledge of her husband, forms a parallel with her own secret marriage in the 1430s, reminding us that she had been prepared to marry for love in defiance of the law. However, Elizabeth's was not just a marriage of love: it was the most lucrative possible match she could have made. Jacquetta may have encouraged her to seize her good fortune and worry about the consequences later.

There is no question of Edward's passion for his new wife, yet his methods appear underhand to the modern eye. Croyland explains that the king was 'prompted by the ardour of youth', and Hearne adds that he was 'lusty'. Philip de Commines described how Edward 'thought nothing but upon women', and Mancini stated he was able to overcome 'all by money or promises'. Elizabeth may have been beautiful, but she 'had only a knight' for her father, and would have been considered 'no wife for so high a prince' as Edward. The Danzig Chronicle has the detail that Edward fell in love with Elizabeth when he 'dined with her frequently', suggesting thay he made more visits to Grafton than just the four days he passed there in May, and that she was more than a pretty face. John Hardyng, writing at the time of the marriage, expressed the opinion of many 'kynges and prynces' that Edward had been 'led rather by blynde Cupyde than by anye reason'. According to Mancini's account, Edward fell in love with Elizabeth in spite of her comparatively humble background because of her 'beauty of person and charm of manner', and his feelings strengthened when he realised 'he could not corrupt her virtue by gifts or menaces'. This last comment sounds rather unpleasant, suggesting Edward attemped to win her favours by force, which cannot be disguised as anything other than rape. Mancini continues:

> The story runs that when Edward placed a dagger at her throat, to make her submit to his passion, she remained unperturbed and determined to die rather than live unchastely with the king. Whereupon Edward coveted her much the more, and he judged the lady worthy to be a royal spouse who could not be overcome in her constancy even by an infatuated king.

At least Mancini acknowledges that his source is a rumour, with the words 'the story runs', which may indicate that the use of the knife is a dramatic embellishment. The contemporary Italian poet Antonio Cornazzano suggests that it was Elizabeth herself who wielded the knife, threatening that she would injure or kill herself if Edward persisted in his attempts to seduce her. Death, Cornazzano wrote, was preferable for Elizabeth than living in 'eternal filth and squalor' after the king's 'vain pleasure were soon over'. It is interesting that no English source bears such a detail, which may have been more suited to Italian literary tastes or meant to blacken the reputation of a king who had rejected the Turin-born Bona of Savoy. Hearne's Fragment has a similar sentiment to Mancini without the unpleasant connotations of violence, stating that after having pursued many women, Edward could perceive 'none of such constant womanhood, wisdom and beauty' as Elizabeth, with her 'constant and stable mind'. No doubt he did admire her very much, but the possibility of violence cannot be ruled out. Elizabeth could have refused him outright, if she intended to enter a convent and was prepared to abandon her sons. She may have suggested legitimate marriage as the condition of her surrender, with little expectation that Edward would take it seriously. Yet that is exactly what he did.

Hearne, Gregory, Fabyan and other chroniclers pinpoint the day as 'the first of May ... [when] our sovereign lord the King, Edward IV, was wedded to the Lord Rivers' daughter ... and this marriage was kept full secretly long and many a day, that no man knew it',[2] while Warkworth tells us the wedding 'was privily in a secret place'. It is far more likely to have taken place in the secluded hermitage on Woodville land than in the Church of St Mary the Virgin in the village of Grafton Regis itself. Excavations at the site of the hermitage in 1964 uncovered a number of late-fifteenth-century floor tiles featuring the white rose of York and the Woodville arms, indicating the building was significant for both families. The notion of the wedding taking place on 1 May ties in nicely with romantic tradition and the playful, carnival nature of May Day. If he deliberately chose this occasion to make his promises, Edward would have been exploiting a centuries-old tradition that allowed normal social relations to be inverted on this day, with women dominating men and servants overruling masters. It was a topsy-turvy time of rule breaking and carnival. Mock kings and queens were crowned from among the servants, presiding over pretend courts and punishing their enemies. They could even be fined if they refused to take part. The social underdog was celebrated, with outlaws such as the legendary Robin Hood featuring in pageants and plays. A degree of sexual licence was also tolerated, with later Puritans critical of it being an excuse for the deflowering of a large number of virgins. Everyone knew that, for a brief window, the normal hierarchy was suspended, but that in a few hours all would return to normal. Edward's marriage was opportunistic, even potentially reversible. If necessary, it could be dismissed as part of the May Day tradition.

Practically, the day makes sense too. Edward's itinerary can be identified through some of this period. In late April, he had been moving north from London, in response to the threat posed by the Duke of Somerset, whose death at Hexham on 25 April, took the impetus out of Edward's journey. He could indeed afford to pass a day or four in hunting or amorous pursuits. From Grafton he travelled north to Northampton and Leicester, having ordered soldiers to be sent there for 10 May. He was in York on 23 May and signed the Anglo-Scots truce on 1 June. It was not until the middle of July that he headed south, and at the start of August he met his advisors in Stamford, ahead of Parliament's session at Reading that September. It is not inconceivable that he managed to snatch a few more days at Grafton during this time, either to be married or to visit his new bride. Yet this day cannot be asserted with certainty. Historian Michael Hicks has suggested a later date of 30 August for the marriage, based upon a grant Edward made of the lordship of Chester to George, Duke of Clarence. Hicks argues that this was a position usually given to the heir to the throne, and that Edward may not have been willing to grant this to his brother if he was expecting to marry and father an heir. However, this creates a very narrow margin for Edward to have changed his mind about the marriage, unless he had not yet decided to own to the Woodville match.

Why did Edward choose to keep his marriage quiet? Clearly, he knew that Elizabeth was an unsuitable match on account of her background, her age and her previous marriage. He knew he was acting against expectations, that Warwick's diplomatic efforts would be wasted and that his family would be angry. In 1460, he, along with Salisbury and Warwick, had expressed the Yorkists' disgust at the perceived pretensions of Richard Woodville and his son, so he could easily anticipate the responses of his allies to his marriage. Through marriage to Elizabeth, he had personally justified Woodville's aspirations and given him something to crow about, but the difference was that Edward was now king. He knew his choice would cause embarrassment and conflict, yet these factors didn't prevent him from announcing it later on. Ultimately, he may have decided that his anointed authority overrode the preferences and politics of all his family and allies. It was a shocking elevation of the private over the public. Yet perhaps the young Edward, still flushed with success, thought there was little point in having fought his way to the throne if he could not allow himself the reward of choosing his own queen.

However, there may have been an alternative reason for the secrecy. It is not too cynical to suggest that Edward intended to repudiate Elizabeth after he had bedded her, or simply exclude her or deny it had taken place. As he appeared to hold her family in such low esteem, he might not have scrupled to insult them further by enjoying a brief fling with their daughter. The indications from some of the chroniclers are that Edward may have used this method before, with Hearne stating that he was a 'lusty prince' and had 'attempted the stability and constant modesty of diverse ladies and gentlewomen'. Gregory wrote that men 'marvelled' that the king had remained unmarried so long, and feared his unchaste living, and Croyland added that Edward was a man of 'vanities, debaucheries, extravagance and sensual enjoyments'. Even the Milanese ambassador noted that Edward's desires bent towards pleasure in both 'festivities of ladies and of hunting'. Two decades later, Commines went further and related the current rumour that Edward had been wed previously, after becoming 'enamoured of a certain English Lady ... [and] promised to marry her, provided that he could sleep with her first, and she consented'. The Bishop of Bath and Wells would later state that 'he had married them when only he and they were present', without any other witnesses, making this a difficult case to verify, which is exactly why it proved so politically useful when it was raised amid the volatile climate of 1483.

The woman in question was an Eleanor Butler, widow of Sir Thomas Butler and daughter of John Talbot, Earl of Shrewsbury. Old Talbot, also Shakespeare's 'brave Talbot', had been Constable of France and Lieutenant of Ireland under Henry VI, but had supported the Duke of York in the 1440s during York's rule in Normandy. Talbot was one of the best generals Henry had and was recalled to help repress Jack Cade's rebellion, but was killed in battle in 1453. He had two daughters from his second marriage to Warwick's sister-in-law Margaret Beauchamp: Elizabeth, who married into the Norfolk de Mowbray family, and Eleanor, born around 1436. At the age of thirteen, Eleanor was married to Thomas Butler, who left her a childless widow at some point before 1461. Her father-in-law seized one of the two manors settled on her at the time of her marriage, but on Edward's succession the Crown confiscated both. Eleanor was also a Lancastrian, with her half-brother being killed at Northampton. Thus, Eleanor's situation as an impoverished widow trying to regain part of her dowry was remarkably similar to Elizabeth's in 1464, and Edward's reaction may have been the same.

Eleanor would have been around twenty-five in 1461, but she died only seven years later, making her conveniently unable to counter the allegations made in 1483. The case raises questions about the formality of the marital contract in terms of canon law and what constituted a legally binding match. John Ashdown-Hill has explored the case for Edward and Eleanor's formal marriage, making Eleanor legally Queen of England and invalidating Elizabeth's marriage. Yet the case is by no means a straightforward one. Papal responses to such cases could vary, depending upon the existence of children and whether the original parties were both still alive. Additionally, it had proved possible for children conceived out of wedlock to be retrospectively legitimised. John of Gaunt's Beaufort offspring, borne by Katherine Swynford, arrived while he was still married to Constance of Castile, yet were subsequently legitimised when Gaunt and Swynford married, after Constance's death. They were even included in the royal succession for a decade, until the new Lancastrian king, Henry IV ruled against this in 1407. Following this example, if Edward and Elizabeth had undergone a second ceremony after Eleanor's death, all their children could have been made retrospectively legitimate. The degree of flexibility in the papal records, though, suggests that the law could be manipulated to suit various political imperatives. We simply cannot know now what promises, if any, Edward made to Eleanor.

However, it is worth noting that even if the rumour about Edward and Eleanor was purely a political invention, it had to be credible enough to secure its success. People must have believed Edward to be a womaniser in 1483, although this may have owed more to his later years than his early ones. Edward did have an acknowledged mistress later in life, who was widely known to be an Elizabeth Shore, the wife of a London mercer, who had left her husband on the grounds of his impotence. Elizabeth was renamed as Jane by dramatist John Heywood, furthering the confusion, but there is little doubt that she did exist. Edward is also believed to have had at least one other mistress, referred to by Thomas More as Elizabeth Lucy, although he credits her with the same history as Eleanor Butler. Either More confused the identities of the two women, or else Edward promised marriage as a pretext for sex to at least two women before he went through with the ceremony at Grafton. There may also have been a woman known as Elizabeth Wayte, although this could be the maiden name of Elizabeth Lucy, just as Eleanor is known by the names Talbot and Butler. Equally, Elizabeth Lucy may have been the daughter of the Hampshire gentleman Thomas Waite. More referred to three mistresses, apparently following a boast by Edward that he had 'one the merriest, another the wiliest, the third the holiest harlot in his realm'. Since then, historians have indulged in a sort of 'guess-the-mistress' game, matching the description of 'merry' to Elizabeth or Jane Shore, 'holy' to Eleanor, who patronised nunneries, and leaving Elizabeth Wayte as the 'wiliest', although some have been keen to give Elizabeth Woodville that epithet. Such retrospective guessing games are unhelpful. The seventeenth-century antiquarian George Buck also named a Katherine de Clarendon among Edward's lovers. There may have been others unrecorded by history, but Edward was by no means the worst of the Plantagenet kings in this department.

But when exactly did Edward's reputation as a sexually voracious king begin? He may have pursued women before his marriage and had a couple of mistresses later in life, but this hardly merits the descriptions of later chroniclers that he was debauched. It seems that this version of Edward suited the political climate of 1483 and spiralled after his death. In the months after his death, the newly arrived Mancini heard a rumour that Edward 'was licentious to the least' and 'had been most insolent to numerous women after he had seduced them, for, as soon as he grew weary of dalliance, he gave up the ladies much against their will to the other courtiers'. Worse still, Edward 'pursued with no discrimination the married and unmarried, the noble and lowly ... he overcame all by money and promises, and having conquered them, he dismissed them'. However, Mancini was writing after Richard III had used Edward's reputed bigamy to claim the throne, when such rumours had become part of a mainstream dialogue about Edward's character. By the time Thomas More was writing during the reign of Henry VII, Edward was being described as a man given to 'fleshly wantonness ... [which] greatly grieved the people.' The existence of one illegitimate child fathered by Edward is certain, with Arthur Plantagenet living until 1542, although his date of birth is unknown. A Grace Plantagenet is also referred to in a single source regarding the arrangements for Elizabeth's funeral in 1492, and a century later the Elizabethan Lumley family would claim descent from a Catherine Plantagenet. Whatever the truth of his private relations, about which little real evidence survives, it remains plausible that the secret Grafton ceremony was intended as a short-term measure to allow Edward into Elizabeth's bed.

It is possible that in May 1464, Edward saw Elizabeth as a conquest rather than as his queen. This is supported by the negotiations the king had initiated to find a foreign bride. As early as 1462, enquiries had been made about a possible marriage with Mary of Guelders, the widow of James II of Scotland and, briefly, regent for her young son. These came to nothing: although Edward was keen to make peace with Scotland, as he recognised that Mary's powers were limited. In the winter of 1464, Edward received a Spanish offer of the hand of Isabella of Castile, the future mother of Catherine of Aragon, which would have been a lucrative match. However, Edward rejected Isabella, probably because at the age of twelve she was too young, but equally it may have been because he was already intending to make Elizabeth his wife. Dynastic negotiations frequently came to nothing and Edward's passion may have been sated or dwindled before he had to commit to a foreign wife. Warwick favoured a French match, with several candidates being considered before the discussions began for Edward to marry Louis XI's sister-in-law. By then, Louis had been married for over a decade to Charlotte of Savoy, whose fourteen-year-old sister, Bona, was proposed as a likely bride for the English king. With royal blood, Italian and French connections, youth and virginity on her side, Bona was a perfect candidate to share the throne with Edward. When Parliament met at Reading that September, they were keen to finalise the arrangements for this marriage, but Edward had other ideas.

II

Bona of Savoy would not be coming to England after all. There would be no grand royal wedding in St Paul's Cathedral or Westminster Abbey, no conduits running with wine, no reception by the mayor and aldermen in their scarlet robes. The chronicler

Gregory describes how 'the lords moved [Edward] and exhorted him in God's name to be wedded and to live under the law of God and church', which may suggest they were aware he was already practising 'ungodly' ways. They implored him to send 'into some strange land to enquire for a queen of good birth, according unto his dignity' and bring her to England. It was at this point that Edward told the truth: England already had a queen. Perhaps he did so upon the spur of the moment, when it seemed the French marriage was reaching an unavoidable conclusion, or perhaps he had intended to confess all along. No doubt the Woodvilles could have protested if he had gone ahead and married Bona, although given that only Jacquetta was at the ceremony and Richard Woodville had not at that point been informed, it may have been difficult to prove. Any witnesses to the May Day event could have been silenced or bought off; they would have been no match for Warwick, had Edward enlisted his help in denying the connection no matter how Jacquetta may have protested. In addition, had he wished to use a prior connection with Eleanor Butler as an excuse, he would have had the perfect advocate in Warwick, as Eleanor was the niece of the earl's wife. But he did not. He told the assembly that he was already married to Elizabeth Woodville, a widow five years his elder with two sons.

An English queen was unusual. Henry VI and Henry V had both married foreign princesses, specifically those with French royal blood. Henry IV's first marriage had been arranged for him before his succession to the throne; he was able to choose his own queen in his maturity, however, Henry's rise to power had been unexpected and his second wife, Joan of Navarre, did not bear him children; all his heirs came from the first match to Mary de Bohun. Yet Joan was still foreign and royal. Before Henry IV, the previous Plantagenet kings – Richard II, Edward III, Edward II, Edward I and Henry III – had all married foreign wives for diplomatic purposes, even though affection certainly developed between some of them, even love. Edward broke this pattern and did not feel obliged to follow through the marital plans with France, instead prioritising his personal choice over the example set by his forebears. The single precedent for such an act was the marriage of Richard, the Black Prince, who was England's heir when he married the widowed Joan of Kent against his parents' wishes almost exactly a century before. However, Richard had died before he became king, so Joan had never become queen. Edward's actions highlight the personal nature of his rule, the strength of his personality and his unwillingness to follow anyone else's rules. Some might call it reckless, immature or lust-driven, but just as his conquest in 1460–1 had demonstrated, Edward was going to do things his own way. Perhaps the speed and success of his rise had given him such a sense of his own authority, his absolute power, that he might have overreached himself with this marriage. One thing was certain: Edward was redefining kingship on his own terms.

The news was received with shock. The obvious objections to Elizabeth's status were raised. The Croyland Chronicler tells us 'the nobility and chief men of the kingdom took amiss, seeing that he had with such immoderate haste promoted a person sprung from a comparatively humble lineage'. Waurin adds that the council recognised Elizabeth's charms but rejected her background, telling the king that 'however good and fair she might be, he must know well that she was no wife for so high a prince as himself; she was not the daughter of a duke or earl but her mother … had married a knight … she was not, all things considered, a suitable wife for him, nor a woman of the kind who ought to belong to such a prince'. A contemporary dispatch from Bruges, dated 5 October 1464, stated that the people of England were 'offended' by the union and the lords were 'very much dissatisfied at this' and were holding meetings 'for the sake of finding means to annul it'. Later, despite Elizabeth's position as ancestress to the Tudors, who were his patrons, Polydore Vergil described her as being of 'mean calling' against whom the nobility 'truly chaffed and made open speeches that the king had not done according to his dignity' and 'found much fault with him'. Thomas More, however, described Elizabeth as 'a widow born of noble blood' and stressed her mother's first marriage to John, Duke of Bedford.

Warwick in particular appears to have been disappointed, having been charged to conduct negotiations for the hand of Bona, and worse, to not have been in Edward's confidence. Warkworth tells us that the earl was 'greatly displeased' and 'great dissension' arose between him and the king, to the effect that 'they never loved each other after'. The Danzig Chronicle stressed the role of Warwick as 'Kingmaker', although this epithet was not applied during the earl's lifetime: 'Warwick and his friends, who helped to make him king, he no longer regarded at all. Because of this Warwick hated him greatly and so did many noblemen.' The Great Chronicle adds that Edward's marriage 'kindled after much unkindness between the king and the earl [and] much heart burning was ever after between the earl and the queen's blood so long as he lived'. It was also a personal insult to the earl: a public rejection of his French aspirations and a break in their previous close conspiracy. Warwick had been a mentor to Edward in Calais and during his early reign, his confidant and ally, who had now not just been excluded from an important decision, but deceived regarding Edward's intentions. Now the young king had asserted his authority and this may have struck the earl as rash and ungrateful. Warwick had previously made his feelings about the Lancastrian Richard Woodville very plain; this marriage must have seemed to him to be a triumph of lust over wisdom. Writing at the time, John Hardyng goes so far as to state that it was Warwick who uncovered the king's secret:

> the erle had sure knowledge, by the letters of his frendes, that the king had got him a wife prively ... [and] he was so ernestly moved with it, that he thought best that the kynge shuld be deposed from the crowne, and as one not worthy of such a kingly office.

However, the French king Louis's hopes that the marriage would prompt Warwick to rise up and rebel against Edward show how out of touch he was. Many of these comments are written with hindsight, tracing the start of later enmities that were actually the result of other factors. Five more years would pass before Warwick would rebel and the Woodville match was not to be the catalyst.

Edward's family were also surprised, as a dynastic marriage had been anticipated for him since his early years. The arrangements for his wedding to Bona of Savoy must have seemed to them to complete the process begun by the Duke of York back in 1444–5, when he requested the hand of Princess Magdalen of Valois. Since then, Magdalen had been married to Gaston, Prince of Viana, in 1461, but Cecily would have equally welcomed the match with the French queen's sister, to validate the new Yorkist regime in European eyes and, hopefully, bring a rich dowry. Mancini's account contains the colourful details of Cecily Neville venting her anger by denying Edward was her legitimate son:

> Even his mother fell into such a frenzy that she offered to submit to a public enquiry and asserted that Edward was not the offspring of her husband, the Duke of York, but was conceived in adultery and therefore in no way worthy of the honour of kingship.

If Cecily did make such a statement, it is testimony to the depths of her frustration. Having been anticipating a royal marriage for Edward as the representative of the Yorkist dynasty, whose hard-won kingship had come out of the loss of his father and brother, Cecily's considerable pride suffered as a result of the Woodville alliance. Equally, until 1464 she had been the leading lady in the land – the queen by rights, who narrowly missed her chance to sit on the throne – and one of Edward's principal advisors. Now she would have to give precedence to the young Lancastrian widow. It would also have been hurtful for Cecily that her son had contracted this marriage in secret and frustrating that it was presented to her as a fait accompli. If such a sentiment was expressed by Cecily aloud, it appears to have immediately been dropped and it does not follow that she did submit to public enquiry. Nor does it mean that she was speaking the truth. It was the quickest and most effective way she had to wound her son and his new wife. When it came to protecting the dynasty her husband had died for, this comment implies that Cecily was prepared to fall upon her sword, sacrificing her own reputation to prevent the inclusion of Woodville blood. She must have felt that her trump card had thrown itself away. If she discredited Edward, the duchess still had two sons to continue the Yorkist line. It seems most likely, though, that such words were spoken in the heat of anger, and their consequences had not been fully thought through. Her good judgement may have been temporarily affected. The terrible irony is that once this seed had been planted, Warwick and George, Duke of Clarence, were able to exploit it against Edward in 1469. Cecily's outburst gave the notion of Edward's illegitimacy enough credence that, when it resurfaced in 1483, Edward's enemies were prepared to use it against his sons.

Whatever their feelings may have been in September 1464,

Warwick and Clarence had to overcome them and make a show of welcoming the new queen. Perhaps they followed Lord Wenlock's pragmatism when he decided that 'since the matter has proceeded before anything could be done about it, one must tolerate it, in spite of ourselves'. There is no contemporary eyewitness account of the response to Edward's declaration in Parliament, but the *Annales Rerum Anglicarum* tells us that when Elizabeth was brought to Reading, she was 'admitted into the abbey church, led by the Duke of Clarence and Earl of Warwick, and honoured as queen by the lords and all the people'. Mancini stated that the marriage offended the nobles, who 'would not stoop to show regal honour in accordance with her exalted rank', but in reality they had little choice. Equally, claims that 'die-hard Yorkists' loathed Elizabeth's Lancastrian connections is probably too simplistic, as only a few years before they had all been in the service of Henry VI, with the Duke of York continually stressing his own loyalty. Although it may have caused shock and disappointment, the marriage was a fait accompli, and with Edward by her side, Elizabeth's position was not overtly challenged; when the fissures between the king and Warwick did appear, in 1468, not 1464, there were plenty of other contributing factors, not least their disagreement over foreign policy.

A painting of the September parliament, made by Ernest Board in 1923 and now hanging in Reading Town Hall, may give an optimistically positive view of the occasion, with the lords raising their swords in an enthusiastic chorus, as if part of an Arthurian scene. Yet something of its very courtesy and loyalty rings true, in the sense of surprise and deference to the large figure of Edward, who wears his power as casually as his ermine robes. Some of those in the background might have been harbouring feelings of resentment, but for now they were concealed by the chivalric veil. Also present in Parliament was the new queen's brother, Anthony Woodville, summoned as a result of his marriage to Baroness Scales, and it is interesting to speculate whether the news was as much a shock to him as it was to Warwick, or whether he had been let in on the secret in advance. Perhaps it was his watchful eyes that prompted the king's confession.

For Elizabeth, the spring and summer of 1464 were a period of transition. It is impossible to recapture the range of emotions that she must have experienced during this time, as she went from the object of the king's passion, to becoming his secret wife, to being an acknowledged queen, but it must have been a tumultuous ride. She and her family may well have entertained doubts about the match, given its secret nature, especially as Richard Woodville would have been aware of the marital negotiations taking place with France. Hindsight tells us that their faith in Edward was vindicated, but they can hardly have been certain of that at the time. The nature of the wedding left them in a state of legal insecurity. If Edward had died or been deposed between May and September, proving the match might have been difficult – that is if, under those circumstances, the family had decided it was desirable to admit it had taken place. Elizabeth was also in a personal and social state of limbo. As a married woman, she was still obliged to live as a dependant under her parents' roof, waiting to see when, or if, she could admit her new position. There was also the possibility that she might fall pregnant, which would have exposed the match and forced Edward to either acknowledge or abandon her. She cannot have known for certain, amid such volatile times, that her future with Edward was secure. There was little Elizabeth could do during the summer months other than wait until he summoned her.

There is also the matter of Elizabeth's feelings. It would be anachronistic to wonder whether or not she was in love with Edward, yet it is a question that has long fascinated readers, especially in recent years. It was certainly the best offer she was going to receive by a long way, and setting the king's status aside, Edward's considerable personal charms made him a very attractive prospect. By May 1464, Elizabeth had been widowed for over three years, so she was out of mourning and had had plenty of time to consider remarriage; as some historians suggest regarding Jocelyn Hardwicke, she was already considering remarriage. She was still young and of childbearing years, and reputedly very beautiful, so a second husband was a distinct likelihood, although she would not have anticipated making quite such an important match. Marriage offered security and a degree of independence from a woman's parents, and although in reality it meant a transfer of legal and domestic power from one man to another, an affectionate husband might treat his wife with a greater degree of respect and freedom than she had experienced as a daughter. The opposite was also true, of course, and unhappy and abusive marriages must have been common.

The connection between marriage and love is a relatively modern concept, with the emergence of the companionate marriage in the eighteenth century, but it certainly was not the norm among the medieval aristocracy. Matches were often made among noble families for financial and political gain, often when those involved were merely children, with formal ceremonies taking place when the young bride reached the age of twelve. If respect developed into friendship or love, or if love inspired the match, it was a bonus, but not a necessity. French historian Francois Lebrun drew a defining line around the time of the French Revolution of 1789, stating that 'in every milieu, marriage was considered as being first an affair of interest, in the largest sense, and, very secondarily, an affair of sentiment'. Marriage was 'too serious an affair to be the result of personal choice. It was generally the parents who worked everything out in the best interest of both parties.'[3] While this may have been too simplistic a model for general use, it was certainly true that the king's marriage was too important to leave to personal inclination. Elizabeth might not have been 'in love' with Edward, however that might be defined, but she could recognise that he would be able to offer her advantages that no other man in the country might. What woman raised among the medieval aristocracy would not have welcomed the opportunity to become queen?

Despite all this, it would be to underestimate the unpredictable nature of human relations to rule out the possibility that Elizabeth did fall in love with Edward. In fifteenth-century terms, he was the 'full package', and she may well have been strongly attracted to him, if not actually in love. This raises another alternative interpretation of her actions in resisting his advances, and draws a parallel with her grandson Henry VIII's future relationship with Anne Boleyn. It would be wrong to assume that Elizabeth's feelings for Edward were constant before their marriage. Although many of the chroniclers comment upon the constancy of her mind, which drew Edward, this implies that she had self-control and a strong sense of her place and piety. She resisted Edward as she did not want to become his mistress, understanding the implications that would have for her reputation and the future of her sons. She may have been aware of the king's record with women, or reasonably doubted his sincerity, and acted to prevent herself being cast aside and her chances of remarriage damaged, if not destroyed. It may be that when she initially refused him, saying that she was not good enough to be his wife, nor low enough to be his concubine, she had no intention of drawing him into marriage. Yet as she saw his affection increase, the possibility of wedlock may have dawned upon her as a reality. Elizabeth does not come across as a femme fatale in the way Anne does, holding out for marriage, but this may be due to the very different circumstances and the way they have been depicted by subsequent centuries of historians. Edward was free to marry, and he found Elizabeth sufficiently captivating to believe she was worth risking the displeasure of his council and family. Whether love was present at the start, or whether it developed from lust, the personal success of their marriage over the next nineteen years proves that there were strong grounds for mutual attraction and affection.

Then there is the question of witchcraft. It was a theme that would emerge at several points during the lives of Jacquetta and her daughter; a theme that was ever-present in fifteenth-century culture, from the burning of Joan of Arc in 1431 to the penance of Eleanor Cobham in 1441. Witchcraft was an easy weapon, a lazy weapon, the tool of those who wanted to destroy reputations through a whispering campaign, and it was almost exclusively used to target important women. A queen or duchess could not be defeated on the battlefield, so she had to be undermined in terms of her reputation. This usually took one of two forms, by attacking her modesty, implying she was sexually voracious or adulterous, or that she had used magic in order to seduce or influence others. Both involved the transgression of male boundaries and both were difficult to prove but practically impossible to eradicate once the damaging rumours were in the public domain. A woman was defined by her reputation, or 'good fame', which was a construct of masculine approval; as such a fragile function of male goodwill, it could as easily be destroyed at the will of her enemies.

However, 'witchcraft' is a difficult concept to define, especially across the centuries. In Elizabeth's day, it was an extension of people's daily rituals, in prayers, astrology, astronomy, charms and medicines. Leechbooks or doctors' books of the era include a pseudoscientific jumble of remedies that fused Catholicism and superstition, often advising patients to imbibe certain herbs at certain times, or to carve or repeat a particular mantra to achieve a desired effect. Many of these remedies were focused on the female realms of love, sex, conception and childbirth. The birth chamber alone was full of such customs, with fires lit to keep out the Devil, lacings and ties kept loose for fear they would strangle an unborn child and violent images removed so that they did not cause miscarriage. That people put such store in these rituals should come as little surprise, when life was often fraught with uncertainties that could not then be explained by science. People put their faith in popular superstitions, like reciting rhymes during childbirth or clutching at a particular stone to ease pain, or believing that washing in a particular herb might make a woman more attractive or that drinking a potion might protect a man from gossip. These made as much sense to the pre-Reformation mind as leaving offerings of flowers, eggs or money at the shrine of their favourite saint. Sometimes popular recipes required ingredients to be collected at dawn, or under a full moon, or on certain days of the year. It is easy to see where the boundaries of folklore and home medicine might blur with that of witchcraft. Sadly, it is also clear that there was great potential for misunderstanding or deliberate misinterpretation. Literally everyone would have relied upon some sort of superstition, if even just the cramp rings that were among Edward's possessions. Jacquetta and Elizabeth would have been no different. They may have mixed herbs to drink or apply to the hair or skin to enhance their beauty. They may have recited charms or burned certain items in the belief that this would keep bad spirits away. This alone does not make them 'witches'. What was needed for an accusation of witchcraft to be made was some evidence of maleficium, or malevolent intent.

Fear of witchcraft was great in Europe in the second half of the fifteenth century. In 1486, a German clergyman named Heinrich Kramer wrote what proved to be a major treatise on the topic, *Malleus Maleficarum*, which formed the basis of the more famous witch trials under Matthew Hopkins, the seventeenth century's 'Witchfinder General'. The book identified witches as predominantly female members of society, engaged with magic after having made a pact with the Devil. Just a cursory glance at the medieval images of hell and Satan, which appear everywhere from manuscripts to church walls, acts as a reminder of just how real such beliefs were, and how strong the fear of hell and the Devil was. May Day was associated with magic and ritual, being the day of Beltane, the old Celtic festival when feasting took place, bonfires were lit, dew was gathered, May branches were decorated and other similar rites were performed, in order to welcome in the new season and keep the forces of evil at bay. The choice of wedding day coupled with Edward's complete infatuation with Elizabeth that led him to make such a seemingly inexplicable decision, was enough to fuel rumours that witchcraft had been used by the Woodville women to ensnare him. When the Yorkist dynasty was at a low point in the years ahead, Edward's enemies would return to this theme and claim that Jacquetta had enchanted the king using lead images of a man and woman tied together with gold thread. In 1464, however, the most common reaction to the marriage was surprise and condemnation, followed by resignation. Edward had chosen his wife and brought her to parliament. England had a new queen, and, with such a strong man at her side, it seemed as if nothing could dislodge her.

The wheel of fortune is a frequent choice of metaphor for the turbulent fifteenth century, and with good reason. Its appearance in contemporary literary works, illustrations and pageantry means that Elizabeth and her peers would have recognised its function and relevance to their lives. One such illustration of the 1460s, in the Harley manuscript 7353, which is housed in the British Museum, shows Edward crowned and seated on top of such a wheel, flanked by his brothers and members of the army and clergy. Having been cast down low by the goddess Fortune upon the death of John Grey and the uncertainty over her future, Elizabeth's luck had raised her high again, just as Edward's had. In 1464, she climbed as high as she could have up the social ladder, to the wheel's apex as her country's queen.

6

QUEEN
1464–1468

'Under the canapye in a mantyll of purpull.'

I

Elizabeth and Edward spent two weeks staying at Reading Abbey after Parliament had been dissolved. It must have been the closest thing they experienced to the modern concept of a honeymoon, given that the secrecy of their wedding meant they would not have had the opportunity to spend much time together until then. For Elizabeth, it was a period of both public and private adjustment. Triumph must have been mixed with apprehension, as she was treated for the first time as a queen, making the transition from being a private individual, the widow of a knight, to being the first lady of the land. The chances are that, due to her parentage, she was not a complete stranger to the ceremony of a royal court, but now she was its controversial focus, operating according to a strict code of conduct to which she had not been raised. In a way, she was following a path Edward had already walked. In spite of his father's claims to the throne, no one had really considered it likely that Henry VI would not be succeeded by his son, as the Lancastrian line had been passed as a result of direct inheritance for the past three generations. In 1461, Edward had forged his own model of kingship, inheriting a system from Henry that represented a regime he was rejecting while carving his own path in terms of the definition of his majesty. Side by side, he and Elizabeth made an unlikely couple, neither destined for the throne, nor for each other.

But Elizabeth was not only adjusting to a new life in the public eye. It is difficult to know just how much she and Edward were acquainted; whether they had known each other since childhood or if their first meeting had taken place in recent years, or even months. She may have been comfortable in the company of an old friend, or she may have been forging a new relationship with a man she knew little about. While their physical attraction appears to have been strong, or at least his attraction to her was, she may initially have known little about his character and preferences. Elizabeth had to undergo a rapid period of redefinition, as a queen and a wife. At the end of October they were at Wycombe, and in November they travelled to Westminster, where they spent the Christmas season. Edward granted her £466 13s 4d 'for the expenses of her chamber, wardrobe and stable against this feast of Christmas next coming', and over the next two years she received the palaces of Sheen and Greenwich, lands worth an annual £4,500 and numerous lordships and manors in England and Wales.[1]

Just how Elizabeth adjusted to these changes is unknown. She may have been uncertain, seeking advice, out of her depth and feeling uncomfortable, or she may have had a sense of occasion and risen to it, easily receptive to the court's deference. Edward clearly believed her capable of fulfilling the role of queen, so must have seen something of a natural nobility or a dignity and poise in her that allowed her to wear her new status well. This does not mean she was arrogant, haughty or cold, as many subsequent historians have concluded, while often praising the same qualities in the men of the era. In fact, Elizabeth's character remains elusive. As a result, she has been redrawn as a caricature by the patriarchal dialogue of historical reconstruction and those who might seek to blame Elizabeth for her marriage, or for subsequent events. This process began early, with sixteenth-century chronicler Edward Hall reducing her to a female stereotype with a 'mutable mind' seduced by 'flattering words', and Francis Bacon adding that she was 'prompting' and 'instructing' the 'stage play' from behind the scenes. A typical example is found in David MacGibbon's 1938 biography, which begins by acknowledging that some accounts paint Elizabeth as a 'person of a cool, calculating decision of character, without any deep affection, but of steady dislikes and revengeful disposition', then proceeds to add that Elizabeth's influence over Edward's mind was a 'most dangerous weapon in the hands of a woman possessed of great cunning and powers of intrigue'. Disappointingly, more modern writers have accepted this reductive process, without looking at her actions and potential motives afresh. To Ricardian Paul Murray Kendall she was 'arrogant and vain', to Geoffrey Elton, 'meddlesome and interfering', while J. R. Lander has her as 'unworthy, arrogant and avaricious'. It is time to set aside such anachronistic assessments, coloured by gender, and consider other possibilities when it comes to Elizabeth's considerable qualities. More than likely she was ambitious, like many of her peers, but was also possessed of dignity, adaptability and poise.

There was also the question of Elizabeth's large family, whose relationship to the new queen required provision. That October, her sister Margaret became the wife of Thomas FitzAlan, heir to the Earl of Arundel, who had been created a Knight of the Bath on the eve of Edward's coronation and would become a Garter knight in 1474. Then, in January 1465, the twenty-something John Woodville caused a scandal by wedding the thrice-widowed Catherine Neville, Duchess of Norfolk, who was then in her sixties. She was a sister of Cecily Neville, and thus the aunt of both Edward and Warwick. In 1466, Katherine Woodville became the wife of Henry Stafford, Duke of Buckingham, and the following year Elizabeth's eleven-year-old sister, Mary Woodville, married William Herbert, heir of the Earl of Pembroke, while her elder sister Anne became one of her ladies in waiting at a salary of £40 a year, before marrying Edward's cousin William Bourchier. The marriage that cause especial annoyance to Warwick was that of Elizabeth's son, Thomas Grey, to Anne Holland, the daughter of Edward's elder sister, Anne. An existing betrothal had been set up between Anne and Warwick's nephew, and Edward had paid his sister 4,000 marks to change her mind and her daughter's bridegroom. Certainly, some of these marriages blocked the

Above left: 1. Medieval Rouen. Edward was born in Rouen on 28 April 1442. Many of the medieval streets still remain in the city centre, with their tall, narrow buildings and churches. A clock that Edward would have known was installed on the Roman walls in this spot in 1409, although this current one dates from the sixteenth century. (Geoff Licence) *Above right:* 2. Ruins of Fotheringhay Castle. The seat of the York family in Northamptonshire, Edward would have lived here much of the time before being sent to Ludlow, and would have returned often. It came into his possession on his father's death and he stayed there frequently as king. It was also the site of the execution of Mary, Queen of Scots, in 1587. Now only this stack of stone remains in situ. (David Noble) *Below:* 3. Falcon and Fetterlock symbol. The heraldic device of the house of York, the falcon and fetterlock was the badge of Edmund of Langley, first Duke of York, who used it with the fetterlock open. Richard of York and Edward adopted it with the fetterlock closed. (Simon Leach)

Above: 4. Ludlow Castle. In the imposing castle at Ludlow, situated on the Welsh border, Edward and his brother Edmund were established in their own household in the 1450s. Two decades later, Edward would send his own son there under the guidance of the prince's uncle, Anthony Woodville, to be educated as the future King of England. (Simon Hayward) *Below:* 5. The wedding of Henry VI and Margaret of Anjou, in a cartoon of 1848. In 1445, Henry VI married the fifteen-year-old Margaret, who was passionate, warlike and driven, making her quite the opposite of her husband. The match was not popular, as Henry had to cede English possessions in France, and the Yorkists later saw her as a focal point for the king's bad advisors. This cartoon tells us more about Victorian perceptions of the couple than the marriage itself. (Library of Congress)

Above: 6 & 7. A page from an illustrated manuscript depicting Henry VI. In the close-up detail the Lancastrian king can be seen enthroned in an illuminated letter 'H'. (British Library Illuminated Manuscripts) *Right:* 8. Henry VI, taken from an engraving of 1743. Henry had come to the throne when he was still a baby, upon the death of his father, the military Henry V. Increasingly, he proved to be an ascetic and gentle personality, unsuited to the realpolitik of medieval kingship. During his bouts of mental illness in the mid-1450s, the Duke of York was appointed Lord Protector. (Library of Congress)

K.HENRY   VI

Above left: 9. Ships outside Calais. After the Yorkists fled from Ludford Bridge in 1459, York headed to Ireland while Edward accompanied Warwick to Calais. There, in 1460, they berated the captured Richard Woodville, Elizabeth's father. The town, and the weather in the Channel, would play a significant part in Edward's history, becoming both a refuge for and a location of rebellion fomented against the king. (Library of Congress) *Above right:* 10. Wigmore Castle. Following the death of his father, Edward inherited his titles and estates. Early in February 1461, bent on revenge, he used the Mortimer property of Wigmore Castle as a base before the Battle of Mortimer's Cross. Edward was swift to interpret the appearance of a parhelion, or sun dog, to his advantage, to inspire his men to victory. (Owen Lee) *Left:* 11. Edward IV. After his success at Mortimer's Cross, Edward was proclaimed king in London before defeating the Lancastrians again in the savage bloodbath of Towton. This Victorian depiction of him as king is taken from the exterior of Canterbury Cathedral. (Amy Licence)

Right: 12. The Choir of Westminster Abbey. Edward was crowned in the abbey on Sunday 28 June 1461, by Thomas Bourchier, Archbishop of Canterbury. He was crowned a second time the next day, as Sunday was considered unlucky, because the anniversary of the Childermass, or Herod's Massacre of the Innocents, had fallen on a Sunday the previous December. (Library of Congress)
Below: 13. Sunburst and white roses, Thaxted Church, Essex. Dedicated to St John the Baptist with our Lady and St Laurence, this magnificent church dates from the 1340s. Edward paid for the building of the north porch, which features his arms, and his personal symbol appears in this stained glass inside. The parish had associations with the Earls of March, who owned the manor. (Letitia Joyce)

Above left: 14. Elizabeth Woodville. This small panel portrait, thought to depict Elizabeth in her widowhood, has been attributed to Edward's court painter, John Stratford of London. Dr William A. Shaw of the Public Records Office identified this as a work by Stratford dating from 1463. (Amberley archive) *Above right:* 15. Elizabeth Woodville depicted in her coronation robes. This illuminated image is taken from the book of the London Skinner's Company's Fraternity of Our Lady's Assumption, a city guild which Elizabeth patronised. It was probably painted around 1472 and employs a range of dynastic devices. (Amberley archive) *Below:* 16. Church of Grafton Regis. After the death of her first husband in February 1461, Elizabeth Woodville returned to her parents' home at Grafton Regis. Although the manor had a hermitage on its site where Elizabeth's secret wedding to Edward is more likely to have taken place, she would have been familiar with the parish church of St Mary the Virgin, which contains the tomb of her great-grandfather Sir John Woodville, Sheriff of Northampton. (Michael O'Donnell)

Above left: 17. Canterbury Cathedral. This cathedral was something of a favourite with Edward, who visited it frequently, especially when en route to the coast. In 1468, when Margaret of York was leaving London, he decided on the spur of the moment to accompany her in order to visit the cathedral. His household accounts include payments to the shrine of St Thomas Becket and he chose to locate a portrait of his family in a window above the site of the martyrdom. (Amy Licence) Above right: 18. Margaret of York. Edward arranged the marriage of his sister Margaret to Charles the Bold of Burgundy in 1468. It marked the special relationship between England and the Netherlands that would have political and cultural influences throughout Edward's reign. (Jonathan Reeve JR1565b13p704 1450 1500) Right: 19. Shield of Edward in his capacity as a Knight of the Order of the Golden Fleece. (Rijksmuseum)

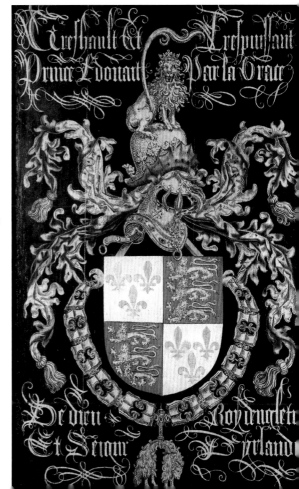

Left: 20. Richard Neville, Earl of Warwick. Having been a mentor of Edward's, whose assistance had been invaluable in 1460–1, Edward's cousin became disaffected because of differences in foreign policy, and over the promotion of the Woodville family at the expense of the Nevilles and other members of the old nobility. In 1469, he joined with Edward's ambitious brother George, Duke of Clarence, in the first of a series of attempts to oust Edward. (David Baldwin) *Below:* 21. Warwick Castle. The stronghold of the Nevilles, in Warwickshire, where Richard, Earl of Warwick, brought Edward in 1469, before realising he had little choice but to release him. On this occasion, the king forgave him and they were reconciled briefly. When Warwick rebelled again in 1470, Edward put a price on his head and the earl was forced to flee to Calais. (Library of Congress)

Above: 22. Tewkesbury Abbey. In 1470, Warwick restored Henry VI to the throne, forcing Edward into exile in the Netherlands. With help from his sister Margaret, Edward returned the following March and defeated Warwick at Barnet, before killing the remaining Lancastrians at Tewkesbury on May 4. The abbey needed to be reconsecrated after the bloodshed, as its sanctuary had been violated. (Simon Jenkins) *Right:* 23. St Mary and All Saints Church, Fotheringhay. The present church was begun in 1434 by Richard, Duke of York. In 1476, Edward arranged for the bodies of his father and brother Edmund to be exhumed and brought from Pontefract, where they were reinterred with full honours. The effigy of the Duke of York featured a crown held above his head by angelic hands, as a symbol of his inherited right to the throne. (Amanda Miller at Amanda's Arcadia)

29. Edward IV. (Ripon Cathedral)

30. Signature of Edward IV. (Amberley archive)

31. Elizabeth Woodville. (Ripon Cathedral)

32. Signature of Elizabeth Woodville. (Amberley archive)

Left: 33. Stained glass window depicting Elizabeth in Canterbury Cathedral. Made in around 1482, the window is situated above the martyrdom site, and also features Edward, with the royal arms in the centre and the personal motifs of sunbursts behind Edward and gillyflowers or carnations behind Elizabeth. (Amberley archive) *Below:* 34. Nineteenth-century illustration of Elizabeth in sanctuary, being parted from her sons Edward, Prince of Wales, and Richard, Duke of York, on the orders of Richard III. This is a dramatised version of events, as in reality Edward was already held by his uncle in the Tower of London. Elizabeth was probably persuaded that her younger son Richard was going to join his brother to prepare for Edward's coronation, or else she surrendered him through fear. (British Library on Flickr)

Above: 35. Tower of London. The Tower was the traditional location for a new king to reside before his coronation. Edward V entered in 1483 and never left; today, historians are divided over their fate and the Tower retains something of a sinister reputation as a result. (George Groutas) *Right:* 36. Richard III. On July 6, 1483, Richard of Gloucester was crowned king instead of Edward V. His two-year reign began with rebellion and was marked by the personal losses of his son and wife. In the spring of 1484, Elizabeth made the pragmatic decision to leave sanctuary on the agreement that Richard swore a public oath to protect her daughters. (Ripon Cathedral)

RICARDVS. III.

Above left: 37. Henry VII. In August 1483, Henry VI's half-nephew Henry Tudor returned from exile in Brittany and landed on the Welsh coast with an army of mercenaries. Richard had been expecting him. Against the odds, the untried Tudor defeated the king at the Battle of Bosworth Field on August 22, and was crowned on the battlefield. This Victorian depiction comes from the exterior of Canterbury Catherdral. (Amy Licence) *Above right:* 38. Elizabeth of York, eldest daughter of Edward IV and Elizabeth Woodville, whose children became kings and queens of England, Scotland and France. (Amanda Miller from Amanda's Arcadia) *Below:* 39. The great hall at Winchester. In the summer of 1486, Elizabeth accompanied her eldest daughter to Winchester and assisted in the delivery of her child, Prince Arthur. The choice of location and name must have been poignant for the widow, given Edward IV's use of the Arthurian legends. (Mark Smith)

dynastic ambitions of other 'overmighty' subjects. However, in 1469 Warwick was given the honour of his nephew's betrothal to Edward's eldest daughter and heir.

Given that in 1460 at Calais, Edward had considered Elizabeth's family to be upstarts, parvenus, who had acted above their station, these many marriages represented a considerable change of policy, but claims that they alienated the established nobility cannot be fully substantiated. The assertion by Henry VII's recent biographer, Thomas Penn, that the 'arriviste' Woodvilles were 'scrabbling' for favour at Edward's court paints too one-sided a picture, while MacGibbon sees this as the new queen's 'grasping haste'. Alison Weir writes that Elizabeth 'knew well how to manipulate her husband' and 'used her considerable influence over him to obtain favours',[2] but although she may have been aware of her power, it need not follow that she exploited this, or that any grants were made unwillingly by Edward. Perhaps he was even the instigator of these gifts. Some historians have suggested that Edward was intending to create an alternative power base to that of the Nevilles, while others assert he was simply acting in the interests of his new family. But, as Edward had found with the Nevilles in 1459–64, a large clan was a distinct advantage, and he was tying in new loyalties to the Yorkist regime with the matches for Elizabeth's sisters. Given that there was a relatively small gene pool of available spouses, the Woodville marriages did claim a number of potential husbands for other hopeful young women, such as Warwick's own daughters, Isabel and Anne, but it is likely that the earl already had his sights upon Edward's two younger brothers as potential sons-in-law. The one source that does stress Warwick's frustration with the Woodvilles is the *Annales Rerum Anglicarum*, but this is fragmentary and inconsistent and has a distinctly pro-Neville flavour.

Edward might have followed Warwick's lead in berating Richard Woodville at Calais, but in March 1466 he appointed his father-in-law as Treasurer of the Exchequer and the following year elevated him from the baronetcy to become Earl Rivers and Lord High Constable of England, drawing a salary of £200. Rivers' eldest son, Anthony, had become Lord Scales upon his 1462 marriage and taken his seat in Parliament. In the coming years, Anthony would be granted Carisbrooke Castle and the right to inherit his father's position as constable. He would prove himself to be an ideal companion for the new king in the Arthurian mode: an urbane, sophisticated patron of the arts, excelling at intellectual pursuits and the joust while remaining humble and devout. With his varied talents, as a patron and man of letters who mortified his flesh with a hair shirt, Anthony was very much a proto-Renaissance man, as much an adornment to Edward's court as his sister. Visiting Elizabeth at Sheen in April 1465, he knelt before her and her ladies gathered round him and 'tied round his thigh a collar of gold and pearls' and dropped a roll of parchment tied with gold thread into his bonnet which challenged him to compete in a tournament. Twenty years later, in the hindsight of Edward's death, Mancini would write that the Woodvilles were promoted 'to the displeasure of the whole realm' and that they were 'detested by the nobles because they were advanced beyond those who excelled them in breeding and wisdom' but there was little evidence of this being anything but short-term in 1464. In fact, Louis of France noted that Edward and Warwick were quickly reconciled. The appointments of Woodvilles to positions of office could suggest Edward's devotion to his new family, or that their merit outstripped their former rank, or both.

Elizabeth's coronation took place on Sunday 26 May 1465. As some commentators have stated, this was a whole year after her secret wedding, but it was just nine months after she had been introduced to the Reading parliament as queen. Edward was not delaying the process: such things took time to organise and he was keen to allow for her Luxembourg relatives to arrive. Safe conduct for Philip of Burgundy and his party was issued as early as October 1464 and coronation invitations were dispatched in January. Shortly before the event, Elizabeth's uncle, the elegant Jacques de Luxemburg, landed with a deputation of 100 Burgundian knights. Edward fully intended to make it a grand event, to deploy his connections and resources in order to emphasise Elizabeth's new status. Yet given some of the criticisms levelled against her birth, it was essential to remind people of her maternal descent from the Count of St Pol and the grand-ducal family of Luxembourg. Again, the concept of magnificence was deployed as a political tool. Costs of over £400 were paid to the treasurer of Elizabeth's household for the event, with £280 spent on cloth of gold, £108 on a cup and basin of gold, £27 on silk for her chairs and horses and £20 on plate for the coronation feast. The heralds were supplied with scarlet and crimson damask robes and summons to attend were sent to the lord mayor and aldermen on 14 April.

Elizabeth's coronation procession was to be enlivened by pageantry. Evidence survives for only a fraction of the payments made to the guilds for their entertainments staged at various points through the city streets. Elizabeth was met by the mayor and conducted into the city, probably from Shooter's Hill or Blackfriars. London Bridge had been fumigated and sprinkled with sand and she was guided across the bridge by a clerk dressed as St Paul, who was paid 20*d* for his part. Angels awaited her in the middle, wearing flax wigs dyed with saffron and wings made of peacock feathers. A choir of twenty-six singers serenaded her from a stage that had been built using 5,000 nails and plastered with gold, red, green, black and white paper. It is to be expected that the usual format followed, of several displays and performances of mythical and biblical figures along the route, with the conduits running with wine and bells pealing out across the spectator-lined streets. London itself had spent 200 marks on decorations and collected a gift for their new queen of 1,000 marks.[3] Ballads were composed and written upon six boards but no longer survive, nor does the welcome speech delivered by the character of St Elizabeth. There would have been more pageants, speeches and song before Elizabeth reached the Tower, where she was to be lodged in advance of the event.

It is worth pausing at this point to draw the comparison between this event and the coronation of Margaret of Anjou exactly twenty years before. The fifteen-year-old Margaret had undergone a very similar reception on 30 May 1445, welcomed as a princess of royal blood by Londoners in 'costeous array' as she rode in a chariot followed by more chariots filled with ladies of rank. London Bridge featured two pageants emphasising the particular hopes for her reign, combining Peace and Plenty, as the future bearer of sons and the bringer of peace with France. There were six other pageants along the route to the Tower, and possibly more the following day as she rode from there to Westminster. Her final journey was made in a litter made of white cloth of gold, drawn by horses trapped in the same material, with the queen's hair hanging loose under a gold coronet of precious stones and pearls. Elizabeth had been around eight years old at the time and it is likely that her parents played key roles during the ceremony and the banquet and jousting that followed. As she travelled the same route, did Elizabeth reflect upon the fate of her predecessor, now languishing in exile?

On the night of 23 May 1465, Edward created a number of new Knights of the Bath in the Tower of London. Elizabeth's brother John Woodville was among them, joining the king's brothers and other figures such as his new brother-in-law Thomas FitzAlan. On the following morning, these knights dressed in blue gowns with white silk hoods and accompanied Elizabeth, who rode in an open horse litter through the streets toward Westminster. The following day, she was crowned in the abbey by the Archbishop of Canterbury, Thomas Bourchier, whose brother was married to Edward's aunt; Bourchier would be made a cardinal two years later. The Duke of Suffolk bore the sceptre of St Edward and the Earl of Essex the sceptre of England. After the ceremony Elizabeth was led to her chamber, where she had a brief moment to catch her breath before being 'new revestyd in a surcote of purpull' and conveyed to her seat in the hall. The King of Arms, William Ballard, left a written account of the banquet that followed. The Duke of Clarence and the Duke of Norfolk, as stewards, rode into the hall to 'avoyde the peple agenste the coming of the queen' with their horses richly trapped in crimson garnished with gold spangles hanging down to the ground. As Elizabeth entered, she was 'under the canapye clothed in a mantyll of purpull and a coronall upon her hede, brought yn between the Bysshop of Durham on her right hand and the Bysshop of Salisbury on her left'.⁴ In attendance upon her were her mother, Jacquetta; Edward's sisters Margaret and Elizabeth, Duchess of Suffolk; along with thirteen duchesses in red velvet and ermine, fourteen baronesses in scarlet and miniver and twelve ladies in scarlet, clearly delineating their status by slight changes of colour and furs. Edward's mother, Cecily, Duchess of York, is not specifically named as being in attendance. There might be significance to this, although it should be noted that Edward would not have attended so as not to upstage his wife in precedence, and that Warwick was absent on a diplomatic mission. At her own coronation, Elizabeth had to be the star of the show.

The elaborate protocol of Elizabeth's banquet has often been cited as evidence of her arrogance and hauteur. Yet these rules would have been established by Edward and his advisors, not Elizabeth herself, with all the members of her court doing her honour. First, she washed her hands, with Clarence holding the bowl and the Earl of Oxford pouring the water. Then she sat in state, crowned, with kneeling countesses holding her veil, flanked by Elizabeth and Margaret of York. Even seemingly menial roles were taken by high ranking officials in an act of deference to her position, so it was not the usual stewards and ushers who bore the cups or carved the meat: the Duke of Norfolk was her server, Lord Cromwell her carver and her brother Anthony carried the cup. The first course, comprising seventeen dishes, was brought to the table by the Knights of the Bath; the second had nineteen and the third, fifteen. Between each course, the trumpeters blew and the king's minstrels played 'full melodiously and in the most solemn wise'. She was served spiced wine, or hippocras, by her brother, then her almoner and chaplain folded the table cloth 'and before her reverently took it up and bore it from the table'. The Mayor of London brought the final cup of wine and Clarence held the dish of spices known as the 'void', which was the traditional ending to a meal. On the Monday following, the Arthurian tradition was continued with a great tournament held at Westminster.

One writer has suggested that the presence of Elizabeth's Luxembourg relations, intended to enhance her status, resulted in the opposite effect. Describing Jacques and his knights as 'rowdy relatives' who 'spoke and understood little English' thus 'marring' the marriage, H. Eugene Lehman paints a picture of guests carousing with 'flamboyant heraldry' that featured Elizabeth in the role of Melusine, the 'bawdy water-witch daughter of Satan himself'. Lehman states that this imagery would have confused the English, who would have been left wondering whether their new queen was engaged in acts of black magic. This is unlikely to have occurred on any level other than that of idle gossip, which Edward would not have tolerated, yet from this Lehman extrapolates that Elizabeth was accepted as Edward's consort, but 'never enjoyed the goodwill of her subjects' because of her witchcraft and that she was a 'common nobody', a 'schemer' and a social climber.[5] This may have been drawn from descriptions that have arisen from historical fiction that Jacques and his men carried shields bearing a creature that was half-woman and half-serpent. Such images and their connotations would have hindered the very occasion that the Burgundians had been invited to support, and do not appear in any contemporary or subsequent sources relating to the occasion. They appear to be yet another example of the entangling of historical fact and myth, which has led to the blurring of Elizabeth's true story.

In July 1465, Edward and Elizabeth were visiting Canterbury when they were brought the news that Henry VI had been captured. Edward ordered a service of thanksgiving to be held and the news proclaimed as Warwick brought the Lancastrian to confinement in the Tower. Henry was paraded through the streets to allow the public to see it was really him, although the London mob jeered and spat and according to Warkworth, Henry's legs were 'bound to the stirrups.' It was an undignified and humiliating journey for an anointed king, but Warwick clearly felt it was necessary in case of attempts to liberate him, or that it was desirable to display Henry's degradation in contrast with Edward's majesty. Elizabeth's son Thomas Grey was among the five men appointed to look after the ageing Lancastrian. It was around this time that Edward reissued the coinage, so that it was his face, his sign of authority, circulating with every transaction throughout the country instead of that of Henry VI. With his rival king in his power, Edward could finally be confident that the external threats to his regime had been eradicated. However, he would soon have to look closer to home for his enemies.

II

By the time of Henry's capture, Elizabeth may have begun to suspect she was pregnant. Having already been through the process twice, she would have spotted the symptoms fairly early, even in an era when conception was difficult to diagnose and physicians resorted to dubious urine testing and external symptoms such as the brightness of the eyes or flushed cheeks. With regular menstruation dependent upon bodyweight, health and nutrition, Elizabeth's diet would certainly not have been lacking the necessary protein; actually, given her record and the existence of at least one illegitimate child fathered by Edward, it may be more remarkable that she did not conceive sooner. It is worth considering the possibility that during the period between her marriage and falling pregnant, which was roughly a year from May 1464 to May 1465, Elizabeth may have mistakenly believed herself to be pregnant, or hoped that she was. Paradoxically, pregnancy was a condition which placed woman at their most powerful and their most vulnerable. Motherhood was the fifteenth century's ultimate goal for a secular woman, elevating her status, giving her purpose and locking her firmly into the patriarchal system of inheritance and dynastic continuity. Illegitimacy complicated the question, but powerful men could still rally around such a child to secure their future, as happened with Arthur Plantagenet. Yet it could easily go wrong for a mother, even an experienced mother, on a social and personal level. Every pregnancy carried a range of risks and the Woodville women would have been aware of this.

There is also the possibility that a potential pregnancy was used to sway Edward's hand in admitting the marriage: perhaps Elizabeth or Jacquetta feared his intentions and hinted at the likelihood to prevent him repudiating the ceremony. With both Richard and Anthony Woodville frequently at court, rumours of Edward's former dalliances and broken promises may well have reached the women's ears. After all, Elizabeth had already produced two healthy sons, and healthy sons were exactly what the new dynasty required. It is not inconceivable that Edward's decision to admit the marriage in September might have been provoked by a suspected pregnancy, which tipped the balance in Elizabeth's favour, but later turned out to be a false alarm.

It seems Edward had no scruples in fathering illegitimate children, as proven by the acknowledged existence of Arthur Plantagenet. However, Arthur's unknown mother may have already been married or deceased or unsuited in some way to being queen, which would have prevented a marriage to solve the problem of illigitmacy. Alternatively, Edward may simply have no longer desired her. No sources actually mention these possibilities – it is pure speculation – but it would provide an alternative explanation for Edward's confession of his marriage to Elizabeth in parliament that September, despite his previous track record of abandoning his past lovers. Regardless of this theory, Elizabeth would have become increasingly confident of her condition as the summer of 1465 progressed. With the arrival of autumn, she would have felt her child quicken.

Elizabeth frequently travelled with Edward to the palaces of Sheen, Greenwich, Westminster, Windsor and other places, but she was granted Ormond's Inn as a London base. It was situated on the corner of Garlicke Hill and Knightrider Street, right next to the corner of Old Fish Street, just beyond the city wall at Smithfield, and had been owned by James Butler, 5th Earl of Ormond, who had been beheaded after Towton. Her household consisted of trusted Yorkists, often members of the extended family, including her chamberlain, John Bourchier; Lord Berners, Knight of the Garter and Constable of Windsor Castle; her brother John Woodville, who was her Master of the Horse; her carver, Humphrey Bourchier; and among her ladies in waiting were her sister Anne, Lady Bourchier; and Anthony's wife, Elizabeth, Lady Scales. She had an additional twelve women, three minstrels, a confessor, chancellor, solicitor, clerk and other legal assistants. Henry and Humphrey Stafford, sons of the Duke of Buckingham who had died at Northampton, also lived in Elizabeth's house as wards, being granted 500 marks a year for their keep and taught grammar by a John Giles.[6] Her physician, Domenico de Serigo, kept a close eye on her as her pregnancy advanced and the royal couple retired to Westminster for Christmas.

Elizabeth would have made a formal retreat into confinement in January. This delivery would be very different from the two she had previously experienced, although some of the practical elements would have been similar. The birth chamber was governed by a set of rules and superstitions that travelled across class boundaries, although status did dictate the way they were applied. With her Grey sons, Elizabeth is likely to have followed the pattern for women of the nobility in delivering her child in a chosen room of her own home, or returning to the home of her parents. The latter was quite common, as medical advice urged women to retreat from the world for around a month, sealed inside their chamber and remaining lying down for weeks after the delivery. This was partly based in common sense, to avoid accidents and allow for a period of recovery, but it did mean a woman needed a support network of family, friends or servants and the female 'gossips' who kept her company and filled essential roles during and after the delivery. With men excluded entirely, the sealed room became metonymic for the expectant womb: kept warm and dark, supplied with food and drink, firewood and blankets for up to a month before and a month afterwards. Of course, predicting a child's due date was not a precise science, and some women experienced early or late arrivals, sometimes even false alarms. However, there was a recognition that once the process began, a woman was in the hands of nature, or of God. Wherever possible, as many plans and preparations were made in advance, although the examples of women being caught unawares show that even the best-laid plans could go awry.

In January 1466, Elizabeth chose to lie in at Westminster Palace. Her royal chamber had already been prepared, probably months in advance, being thoroughly cleaned, repainted, redecorated and provisioned. It is likely that her bedchamber was among the queen's apartments in the southern range, overlooking the Thames and Lambeth Palace set in the fields of the south bank beyond. This may have been the White Chamber built by Henry III for his queen, or part of a later remodelling in the fifteenth century, but it would certainly have been secluded and sheltered, away from the social, legal and financial hub of the palace. There would have been a process of formal retirement, signalling Elizabeth's retreat, marked by her attendance at Mass, special prayers for her safety, a ceremonial procession and the partaking of wine and spices. The door was closed upon her and her ladies, and the stream of female visitors was carefully monitored. Inside the room, two beds were provided; a straw pallet for her labour and a bed for her rest. The following year, Elizabeth would order a featherbed with bolsters and cushions, furnishings of damask and washable fabric, fine linen cloth from Brittany and unbleached, thick fustian, so it is likely she made similar provision in late 1465. There were also two cradles, the fires were built up, the 'cup-board' stocked with artefacts and talismans and a portable altar with religious objects and relics. Curtains or tapestries were hung over the windows, with just one left unsealed to allow her to look outside. These were chosen carefully, with all scenes of hunting or violence removed: anything that might be considered shocking might imprint itself upon the unborn child. It was clearly not the series of tapestries depicting the Trojan Wars that graced the king's chamber later in Edward's reign.

Along with most royal physicians, Dr Serigo had predicted the arrival of a son and was keen to gain admittance to Elizabeth's chamber while she was in labour. Fabyan's Chronicle described him waiting in an antechamber in order to spread the news. However, he was denied entry to Elizabeth's bedroom and had to sit and wait as the midwife, Margery Cobbe, along with Elizabeth's mother, Jacquetta, and 'gossips', friends and sisters, were put to more practical use. It is not impossible that Edward's mother, Cecily, was also present, as the survival of mother and child could depend upon the accumulation of female wisdom, in generations of experience passed down in an oral tradition from mothers to daughters. Some would have played a fairly hands-on role, but the younger ones may have been present to read aloud to Elizabeth, to sing and dance, or play games to divert her, or to pray with her. With little pain relief beyond herbal remedies containing mint or willow bark – from which aspirin is derived – or the dulling effects of spiced wine, Elizabeth braced herself against her labour pains. As a good Catholic, she would have also relied upon the power of prayer and holy relics; later, her daughter would use the girdle of the Virgin Mary, kept in Westminster Abbey, as a pain reliever during childbirth, so Elizabeth may also have clung to this, or a phial of holy water or wax Agnus Dei: anything that would have given her the placebic illusion of control.

Finally, on 11 February, Elizabeth delivered her baby safely. It was a girl. She was cleaned, probably in a mixture of white wine and herbs, swaddled and laid in the cradle. It was not the boy that had been predicted, but she was healthy enough and girls were always important for dynastic marriages. Her survival allowed Edward and Elizabeth every hope that they would have more children in the future, of both genders. Edward rewarded his wife with a jewelled ornament worth £125; perhaps he was allowed into the darkened room to present it in person, as Elizabeth lay recovering in bed. She would have been advised to remain lying down for between forty and sixty days, depending on how easy the birth had been. During this time, her daughter was carried out to the church and baptised Elizabeth, with her two grandmothers, Jacquetta and Cecily, standing as godmothers and Warwick as godfather. When the queen was ready, high-ranking women would have assisted her to rise and dress, in advance of the churching ceremony of purification. This marked her re-emergence into society and her return to her duties and her husband's bed. It was also a process of welcoming her back into the Church: a blessing to remove the dangerous influences that were thought to hover around the birth chamber and to celebrate her survival.

Elizabeth's churching was famously witnessed by the Bohemian visitor Gabriel Tetzel, who was visiting London with his master, Leo of Rozmital, and left a detailed account of the occasion. It gives an idea of the elaborate ceremonial of the court and its emphasis on order and precedence, while also shedding light on the origins of the queen's reputation for being aloof and haughty. Elizabeth walked in procession from her chamber to either the abbey or St Stephen's Chapel, 'accompanied by many priests bearing relics and by many scholars singing and carrying lights'. Behind her were a 'great number of ladies and maidens from the country and from London' and a 'great company of trumpeters, pipers and players of stringed instruments'. After them came the king's choir, comprising forty-two singers, then there were twenty-four heralds followed by sixty counts and knights. Then came Elizabeth, walking under a canopy, escorted by two dukes. Sixty women walked behind her, including her mother. After the service had been performed, all those involved were feasted in the palace, 'men and women, ecclesiastical and lay, each according to rank, and filled four great rooms'. According to Tetzel, 'one of the King's most powerful earls sat at the head of the King's table on the King's chair in his stead', and this may have been Warwick. 'Everything was supplied for the earl, as representing the King … [with] carvers, buffets and side tables in profusion'. It is likely that, along with the coronations and funerals of royal spouses, Edward was not present in person at the ceremony, so as not to upstage his wife.

Edward may not have physically been there, or else may have followed the custom of observing from behind a screen, but his presence was felt in the distribution of royal gifts to the musicians and heralds. When Rozmital's retinue had finished eating, they were conducted to an 'unbelievably costly apartment' and seated in an alcove to observe the queen dining. Elizabeth was seated at a table alone, on a 'costly golden chair'. Her mother and Princess Margaret were standing at a distance, kneeling whenever they interacted with the queen – 'not until the first dish was set before the queen' could they be seated. Tetzel commented that all the women present 'were of noble birth' and he found it remarkable that they 'had to kneel so long as the queen was eating'. The meal lasted for three hours in total, during which 'everyone was silent and not a word was spoken'. It is this elaborate ritual that has been interpreted as haughtiness on Elizabeth's part, but in the context of the entire account, it was merely the pinnacle of the extensive social triangle, each section of which was governed by similar restrictions. This was not imposed by Elizabeth, who would hardly have chosen to treat her mother in such a manner had there not been good reason or mutual agreement. The account continues with the detail that once the dancing began the queen bade Jacquetta to rise.

Such 'courtly reverence' being paid to the queen was important in the projection of majesty by which the new regime defined itself, particularly given the criticisms levelled at Elizabeth's origins in 1464. Observation by visitors and the public of the royal ritual was an effective tool to both connect with and distance the populace. Yet it was a conscious performance: a public show designed to impress, with each playing their part. It was not a glimpse into their private world. When on display, Edward's court presented itself at its best, and, according to Tetzel, everything was superlative. The women were 'exceedingly beautiful', the courtiers paid reverence 'such as [he had] never seen elsewhere', and at mass he 'did not think [he had] heard finer singing in this world'. The visitors were then treated to another carefully stage-managed scene, as Edward showed them his collection of holy relics. This display of ownership, of curatorship, established Edward as a conduit to the divine: as a guardian figure, appointed by God to oversee such precious items in his role as divine representative on earth. Just like these glimpses into his court, he controlled who saw the relics, when and how, just as he controlled what people wore through his sumptuary laws of 1463 and 1465. Tetzel and his companions certainly did not get to glimpse the royal family in their private apartments behind closed doors. The clear demarcation between public and private was one of the ways in which Edwardian magnificence was projected.

Another way in which Elizabeth acted as a conduit for majesty was in her patronage of Queens' College, Cambridge. The college had previously been established by Margaret of Anjou, but was refounded by Elizabeth at some point before March 1465, when she was referred to as the college patroness upon the grant of a licence for the president and fellows to purchase lands to the value of £200, and for the appropriation of churches so that they might pray 'for the good estate of the king and his said consort and for their souls after death'. Margaret had issued the college charter seventeen years earlier, on 15 April 1448, the day that the foundation stone was laid. By refounding the institution instead of simply taking it over, Elizabeth was making a point about the legitimacy of the York regime in comparison to the Lancastrian line, echoing similar sentiments used by Edward and his parents, and becoming its 'true foundress by right of succession'. Elizabeth issued the college with its first statutes in 1475.

With the primary role of a queen being motherhood, Elizabeth fell pregnant again just nine months after delivering her first daughter. In July 1467, the queen went into confinement at Windsor Castle, where she gave birth to a second girl, who was named Mary. Less than a year later, she conceived for the third time in four years, and returned to the palace of Westminster for her lying-in. She and Edward must have hoped that this time she would bear a son, but another daughter came on 20 March 1469, whom they named Cecily. Two barrels of hippocras and a pipe of Gascon wine were 'delivered into the king's cellar' to celebrate her christening. Elizabeth had more than proven her fertility, but with three girls in the royal nursery, a question still remained over the future of the Yorkist dynasty. Until such time as she could produce a son, Edward's immediate heir was his brother George, Duke of Clarence. Edward was strong and apparently healthy; in April 1469 he marked his twenty-seventh birthday, but the recent years had proven the propensity of powerful men to die young. Accidents, illness and foul play could also carry people away overnight. That year, George turned eighteen, the very age at which Edward had led an army back into England and won the battles of Northampton, Mortimer's Cross and Towton. George was still unmarried, but in the event that he took a wife and fathered a son, he would stand a good chance of inheriting the throne. He found a powerful ally in the Earl of Warwick, who had become increasingly disaffected by the division between his foreign policies and those of Edward, to whose plans he was no longer privy. By 1469, Warwick's elder daughter was of marriageable age, and frustration combined with ambition united Edward's two closest allies in a rebellion intended to oust him from his throne.

7

TROUBLE AHEAD
1468–1469

'Especially astute and cunning.'

I

By the late 1460s, Edward and Warwick were set on a collision course over France and Burgundy. Edward may have been born in Rouen, but it had then been an English-controlled city and had fallen to the French in 1449, after the Yorks had left. The complicated Anglo-French struggles of the Hundred Years War had technically come to an end four years later, with the defeat of the English at the Battle of Castillon. Edward may have signed a treaty of peace with Louis XI in 1463, but he would soon come to consider reopening the breach and invading France to reassert the English crown's historic claims. Warwick had been keen to promote a French marriage for Edward in 1464, and refused to be deterred in his pursuit of a closer alliance despite the king increasingly favouring Burgundy. By looking towards the elegant and highly ritualised culture of the Netherlands, with its flourishing arts, Edward was taking a new direction, towards a northern-European Renaissance. Essentially, he may have seen France as representative of the past – of the Lancastrian regime – while Burgundy presented an exciting future.

The Milanese state papers highlight the developing tensions between the king and earl over foreign policy. Understandably, Louis was reluctant to trust English intentions after the revelations of Edward's marriage had rendered the potential alliance with Bona of Savoy invalid. Like Warwick, Louis may have felt duped, even insulted, sympathising with the earl as someone who 'had always been a friend to his crown' while he suspected the other ambassadors of 'deceit or double dealing'.[1] Louis was particularly annoyed, as he had sent a contingency of men to fight alongside the Yorkists at Towton and had hoped to cement this with an alliance with the new regime. As Louis met Warwick in Rouen, the French king was aware that Edward was negotiating for his sister to marry Charles the Bold, son of Philip of Burgundy. Louis had offered the hand in marriage of his own daughter Anne to Charles, but it had been refused because the girl was only eight years old. 'If this takes place,' the Milanese dispatch continued, referring to the match of Charles and Margaret, '[Louis had] talked of treating with the Earl of Warwick to restore King Henry in England, and the ambassador of the old queen in England is already here.' This was treasonous talk, imagining Warwick opening the back door to a French invasion to restore the Lancastrian line, dating from as early as the summer of 1467. In such circumstances, a restored Margaret of Anjou could not be expected to be forgiving. It could only mean the death or exile of Edward and his family. The Croyland chronicler stated, 'For some years [Warwick] had appeared to favour the French against the Burgundians, [and] was deeply offended ... this in my opinion, was the real cause of dissension between the king and the earl rather than the marriage between the king and queen.'

Then, in June that year, George Neville was deprived of the royal seal. Just two years had passed since his inauguration as Archbishop of York, when his 6,000 guests at Cawood Castle had entered historical legend by feasting upon 4,000 pigeons, 2,000 chickens, 2,000 pigs, 1,000 sheep, 4,000 tarts, 2,000 custards and much more. Edward refused to let Neville open parliament on 3 June, and five days later had decided that he was obstructing royal policy to the extent that he paid him a visit in person, accompanied by twelve lords, carrying away the seal in his own hands. George was no longer chancellor and Edward backed the nomination of

Thomas Bourchier to a senior position that Neville had hoped for. It might have been taken as an ominous sign that, like his secret marriage, the king was asserting his autonomy and that his intentions did not always coincide with those of the Nevilles. Perhaps this was a conscious policy to limit the family's power, or a reaction to Edward's perception that Warwick's relatives were not willing to accept his ultimate authority, instead feeling that they shared it equally. George's demotion marked an important point in the family's declining influence over the king: on 20 June, Robert Stillington, Bishop of Bath and Wells, was appointed chancellor instead.

Warwick had been in France, but learned of this event upon his arrival in Sandwich four days later. 'This troubled the Earl very much,' explained Waurin, 'but he did not show his anger because he was especially astute and cunning.' Yet, after being reunited with Edward, who was in the company of Anthony Woodville and Lord Hastings, he could not conceal his anger, asking the Admiral of France, 'Have you not seen the traitors who surround the king? ... Know that these are the men by whom my brother has been deprived of the office of chancellor and of the seal.' After this, Edward and Elizabeth left Westminster for six weeks and went to Windsor, so that Edward did not have to see the French ambassadors. It was a deliberate and calculated slight and Warwick felt it deeply. In their absence, the earl met with George, Duke of Clarence, and complained that there were 'scarcely any of the blood royal at court, and that Lord Rivers and his family dominated everything.' According to Waurin, when George asked how the situation could be remedied, Warwick replied 'that if the duke would trust him, he would make him King of England, or governor of the whole realm, and he need be in no doubt that most of the country would support him'. This was treasonous talk, but no less than Warwick's previous scheming with Edward against the hapless Henry VI.

Warwick may have been considering a marriage between his elder daughter Isabel and George, Duke of Clarence, for years. It would seem like a suitable alliance in terms of age and status, and as a reward for the loyalty displayed by the earl during the Yorkist nadir of 1459–61. By this point, though, Edward was hoping to make a more lucrative foreign match for George, and early in 1466 had proposed to the Flemish ambassadors that his brother marry Mary, daughter of Charles the Bold. Mary was then nine years old, but, unless her father produced a son, she was the sole heiress to the duchy of Burgundy. Mary was too valuable a prospect to be married off to a younger brother, so Charles rejected this match, but did propose that he take Edward and George's sister Margaret as his wife. Margaret was then twenty, comparatively old to be a first-time bride, given that husbands had been found for her elder sisters, Anne and Elizabeth, when the girls were in their early teens. Several bridegrooms had already been proposed, including James III of Scotland and Don Pedro, a Spanish Prince to whom Margaret was betrothed in 1465, but whose death soon afterwards freed her to marry Charles. Edward was keen to accept the Burgundian offer and cement what was to become a conduit of cultural exchange which had a lasting effect upon English culture. However the news came as a blow to George, who was 'young and trusting' and agreed to marry Isabel Neville as part of Warwick's plan to overthrow Edward.

Why was Burgundy such an attractive prospect to Edward? An Anglo-Burgundian alliance was nothing new and made geographical sense given the common enemy of France. Back in 1420, Philip the Good had allied with Henry V against France at the Treaty of Troyes, and three years later the duke had married his sister Anne to John, Duke of Bedford. This pact had been shaken by the Burgundians' withdrawal at the 1435 Treaty of Arras, by which time both John and Anne were dead and Philip was reconciled with the French against the Lancastrian regime. Yet any enemy of Lancaster might seek out the Burgundians as an ally, and this proved an advantage to the Yorkists. The experienced Philip was a strategically important figure, ruling across a wide and varied collection of territories, and with its trading hubs of Brussels, Bruges and Ghent, Burgundy had reached a peak of commercial prosperity, allowing for the flourishing of the arts. Philip had established a cultural path of pageantry and tournaments similar to that which Edward was pursuing. In 1430, he had founded the chivalric Order of the Golden Fleece with its distinctive gold chain, with membership initially restricted to twenty-four knights, much as Edward III had created the Order of the Garter in 1348. Even before Philip's death in 1467, Anglo-Burgundian friendship had been furthered by the tournament at Smithfield and discussions were already underway for a marriage alliance between Margaret of York and Philip's son, Charles. The Burgundian diplomat Commines, who was a knight in Charles's household, certainly thought the match was arranged in order to strengthen ties against France. In addition, there was the family connection established by Edward's marriage to Elizabeth, through her mother's descent from a cadet line of the house of Luxembourg. In 1443, the main dynastic line was dwindling and the remaining senior member, Elizabeth of Gorlitz, had sold the duchy to Philip the Good, absorbing Jacquetta's extensive family into the Burgundian fiefdom.

As a young man, Charles had been keen to marry Anne of York, Edward's elder sister, but his father insisted he honour the French alliance outlined in the terms of the Treaty of Arras, so instead he was married to Isabelle of Bourbon. She produced one daughter, Mary of Burgundy, but died in the autumn 1465. Charles was then thirty-three. His envoy arrived in England early the following year. A surviving portrait of Charles, who was given the epithets of 'the Bold', 'the Terrible' and 'the Warrior' by his peers, was painted by the early Renaissance Netherlands artist Rogier van der Weyden. Given that Weyden's death occurred in June 1464, the image is likely to have been completed before Charles's thirtieth birthday and depicts a striking and distinguished, but not unsympathetic, face, with mild eyes, long nose and prominent mouth. Charles's reddish brown hair is slightly curling, cut in a fairly modern-looking style, and he wears a dark-blue doublet with high collar and puffed sleeves, over which hangs the necklace of the Order of the Golden Fleece. In 1468, in anticipation of the match, he conferred this order upon Edward himself.

That year, arrangements slowly advanced. Margaret appeared in person to give her consent to the match before the Great Council at Kingston-upon-Thames. A treaty was signed at Brussels on 16 February and, a week later, Charles wrote to Edward regarding the match: '[For] the giving of mutual aid for the defence and safeguard of countries and dominions … we offer and promise to protect and defend for ever, to our power, the realm of England.' Edward made a corresponding promise on 24 March and the treaty was ratified, meaning that plans for the marriage could proceed. Margaret's dowry was fixed at 200,000 gold crowns, of which a quarter was to be delivered on her wedding day, guaranteed by London city merchants and the merchants of the Calais Staple. Despite his show of magnificence, Edward's coffers were not overflowing and it was difficulties encountered while raising this large sum that led to the wedding to be delayed from 4 May to 3 July. Edward did, however, establish a special committee with responsibility for the marriage, under the leadership of Lord Hastings, Lord Wenlock and none other than Warwick himself. Still Warwick did not give up, and that April, as Edward summoned trusted servants who would accompany his sister to Burgundy, he was still proposing rival candidates for Margaret's hand, most of whom were French. This set him into direct conflict with the Woodvilles, who were actively backing the union with Charles. With the arrival of a papal dispensation in May, removing the obstacle of the bride and groom's relation in the fourth degree, Edward announced in Parliament that Margaret was to be married to 'oon of myghtyest Princes of the world that bereth no crown'. The princess's trousseau was ordered and Warwick was forced to concede defeat.

It was at this point that the scandal of Sir Thomas Cook broke. His sad story is related in the London Chronicle, and it is likely that its author, Robert Fabyan, was at the time serving an apprenticeship in Cook's household. Sir Thomas was a draper who had risen to become Lord Mayor of London in 1462, but is said to have made enemies of the Woodvilles. One of his roles was to supply the court with fabrics and furnishings, but he refused, or was unable, to sell Jacquetta a particular arras she desired. It may have been the 'Life of Alexander', or 'The Last Judgement of the Passion of Our Lord', which were itemised among his possessions at a combined value of at nearly £1,000.[2] Cook was among those who had pledged to guarantee the loan of money to Edward to pay for Margaret's dowry, but that June a Lancastrian servant had been arrested carrying a packet of letters from exiled supporters of the old regime to their friends in England. Under torture, the man named Cook as being sympathetic to Henry VI.

Cook was arrested on charges of treason, and during his absence Woodville servants ransacked his houses in London and the country, removing valuable items including jewels and plate worth £700, as well as the tapestries.[3] Cook was put on trial, but was only convicted of the lesser offence of not declaring treasonable activities that he was aware of, rather than of committing treason himself. It appears that Margaret personally intervened, disliking the scandal attached to one associated with her coming marriage. Cook was given a huge fine, but this was offset against the damage done to his house, although Elizabeth claimed the additional £800 she was entitled to under the rule of 'Queen's gold'. The facts of the case are difficult to establish, with the chronicle's sympathies clearly lying with Cook and the Woodvilles' involvement being used against them by their enemies; going on the surviving accounts, it does not appear to be an episode which covers them with glory. It must be remembered, however, that their side of the story remains untold.

Margaret's trousseau reflected the magnificence of her brother's court. It included silks to the value of £1,000, bedding, cushions and carpets worth £100 and gold, silver and gilt dishes costing £160. In addition, she was granted £200 for her food on the journey to Burgundy and £900 in cash for other expenses. She also took with her a specially made gold coronet, with enamelled white roses interspersed with pearls and precious stones, and red, green and white enamelled letters spelling out her name. With everything ready, Margaret left London on 18 June, riding pillion behind Warwick to St Paul's Cathedral, where she made an offering. Along Cheapside, the new mayor, Thomas Oulegrave, gave her a pair of silver-gilt bowls worth £100. She crossed London Bridge for the last time and spent the night with the court in Stratford Abbey. Here, she was supposed to bid goodbye to Edward and Elizabeth, but her brother decided to ride down to the coast with her and revisit the Canterbury shrine of Thomas Becket, a journey of three days which involved overnight stops at Dartford, Rochester and Sittingbourne. Along with her three brothers, Edward, George and the sixteen-year-old Richard, Margaret visited Canterbury, but it was Anthony and Edward Woodville who embarked with her on the *New Ellen* at Margate the next day. They arrived at Sluys, after possibly being attacked by French ships, on the evening of 25 June.

It is lucky that one of the most prolific letter writers of the age was directly involved in Margaret's marriage. John Paston II of Norfolk had been born in the same year as Edward, less than two weeks before the king's birth in Rouen. He had become one of the henchmen courtiers in Edward's service in 1461, one of the young men for whom the advice manuals of manners and conduct were produced, perhaps waiting at table while being educated and learning the chivalric codes. He was knighted when he came of age in 1463 and took part in the Burgundian joust of 1467, but had to defend his family's inheritance of properties left to them by Sir John Fastolf, which was challenged by such influential figures as Edward's brothers-in-law Anthony Woodville and John de la Pole, Duke of Suffolk. Unswayed by family ties in this case, Edward confirmed John's possession of Caister Castle and made him an MP for Norfolk and a Justice of the Peace. John was betrothed to Anne Haute, a cousin of Elizabeth Woodville, although their marriage never took place. Edward clearly trusted and valued Paston, to the extent that he chose him to be among the retinue accompanying Princess Margaret to Burgundy. A letter from the king to John dated 18 April stated, 'It is accorded between us and our cousin the Duke of Burgundy that he shall wed out dearest sister Margaret and in a short while we intend to send her into Flanders for the accomplishment and solemnization of the marriage ... our pleasure is [that] you will dispose yourself to the said intent and purpose.' What Edward did not know is that Paston had made a wager on the wedding, agreeing to pay eighty shillings for a horse if it took place within two years and only half the amount if it did not.

If Edward's wedding to Elizabeth had been marked by secrecy and a lack of ceremony, Margaret's was the opposite. It was recorded by a number of witnesses, not just John Paston, but some who were specifically commissioned to report details for those who could not attend. Their accounts give a flavour of the Burgundian attention to detail that was to so impress Edward that he later sought to emulate it in his own court. Dressed in crimson and black, Margaret was met by musicians on a barge, playing trumpets and clarions, and led to a reception hosted by Charles's half-siblings, who had previously sheltered Richard of York and his son George during their exile after the Battle of Wakefield. The householders of Sluys were standing in their doorways holding tapers to light her way to the Watergate, where she was presented with a purse containing twelve gold marks. The streets in the town were carpeted, leading her to the marketplace, where she was lodged in the house of the merchant Guy van Baenst. There she met her future husband for the first time and their formal betrothal took place. She stayed there for a week, being entertained by pageants enacted on a stage erected opposite the house, before departing for Damme, where she was married. Paston wrote to his wife, Margaret, from Flanders on 8 July:

My Lady Margaret was married on Sunday last [3 July] in a town near Bruges, at five o'clock in the morning and she was brought the same day to Bruges for her dinner; and there she was received as worshipfully as all the world could devise … many pageants were played on her way to Bruges to welcome her, the best that I ever saw. And the same Sunday my lord the bastard [Antoine] took upon him to tourney and they that have jousted with him have been as richly apparelled, and himself also, as cloth of gold, silk and silver and goldsmiths' work might make them.

In Bruges, more pageants awaited her, featuring historical, classical and biblical figures, although the three main themes were the Legend of Troy, the story of Esther, and Jason and the Golden Fleece. Margaret arrived in a gilded litter draped with crimson cloth of gold, drawn by white horses. Her hair was loose, topped with the golden coronet bearing her name. The Knights of the Golden Fleece accompanied her in procession through the streets, as minstrels played until they reached the ducal palace. The city's mayor presented her with a gold vase filled with gold pieces, candles, wine and a statue of St Margaret. Then came the bishops and abbots, carrying six large crosses, then the merchants, dressed in bright colours, who presented her with four large, white horses with blue and white saddles. Then she was met by the members of her household, in the Burgundian colours of purple, black and red. Paston described the windows draped with flowers and the ten pageants, which were the 'best [he] ever saw'. A team of craftsmen had been employed for the occasion, including painters, jewellers, sculptors, carvers and workers in wax and leather, and inventions were on display in the palace, such as a forty-foot mechanical tower featuring monkeys, bears and wolves.

The ducal palace had a new addition that was used for the wedding. In preparation for the recent meeting of the Order of the Golden Fleece that May, a large wooden hall had been built in the courtyard, with turrets, glass windows with fitted shutters and upper galleries hung with gold-and-silver tapestries, while the roof was draped in blue and white. The wedding banquet was held inside, with the high table covered in black, purple and gold, and gold plate displayed on specially made cupboards featuring 'unicorn horns' and an intricate system of mirrors and candelabra shedding light upon all. There were nine days of feasting, the finest food being accompanied by more mechanical surprises, pageants and plays, unicorns, dragons, griffons, ogres and other mythical beasts. One detail in particular which impressed the onlookers was a buffet in the shape of a lozenge rising in tiers, with large pieces of gold and silver plate displayed on the lower levels, rising to smaller items decorated with precious stones.[4]

Charles himself wore a gown of gold, encrusted with diamonds, pearls and other stones, and a black hat set with a famous jewel called the Ballas of Flanders. 'As for the Duke's court,' wrote John Paston, 'I heard never of none like to it save King Arthur's court ... for such gear and gold and pearl and stone they of the Duke's Court, neither gentlemen or gentlewomen they want none.' Edward would particularly have enjoyed hearing the reports of the Tournament of the Golden Tree, at which Antoine, the Bastard of Burgundy, endeavoured to accomplish three tasks and the participants were dressed as legendary heroes. Antoine broke his leg during the fighting and, finally, Edward Woodville was declared the winner of the tournament. It was the middle of July when the English party returned home and relayed all the details to Edward and Elizabeth.

II

In the spring of 1469, a series of uprisings broke out in the north. Under an anonymous figure, 'Robin of Redesdale' or 'Robin Mend-All', they initially appeared to be a continuation of the minor Lancastrian rebellions of the previous year, such as the mob which had attacked Lord Rivers' estate at the Mote, Maidstone. The past year had witnessed a number of cases of high-level treason: the case of ex-mayor Thomas Cook, the uncovering of the

Earl of Oxford's plotting with the Lancastrians and the executions for treason of Lord Hungerford and William Courtenay, heir to the Earl of Devon. Edward saw this latest episode as the continuation of such dissent, especially as their intention appeared to be to 'compile various articles' to send to the king. He turned to Warwick's brother John Neville, Earl of Northumberland, to suppress it. Northumberland did not share Warwick's discontent and was effective in quashing the rebels. For this, Edward would reward him with a betrothal between the earl's eight-year-old son, George, and the three-year-old Princess Elizabeth. It is unlikely that Edward expected Elizabeth to remain his main heir, anticipating the birth of his own sons, but George was created Duke of Bedford to make him a suitable match for a royal princess. However, the threat in the north had not gone away. While Neville was busy in Yorkshire, the rebels regrouped in Lancashire and joined a new force headed by a figure known as Robin of Holderness. The name Robin was common in the north as a symbol of popular rebellion and power struggles against authority, especially given the mythology of the Robin Hood legend. These may have all been part of the same uprising, or else, as suggested by historian Cora Scofield, there may have been as many as three different foci of discontent.

Edward did not initially connect the rebels with the Earl of Warwick. Two later chroniclers, Hall and Vergil, both saw the uprising as a response to a tax levied upon the people by a York hospital, which was seized upon by 'certain evill disposed persones of the Erle of Warwicke's faccion', and certainly the figure of Robin of Redesdale has been identified by many later historians as Sir John Conyers, steward of Warwick's castle of Middleham and his brother-in-law by marriage. Also involved was another of the earl's brothers-in-law, Lord FitzHugh, and Warwick's cousin Sir Henry Neville of Latimer. Yet there were Percy family connections in Sir Hugh Hastings and Robert Hillyard too, traditionally the enemies of the Nevilles, so their motivation is not entirely clear and is suggestive of disparate elements. Whatever the driving force behind the rebellion, it almost broached the walls of York, posing a serious enough threat to draw Edward north. This may have been the plan all along, to leave the south clear, or else it provided an excellent opportunity for Warwick to exploit.

Edward had been slow to recognise the threat. As late as May he had been at Windsor for the annual Order of the Garter service on St George's Day, where Charles, Duke of Burgundy, had been admitted to the order by proxy. Following the ceremony, he had set out with Elizabeth, Richard of Gloucester and Anthony and John Woodville on progress into East Anglia, to visit the shrines at Bury St Edmunds and Walsingham; the royal seal was used at Bury on 15 and 16 June and at Norwich on 19 and 21. John Paston had equipped his retainers in a livery of tawny and brown and entertained the Woodville brothers at his mother's house with 'right good cher'. By that point, Edward was realising that he needed to take action. He ordered the royal wardrobe to equip 2,000 men with armour, jackets, banners and the royal standard, before visiting the shrine of Our Lady at Walsingham, perhaps to pray for guidance and success. His seal was employed there on 21 and 22 June. Elizabeth remained behind to fulfil their royal obligations in Norwich, while Edward rode to Fotheringhay Castle. According to Waurin, Lord Mountjoy advised Edward that 'it would be well to send away my Lord Rivers and his children when they have done speaking with you,' as 'no one wishe[d] his person ill' but Elizabeth's relatives were potential targets of the rebels. Rivers is reputed to have responded that he was ready to do the king's will, as he did not wish, on his account, that 'there should be any discord between you and those of your blood'. Rivers and Sir John Woodville retreated to Grafton, while Anthony went to escort Elizabeth home from Norwich. Edward rode to Northampton, where he summoned supporters to raise troops for a royal army, including two of his right-hand men, Warwick and Clarence. The days passed as he waited for them in Nottingham Castle, not knowing that by this time the pair had already left England for Calais.

On 11 July, Archbishop George Neville performed the ceremony of marriage between George, Duke of Clarence, and Isabel Neville. It may have taken place in the chapel of Calais Castle, where the party remained for the next five days, ostensibly celebrating the wedding, although the time was also used in plotting. Waurin suggests the match had been proposed as early as 1464, but it had been rejected by Edward on grounds of the couple's kinship, of Warwick's ambition, of his own intentions for George and of the potential threat to his own future heirs. Yet Warwick had gone ahead and defied the king, applying for the necessary papal dispensation, which he received on 14 March. Cardinal Bourchier then issued them with a licence on 30 July. But there was little occasion for lovemaking in Calais. The day after the wedding, a rebel manifesto was issued, accompanied by a letter signed by Warwick, Clarence and George Neville, much in the way the Yorkists had done in 1460. It followed the earlier precedent by complaining about high taxation, lawlessness and the corruption of great men. Significantly though, it made reference to the depositions of Edward II, Richard II and Henry VI, two of whom had met their deaths soon after losing the throne, and made criticism of Edward for advancing the Woodville family. The chronicler Warkworth included the rebels' text and list of enemies:

> The king our sovereign lord's true subjects of divers parts of this his realm of England have delivered to us certain articles [remembering] the deceitful, covetous rule and guiding of certain seditious persons, that is to say, the Lord Rivers, the Duchess of Bedford his wife, William Herbert, Earl of Pembroke, Humphrey Stafford, Earl of Devonshire, Lords Scales and Audley, Sir John Wydeville and his brothers and others of their mischievous rule, opinion and assent, which have caused our sovereign lord and his realm to fall into great poverty and misery, disturbing the administration of the laws, only tending to their own promotion and enrichment.

There was no escaping the direct threat against Elizabeth's parents and brothers, which she must have felt keenly as the fruition of Warwick's long-standing hostility. Finally, the manifesto issued a rallying cry for all its supporters to meet the earl and duke in Canterbury on 16 July. From there, Warwick and Clarence marched towards London, which opened its gates and loaned them £1,000. Did the citizens think this amount was to be used in support of their king or against him? The mood in London was so confused that, on 20 June, the armourer's company had been forbidden to issue any arms out of the city without a specific licence from the mayor. Charles, Duke of Burgundy, also wrote to the mayor to promise the city assistance if they should require it.

Edward had reached Newark, where he received the news of

Warwick and Clarence's treachery in disbelief. He must have wondered what their intention was. Through a failure of timing, he did not connect with the armies of William Herbert, Earl of Pembroke, and Humphrey Stafford, Earl of Devon, who met the rebel forces at Edgecote on 26 July. As Warkworth relates, the king's armies 'fought strongly', but some disagreement between the earls about how to deploy their troops may have weakened their cause. Devon arrived to relieve Pembroke as Warwick himself caught up with the rebels, boosting their morale considerably. Warkworth explains 'at that time was Lord Rivers taken, and one of his sons, in the Forest of Dean, and brought to Northampton and [along with] the Earl of Pembroke and Sir Richard Herbert his brother were beheaded by the command of the Duke of Clarence and the Earl of Warwick.' The news of their father and brother John's deaths probably reached Elizabeth and Anthony in Norwich. Uncertain of Edward's whereabouts, they immediately set out for London, believing that Anthony would have met a similar fate had he been with them. They arrived in the capital on 21 July, keeping such 'scant state' that the mayor and aldermen voted to gift her some wine ten days later.

Edward and his army were still camping in a village near Northampton when the news of the defeat at Edgecote reached them. What followed was a strange interlude during which Edward was temporarily in the custody of Warwick and his faction, under the guise of loyalty, but in a strange political stasis which could have ended in a number of different ways. Warkworth says it was George Neville who found Edward 'in a village beside Northampton' and took him to Warwick Castle and then on to York, where, 'by fair speech and promise, the king escaped out of the bishop's hands and came to London'. Historian Michael Hicks places the arrest at Warwick's own manor of Olney, where the king was discovered by George Neville. The Croyland Chronicle has Edward captured near Coventry and his attendants dismissed before he was 'held prisoner' at Warwick Castle and then transferred to Middleham, as the earl feared reprisals from his 'faithful subjects in the south'. A Milanese envoy in London was clear that Edward was under the earl's control; Warwick, 'as astute a man as ever was Ulysses, is at the king's side, and from what they say the king is not at liberty to go where he wishes'. What exactly

Warwick intended is unclear. Perhaps he hoped to re-establish his influence over Edward and disconnect him from the Woodvilles and others of his close friends. It does not seem at this point that he intended to overthrow the king, replace him with Clarence or kill him, although rumours that circulated that summer about Edward's reputed illegitimacy may have originated with Warwick. For now, though, he had another target in mind.

Warwick used the most powerful weapon he could in an attempt to discredit and destroy Rivers' widow. Jacquetta was probably at Grafton when she learned of the deaths of her husband and son; she may even have been told the news by Warwick's retainer Thomas Wake. Yet worse was still to come: Wake had been sent to Grafton to accuse Jacquetta of witchcraft. Allegedly, he had in his possession a leaden figure in the shape of a man, broken in the middle and bound together with wire. This was supposed to represent Warwick, while two other effigies, bound together, represented Edward and Elizabeth, bound by love. Again, the implication was that Jacquetta had brought about the king's marriage by means of sorcery and was attempting to harm the earl as an enemy to the match. An examination or trial of some sort must have taken place, either at Grafton, Warwick Castle or in London, where Wake claimed he had found the effigies in the keeping of the nunnery of Sewardsley, which was in the parish of Easton Neston in Northamptonshire, five miles up the road from Grafton. Presumably he had a story about how it ended up there. Jacquetta was powerless, with her husband and son John dead, her son Anthony in London and her son-in-law and king in Warwick's control. Without powerful male defenders she was vulnerable, but she was not defeated. She was still the mother of an anointed queen, who was then at liberty in London, a city well disposed towards Edward and his family. Jacquetta appealed to the mayor and aldermen of the city to investigate the claims, buying herself some time by broadly placing authority in their hands, rather than Warwick's. When the mayor summoned witnesses, it transpired that Wake's story was dependent upon the testimony of a parish clerk named John Daunger, who suddenly proved reluctant to comply. Fortunately for Jacquetta, Warwick's brief grasp on power was about to loosen.

Warwick soon discovered that he could not rule without

Edward: he was unable to raise troops to suppress trouble caused by Sir Humphrey Neville, and so was forced to allow Edward to appear in public in York to rally the men. Soon after this, Edward made 'fair speech and promise' and was again at liberty, either by Warwick's design or accident. Vergil states that he convinced his guards to let him go, while Edward Hall explains that he was 'allowed' to escape while on a hunting expedition. Edward's army then defeated Humphrey, who was beheaded before the king in York, underlining the necessity of his presence. Summoning Richard of Gloucester and his brother-in-law John, Duke of Suffolk, Edward returned to London, entering the city in state in the company of 1,000 men. John Paston wrote home to his wife to describe their return, with 200 of the city's dignitaries turning out in their scarlet robes to welcome their king, who was soon reunited with his wife. Warwick and George remained in the country. Their rebellion had registered their discontent, some of their enemies had been removed and the match between George and Isabel could not be undone. However, it now put the duke and earl in a difficult situation: they would either have to move against the king decisively or submit to his authority. They chose the latter.

Luckily for them, Edward chose to forgive the treason of his brother and cousin, although it would not be forgotten. Warwick and Clarence were omitted from the commissions of array issued at the end of October and from the summons to the Great Council which met from 6 November and was very well attended as a mark of support for the king. A formal reconciliation finally took place when the pair came to London in early December 'and it was agreed that all disagreements should be abandoned'.[5] Paston wrote that the king had had 'good language of the lords of Clarence and Warwyk ... seyng they be hys best frendys', but that behind the scenes 'the household men have other language'. Croyland described Edward's 'outraged majesty' in comparison with Warwick's 'guilty mind, conscious of an over-daring deed', while Vergil claimed the earl 'ragyd, fretyd and fumyd extremely'. Warwick was deprived of offices he had granted himself during the period of Edward's capture and Anthony Woodville inherited the title of 2nd Earl Rivers.

George though, in recognition of his marriage, had a set of ordinances drawn up to accommodate his duchess. On 9

December, instructions were given to the various departments of his household, including the pantry, cellar and spicery, the kitchen, scullery and butchery. The allowances for his stable were clearly laid out, down to the number of horses to be kept, which were eight coursers for riding, two ambling palfreys, one for the mail, one for bottles, seven chariot horses, a cart horse and those owned by servants. Perhaps this was to ensure George did not have enough horses at hand to make up a sizeable force or carry much if he intended to flee again. When George was at home, his 'standing' household numbered 144, but he was allowed a 'riding' household of 188 for when he was abroad. The lists of supplies for his court and their costs allowed him a princely diet of sweet wine, ale, a variety of meats, fish, condiments and spices, salt and sauces, wax and candles, linen and wages, liveries, stable and barge. The total estimated expenditure for a year in his household was just over £4,500. As well as accommodating Isabel, these measures reflect an increasing interest the Yorks showed in running their households efficiently, without waste. Such rules also survive from Edward and Cecily's establishments, each reflecting a period of redefinition in their lives that is illuminated by the details of their domestic life, the arrangements for their staff and the daily rituals mentioned therein. In Clarence's case, it may also have been a means of Edward establishing his authority over his unruly brother and reminding him of his subservient position. If this was Edward's intention, it was either unsuccessful or it backfired.

Edward and Elizabeth celebrated that Christmas season at Westminster. The following January, Jacquetta was formally cleared of any charges against her. It was less a victory than a long-overdue restoration of justice. A temporary peace may have settled, but the losses suffered by Elizabeth and her family, as well as Edward's temporary loss of power, must have shaken them all. The Lancastrian threat had been a visible, predictable force which justified its own annihilation, but this enmity among family was another thing entirely. And it had not gone away. The following year, these two damaging forces, these bitterest of old enemies, were to combine in a way which would nearly cost Edward his life and his crown.

8

REBELLION IN THE FAMILY
1470–1471

'I cannot tell you what will fall of the world.'

I

Early in the New Year, Elizabeth fell pregnant again. For a few weeks the family were reunited to share their mutual grief, their shock at the betrayal and their sense of relief that the danger had been averted. It must also have been a period of reflection for all, including Cecily Neville, whose sons were in conflict, one pitted against the other, tearing her loyalties and those of her youngest son, Richard of Gloucester. With their three small daughters, the personal aspect of Elizabeth and Edward's marriage was able to come to the fore again in the privacy of their chambers, after they had feasted, celebrated and prayed. Yet Elizabeth would barely have had time to become aware of her condition before a quarrel erupted in Lincolnshire that was to have important ramifications.

It started small, as if it was merely a local dispute. Thomas Welles, the son of Lord Welles, had driven Edward's knight Sir Thomas Burgh out of his house and confiscated his goods in the name of Henry VI. Edward summoned Welles to him 'in courteous manner', but, according to Fabyan, Thomas 'disobeyed the king's commandment'. Edward responded swiftly, and, 'being then well furnished with soldiers, made good speed towards him'. However, rumours circulated that Edward was not simply coming to deal with Welles, but that he had decided upon reprisals for those involved in the uprisings the previous year. Thus, a degree of panic spread, sending more supporters over to Welles's side than might otherwise have joined the king, drawn by Welles's proclamations 'to resist the king in coming down into the said shire'. Hearing reports of the size of the opposition, Edward summoned Warwick and Clarence, the latter of whom wrote reassuringly that they were on their way to support him. They were not. Edward urged them to gather more men and meet him at Fotheringhay. They did not. There was some confusion about Warwick's intentions and whereabouts, which must have reached Edward's ears. John Paston wrote, 'I cannot tell you what will fall of the world, for the king verily is disposed to go into Lincolnshire and men know not what will fall thereof, nor thereafter ... [My] lord of Warwick, as it is supposed, shall go with the king into Lincolnshire, some men say that his going shall do good, and some say that it does harm.' But Warwick had no intention of appearing in Lincolnshire. He was awaiting developments at a distance: if the rebels succeeded, he could capitalise on their advantage, but if they failed, he could claim that he had no connection with them. Or so he thought.

The rebellion was easily crushed. When Edward's troops arrived at Empingham in Rutland, the sight of the royal standard caused Welles's men to scatter, but not before they had implicated the true instigators of the chaos. Traditionally, it was in fleeing the battlefield, attempting to shake off their incriminatory livery, that the encounter was named after those men losing their coats. Before long the real culprits emerged. According to the *Chronicle of the Rebellion in Lincolnshire,* as the rebels advanced, 'their cry was A Clarence! A Clarence! A Warwick! that time being in the field divers persons in the Duke of Clarence's livery'. Warkworth tells us there were 'very many slain' although Croyland adds that Edward 'spared the majority who were rough and simple'. After Welles was defeated, 'his casket [was] taken, wherein were found many marvellous bills, concerning matters of great seduction and subversion of the king and common weal of all this land, with the most abominable treason'. Other incriminatory letters were found in a helmet which had been discarded in the frantic dash of the escaping traitors. Welles and the other surviving rebel leaders were brought before Edward at Grantham, and 'severally examined of their free wills uncompelled, not for fear of death nor otherwise stirred, acknowledged and confessed the duke and earl to be partners and chief provokers of all their treasons ... Their purpose was to destroy the king and to have made the Duke king.' The chronicle acknowledged this, as did Welles in his confession:

> My lord of Clarence's servant [who] came to us at Lincoln exhorted and urged our host many times and in many places that, when the matter should come near the point of battle, they should call upon my lord of Clarence to be king, and to destroy the king who was thus about to destroy them all and all the realm ... I have well understood by many messages, as well from my lord of Clarence as of Warwick, that they intended to make great risings [and] make the Duke of Clarence king.

This time, Warwick and Clarence could not fail to escape Edward's justice, and they knew it. They ignored a third royal summons and asked instead for a guarantee of forgiveness for themselves and all their men. This was pushing their luck too far and Edward threatened to deal with his brother 'according to the nighness of our blood and our laws', yet it raises interesting questions about the dynamic between Edward and Warwick. It is easy, with hindsight, to see the earl's rebellion coming, with the way he had been humiliated over the Bona of Savoy match, Edward's Burgundian preferences and Warwick's sense that his family had been slighted and favours given to the unworthy Woodvilles. Warwick did not go unrewarded in the late 1460s, but it would appear that Edward failed to recognise the threat he posed, or his own contribution to that. He made a deliberate choice to curtail the Neville influence, perhaps in an attempt to prevent them from becoming too powerful, which backfired, but perhaps this was also a clash of egos at the top. Ultimately, Edward was king, not Warwick, and even though the earl had helped him to that position, he felt compelled to underscore the difference. Edward ruled by personality and was a supremely powerful and capable individual;

he did not want to share his power with another pseudo king. If he pushed Warwick too far, he dealt with the consequences.

The earl and duke fled, gathering troops along the way in anticipation of attack. Edward declared them both to be traitors 'contrarie to natural kyndeness and dutie of allegiance', and headed south, intent upon pursuit. By 3 April, the traitorous pair had reached Exeter, and six days later they boarded ship at Dartmouth, along with Warwick's wife, daughter Anne and the heavily pregnant Isabel. Their hope was to sail for Calais, which was still technically under Warwick's control. Edward anticipated this move, however, and decisively undermined it. Instructions were issued to Lord Wenlock in Calais to refuse the traitors permission to land; Warwick's ships were requisitioned and the ports along the south coast put on alert. It was while they were sailing up and down the French coast that Isabel gave birth to a stillborn child about whom few details are known. The baby's gender is unclear, and it may have been buried at sea or once they were finally allowed to land at Honfleur on 1 May. Warwick headed to the court of Louis XI at Angers, determined to destroy Edward once and for all by committing the unthinkable and throwing in his lot with the exiled Lancastrians.

Once again, Edward had successfully repelled a serious threat to his regime. The efforts of Welles had posed him little danger, but the underlying treason of two of his closest companions, both so connected to the Yorkist bloodline, must have left him shaken. It also exposed the hypocrisy of the peace made the previous December and the extent to which Warwick and Clarence had held Edward's offers of forgiveness in contempt. Just three months after being allowed to take their places on the king's council, they had engaged in active rebellion and, this time, they had pushed Edward too far. Warwick's ambition was no surprise to the king: the parallels between the earl's actions at this time and those of 1460 showed that little had changed in terms of his ruthlessness, and it was the long-standing nature of his position as Edward's mentor that made his betrayal not only difficult to bear, but also permanent. There was to be no way back for Warwick now. The twenty-one-year-old George, though, was another matter. Still technically Edward's heir, his younger brother has been cast as something of a caricature of reckless youth and ambition, easily led and disloyal when he believed the rewards made it worth his while. There was more to George though. He had cast in his lot with Warwick at a moment of disaffection and, perhaps, wounded pride. Like the rest of his family, he had the Yorkist conviction in his right to rule, and the position of being next in line, so near and yet so far, was a difficult one for George to be content with. Yet he had his limits. What Warwick would propose next would remind George of his roots and where his real loyalties lay.

While Edward and Elizabeth were at Canterbury with Anthony Woodville and Princess Elizabeth, hearing Mass on Whit Sunday, Warwick was making a deal with his old enemy. Despite considerable pressure from Charles the Bold and the Count of St Pol, Louis finally agreed to receive Warwick and Clarence, even though this contravened a treaty he had signed with Burgundy. He received them in 'honourable and distinguished manner', and the French lords embraced the fugitives 'in the most friendly way'. They were then taken to meet Charlotte of Savoy, the French queen, at Valognes Castle. Following that, Louis and Warwick withdrew into the royal chambers, where they remained for two hours 'most privately and [with] great familiarity', engaged in 'long discussions'. This was followed by feasts, 'tournaments and dancing and everything else that distinguishes'. Milanese ambassador Sforza de Bettini wrote home in a newsletter that the king and earl were still closeted in secret discussions a week later, as Louis was trying 'by every means in his power to get him to return to England'. Eventually, it was Louis who proposed that Warwick meet with Margaret of Anjou and arrange a marriage between her son and his daughter.

Prince Edward of Westminster was then sixteen years old. Having spent the last decade in exile with his mother in Scotland and France, he was the most credible focus of the Lancastrian dynasty while Henry VI remained in captivity in the Tower. Something of a court-in-exile had been established by Margaret and the remaining Beaufort brothers, with young men centred round Edward learning chivalric skills in anticipation of the day they would return and recapture England. In fact, the Milanese ambassador referred to him as the 'God of Battle'. Little is known about his character, but his early years had been typical of the chaotic changes of power experienced by his peers. His father had been unable to recognise him until he was around a year old, giving rise to rumours about his paternity. As a child he had been invested as Prince of Wales, described at the age of five as a 'most handsome boy' who understood the ways of the court. Yet the Act of Accord had disinherited him in favour of York, leaving him and his mother uncertain about his future. In such circumstances, living in penury, Margaret came to recognise Warwick as her son's best chance. However, she was not prepared to forget the earl's role in their downfall and their former fierce enmity.

According to *The Maner and Guyding of Earl of Warwick*, the former queen was initially furious and 'right difficult' at the prospect of such an alliance, distancing Warwick with the surprising news that she was hoping to marry Prince Edward to the young Elizabeth of York. She stated that she could see 'no honour nor profit in' the union, but would listen to the advice of Louis and her father, René of Anjou. Undeterred, Warwick remained on bended knee before her for a full quarter of an hour, retracting all his former 'slanders' until she was satisfied with his submission. Vergil described their lengthy discussions, as 'many moe conditions wer entreatyd upon emongst them, which both the reason and weight of the cause requyryd'. Yet Margaret was prepared to unite with Warwick, who might prove the most powerful advocate she could hope for, and the earl recognised his former enemies as allies in his fight against Edward. On 25 July, Prince Edward and Anne Neville were betrothed at Angers Cathedral, making their oaths upon a piece of the true cross.

Warwick may have arranged an audacious and unexpected match for his youngest daughter, but in the process he had also made a new enemy. This new marriage distanced Clarence from the throne; it was an acknowledgement that his chance of becoming king was slight, and if it came to a choice between York and Lancaster, George was always going to choose York. Around this time, Edward sent his brother a message through a woman attending on his wife, offering him a free pardon and asking him not to ally with the Lancastrians. In return, feeling betrayed by Warwick, Clarence began to inform his brother of the earl's movements and promised to defect to his side once they reached England. When another rebellion broke out in the north that July, under a Lord Fitzhugh, Edward headed north once more, leaving a heavily pregnant Elizabeth with her mother for company in the safety of the Tower. He had still not returned to London when Warwick and Clarence landed at Plymouth and Dartmouth on 13 September, accompanied by 2,000 troops financed by Louis. Edward was given the news at York on 25 September. He summoned Northumberland again, who was close at hand, but on this occasion the earl turned his 6,000 men against the king, perhaps in disaffection after having been forced to resign his title in favour of the Percy family. Trying to make his way south to reunite with George and repel Warwick, Edward had retired for the night at Doncaster when the sergeant of his minstrels informed him that his enemies were 'coming for to take him' and that he had better flee.

It was an undignified exit, but a necessary one. After Empingham and Warwick's new Lancastrian support, Edward could have been in little doubt that his life was in danger for all Clarence's new protestations of support. It had happened quickly and decisively, but Commines blamed it on Edward's 'sloth and negligence', as the king had not perceived the danger he was in, nor taken steps to discover it. However, Edward could hardly have predicted Montagu's defection, which seems to underpin the collapse of his support in the north. He hurried to the coast, in the company of his brother Richard of Gloucester, Lord Hastings and Anthony Woodville, with a retinue of around 800 loyal men. They were almost drowned crossing the turbulent waters of the Wash, but reached King's Lynn safely on 30 September. Geographically and politically, the most obvious location for exile was Burgundy, but with no money or resources, Edward had to pay the sea captain with the coat off his back: a gown lined with marten's fur. There was no chance to say goodbye to Elizabeth or his daughters, he simply had to trust that they would be safe in the Tower until he could find a way to return.

By this point, Elizabeth was around eight months pregnant. Hearing the news of Edward's flight, she realised the danger posed to her, not just because of her marriage and status, but as a result of the presence of another royal who was then housed in the Tower. With Warwick on his way to liberate and restore Henry VI, the Tower of London was likely to prove a significant location in the coming days. Although it had been chosen as the safest location for her to deliver her child, changing circumstances meant that she was now in the wrong place. That night, Elizabeth gathered a few possessions and fled with her three daughters and Jacquetta for the safety of Westminster Abbey, where they signed the register as 'sanctuary women' on 1 October. From there, Elizabeth sent the Abbot of Westminster to the mayor, to inform him that she was surrendering the Tower because if she did not, 'the said Kentishmen and others would invade the sanctuary of Westminster to despoil and kill her'. The Tower was surrendered two days later. Warwick and Clarence entered London on 6 October.

Sanctuary offered Elizabeth and her family a theoretically inviolable safe place, but its conditions were far from those she had become used to. The two-storied building, with its single entrance and massive ragstone keep, was something of a castle within the palace, surrounded by fifty tenements bounded by marshland on one side and Thieving Lane on the other. Elizabeth arrived 'in great penury and forsaken of all friends', lacking even 'such things as mean men's wives had in superfluity'.[1] The poem 'The Recovery of the Throne by Edward IV' describes her sympathetically, in 'langowr and angwiche ... when hir lorde and sovereyn was in adversite to here of hir wepyng it was grett pete [pity]'. She was offered lodgings in three rooms of a house called Cheneygates, the residence of Abbot Millyng, surviving parts of which are now known as the deanery. Elizabeth had no way of knowing whether she would see her husband again, or what the future might hold for her and her children. She was right to have fled the Tower, as Warwick hurried there to visit Henry VI, finding him 'not worshipfully arrayed as a prince, and not so cleanly kept as should beseem his state', and moving him into the apartments that Elizabeth had prepared for her lying-in. Warwick then orchestrated the restoration or 'readeption' of the Lancastrian king, leading him through the streets to St Paul's Cathedral, after which he was lodged in the nearby Bishop's Palace. Warwick undermined his own efforts though, as he failed to employ the sense of majesty that Edward had understood so well. With Henry looking shabby, as if he did not even own a new gown, the Lancastrian king's cause was damaged.

Despite Warwick's former attack upon Jacquetta, Elizabeth's enemies showed her mercy. A proclamation was issued by Henry, forbidding any man, on pain of death, to 'defoul or distrouble' the churches or sanctuaries or anyone in them, and he allowed John Gould, a London butcher, to supply Elizabeth and her party with meat. Henry also appointed Elizabeth, Lady Scrope, to go and assist the queen, along with her former midwife and physician, Margery Cobbe and Dr Serigo. Elizabeth gave birth on 2 November to a son she named Edward.

II

The exiled Edward was fortunate enough to arrive in the Netherlands comparatively unscathed. Having narrowly escaped an encounter that was likely to have resulted in his imprisonment at best, his death at worst, he survived the perilous conditions of the North Sea, being pursued by Hanseatic ships who only gave up when the English fleet neared the city of Alkmaar. Here, Edward experienced another piece of good luck. Charles the Bold's Governor of Holland, Louis de Gruuthuyse, was in Alkmaar at the time; he was a member of the ducal retinue who had visited Edward's court for the 1467 Smithfield tournament, and was known personally to the king. It must have been a relief for the penniless exile to see an old friend. Louis offered to pay Edward's expenses and conducted him to the Hague, which they reached on 12 October. After this, Edward was a guest in Louis's home in Bruges, where he had collected one of the finest libraries in Europe.

Edward's presence in Burgundy compromised the terms of the Treaty of Peronne, which agreed friendship between Louis XI and Charles the Bold. In December 1470, Louis lost patience with Charles and renounced the treaty, declared war on Burgundy and moved troops into Picardy. Until this point, Charles had been cautious regarding Edward's presence, tolerating his stay in Bruges, but not summoning him to his court. However, Louis's hostility forced his hand in favour of Edward, and on 26 December Charles arranged a meeting with his brother-in-law. No doubt Margaret of York had also been influencing her husband behind the scenes. They met at Aire near St Omer between 2 and 4 January and then moved to St Pol on 7 January, where Edward was a guest of Jacquetta's brother Jacques de Luxembourg. As a result, Charles agreed to support the Yorkist dynasty, offering Edward 50,000 florins, three or four large ships and fourteen smaller vessels which were docked at Veere. On 16 February 1471, Warwick signed a peace treaty with France, along with a commitment that he would personally lead troops of between 8,000 and 10,000 men against Charles of Burgundy. Orders were issued to the garrison at Calais to commence attacks upon its borders with the Netherlands. In the meantime, Edward was planning his return. He managed to secure assistance from Francis, Duke of Brittany; the Hanseatic League, who offered him fourteen ships; Warwick's traditional enemy Henry Percy, Earl of Northumberland; and his own brother George, with whom he had been in contact throughout his period of exile. Anthony Woodville hired more ships in Bruges and further support was raised from the merchants there. A few English ships crossed the North Sea in readiness for the return of the king. No doubt Edward had heard reports that Margaret of Anjou was waiting with her son to cross the Channel and reclaim her kingdom, making the restoration of the Lancastrian dynasty complete. On 16 February, Edward left for Flushing. There, he boarded the *Anthony* and sailed for England on 11 March, after a week of delay caused by bad weather.

The next day, Edward's ships sighted the coast of Norfolk. After an absence of six months, it was a bittersweet moment: a return to the kingdom he had ruled for a decade, a return to his Camelot, which was now being ruled by his old mentor, far removed from the glorious return from exile in 1460. Edward was now almost thirty and he was fighting for his realm and his family. It was unprecedented for a deposed king to return and conquer his kingdom for a second time: the Milanese ambassador compared it to leaving by the door and climbing back in through the window. Edward knew he would have to tread carefully. A party of local men were sent ashore at Cromer, including two East Anglian knights. They quickly established that the Earl of Oxford was in the area, so it was not safe to land. Additionally, Warwick had been expecting Edward's return and predicted his arrival on the east coast, so had arrested any Yorkist sympathisers in the area, such as the dukes of Norfolk and Suffolk, the Bourchiers and other local loyalists. Warwick had also set the Bastard of Fauconberg to patrol the coastline, but a number of his ships had been diverted to escort Margaret of Anjou to England and threatened by the presence of Breton vessels in the Channel. The invasion fleet headed up the coast to Yorkshire and sailed through a three-day storm into the small port of Ravenspur. By coincidence, this was also the spot where Henry Bolingbroke, the future Henry IV, had landed in 1399 before dethroning Richard II. Just as Henry concealed his true purpose by asserting he was merely returning to claim his duchy of Lancaster, Edward gave the reason for his return as his desire to repossess his duchy of York.

Edward's first success was the city of York itself. Hull and Beverley refused to admit him, but despite warnings sent to York he was allowed to enter the city with a small retinue of men while the remainder of his army waited outside the walls. Warkworth stated that Edward declared his loyalty to Henry VI and wore the livery of the ostrich-feather badge, pledging allegiance to Edward, Prince of Wales. Following this, he marched south, through Tadcaster and Wakefield, Doncaster and Nottingham. Loyal Yorkists joined him along the route, so that by the time he reached Leicester, his army had doubled in size. On 29 March, he headed to Coventry, where Warwick was installed inside the castle, awaiting re-enforcements from Oxford, Montagu and Clarence, little knowing that the latter was planning to support Edward. According to Warkworth, Warwick was in possession of a letter written to him by George, 'that he should not fight with [the king] until he came himself'. So Warwick waited. When George did finally arrive, though, he gave his support to his brother. The two were reunited on 3 April near Banbury. 'All convenants of fidelity made between the Duke of Clarence and the Earl of Warwick, Queen Margaret and Prince Edward her son [were] clearly broken and forsaken, which in the end, brought destruction both to him and them.'[2] As Croyland relates, the reunion was brought about by the influence of women: the duke 'quietly reconciled to the king by the mediation of [their] sisters, the Duchesses of Burgundy and Exeter. The former, from outside the kingdom, had been encouraging the king, and the latter, from within, the duke, to make peace.'

On 10 April, Henry VI and George Neville, Archbishop of York, rode through London, urging the citizens to remain loyal to the reinstated Lancastrian regime. However, the pitiful procession, headed by a man with fox tails on a pole and the king in his old blue gown, seemed 'more like a play than the showing of a prince to win men's hearts, for by this means he lost many and won none or right few'.³ The draper Thomas Cook, who had fallen foul of the Woodvilles in 1468, now stepped in to replace the mayor and added his voice to the campaign to keep Edward out of the city. However, as Warkworth relates, the London recorder and aldermen dismissed the armed crowd 'to go home to dinner; and during dinner time King Edward was let in'. Commines believed this was due to three things: 'First the men, who were in the sanctuaries, and his wife the queen who had given birth to a son, secondly, the great debts he owed to the city, which made his merchant creditors support him; thirdly, several noblewomen and wives of rich citizens with whom he had been closely and secretly acquainted.' Whatever the truth of this suggestion, whether or not Edward retook the city on the basis of his amorous exploits, he was 'very joyfully received'. Edward went to the palace of the Bishop of London and took Henry back into his custody. He then headed to the Westminster sanctuary, where he 'comforted the queen, that had a long time abided there ... in right great trouble, sorrow and heaviness, which she sustained with all manner patience that belonged to any creature, and as constantly as hath been seen at any time so high estate to endure'. Edward was able to meet his infant son for the first time, little Prince Edward, who was five months old, 'to his heart's singular comfort and gladness and to all them that truly loved and would serve'. The next day, having bid his wife farewell again, Edward headed north to meet Warwick, taking King Henry with him. None of them knew that Queen Margaret was about to land off the coast of Weymouth.

On 14 April, Edward's army met that of Warwick at Barnet just to the north of London. Overnight, the earl's cannons had been firing at the spot where he believed Edward to be, but the Yorkist army had crept closer than thought, so were untouched by the attack. When dawn broke on a foggy morning, neither side could fully grasp the whereabouts of the other, leading to much confusion. The three parts of Edward's army were commanded by himself, with Clarence in the middle, Richard of Gloucester on the right and William, Lord Hastings, on the left, but Warwick's forces were much larger, including Montagu, Oxford and Edward's estranged brother-in-law Henry Holland, husband to Anne of York. Oxford managed to push back Hastings' men, but in the mist his livery badge of the sun with rays was mistaken by his own side for that of Edward's sun in splendour, and Warwick's troops turned upon themselves. The contemporary poem 'Battle of Barnet' in Trinity College Library, Cambridge, compares Edward's feat in this battle to those of King Arthur: 'Of a more famous knight I never rad syn the tyme of Artors dayes; he that loveth hymn nat, I holde hym mad.' Likewise, 'The Recovery of the Throne by Edward IV' has 'nothur Alisaunder ne Artur, ne no conquerouere no better were acomoenyd with nobill men. Like none of the rounde tabull were beseyn ryally horsid and aparelde in the fere of thayre foo. This victoriously he come.'

Amid the chaos, Warwick witnessed the death of his brother, Montagu, and was forced to admit defeat. He usually kept horses ready, to allow him to escape the field in just such an eventuality, but by this point it was too late. John Paston was injured during the fighting, having been 'hurt with an arrow on his right arm beneath the elbow', although he was 'in no peril of death'. However, others were not so fortunate. Edward had given orders that Warwick be taken alive, but the earl was killed and his body and that of Montagu were taken to St Paul's Cathedral, where 'they lay two days after naked in two coffins, so every man might behold and see them'.[4] Edward returned to London with George and Richard, along with 'an escort in his honour of large numbers of magnates and common folk.' However, as Croyland wrote, 'No sooner was one battle over in the east than he had to prepare himself and his men in full strength for another in the western parts.' The final Lancastrian threat was still to come.

Warwick's expulsion of Edward in the autumn of 1470 had been swift, but Edward's regaining of his realm was just as speedy and decisive. As Commines wrote, 'In eleven days the Earl of Warwick had won all of England, or at least got it under his control. In twenty-one days King Edward reconquered it, though there were two desperate and bloody battles.' Edward's return of 1471 was just as glorious as his conquest of the realm in 1461, but he was not prepared to spare his enemies, executing 'those who had banded together against him'. It was time to expel the final threat so that he could govern the country without fear of treachery. On 4 May, King Edward IV met the army of Prince Edward to the south of

Tewkesbury. Having heard of the death of their champion, the Earl of Warwick, the Lancastrians had decided to go ahead and fight anyway, with the support of the surviving Beaufort brothers, . Lord Wenlock and the Earl of Devon. Edmund Beaufort, Duke of Somerset, commanded a force of around 6,000 men compared with Edward's 5,000, but the king's approach meant that Beaufort engaged his troops early, without waiting for re-enforcements to arrive with Jasper Tudor. The fighting took place on uneven ground, in the fields leading up to Tewkesbury Abbey. Edward's forces overcame those of the Lancastrians, with Beaufort turning upon Lord Wenlock and smiting him down, in the belief that he was defecting to the Yorkists.

The question of where Prince Edward died has caused some controversy since. Some accounts have him dying in battle, or as he attempted to flee the scene. Commines, Croyland and Benet agree that he was killed on the field, as does the *Historie of the Arrivall of Edward IV in England and the final recouerye of his Kingdomes from Henry VI*, and Warkworth adds that the prince was 'taken fleeing … townwards, and slain in the field'. Yet Fabian described how he was captured and brought before the king, where he begged his brother-in-law, George, for mercy. However, according to Fabian, 'after the King had questioned the said Edward, and he had answered him contrary to his pleasure, he then struck him with his gauntlet on the face; after which stroke by him received, he was by the king's servants incontinently slain on the 4th day of May'. This was corroborated by the Italian Bettini, who wrote to the Duke of Milan that the Yorkists had 'not only routed the prince but taken and slain him, together with all the leading men with him'. In 1473, a French chronicle, the *Histoire de Charles, dernier duc de Bourgogne,* stated that the prince had been surrounded and killed in cold blood, while Vergil had Edward waving the prince away to be 'cruelly butchered' and Elizabethan chroniclers Hall and Holinshed followed suit. Whether or not he died on or off the field is somewhat immaterial, and does not reflect upon the chivalric values or fairness of a king who had twice almost lost his realm and his life. It would be naïve to expect that Edward IV would not have killed his opponents, following the precedents set over the previous sixteen years. As the Lancastrian heir, the Prince of Wales simply had to die. So did his father, Henry VI, who was killed in the Tower of London on 21 May. There seems to be little doubt that this was the result of Edward's orders: he simply could not risk leaving the former king alive as a focus for future malcontents.

The Bastard of Fauconberg raised an army in Kent and Essex, which he marched to London with the intention of assisting the Lancastrian armies at Tewkesbury. When they reached the city, though, lawlessness broke out, with looting and burning, so the citizens came out to defend their property and killed a number of the rioters. This only served to re-enforce London's Yorkist sympathies. Later, Fauconberg was captured at Southampton and beheaded. Warwick's brother George Neville was initially pardoned for his role in the readeption of Henry VI, after he swore loyalty to Edward, but he was rearrested in 1472 on a charge of treason. He was imprisoned for over two years in the castle of Hammes, near Calais, before his release and return to England in 1474. He died soon afterwards. Queen Margaret, broken by the loss of her husband and son, was imprisoned in the Tower, then in other Yorkist-controlled castles until she was ransomed by Louis XI in 1475. Finally, the Lancastrian threat had been silenced.

One poem of the time suggested that Edward believed the struggles of 1470–1 were a punishment for 'wickyd lyvyng', with his people punishing him and denying him 'mete, dryncke and logynge'. 'On the Recovery of the Throne by Edward IV' begins,

> At his londyng in Holdyrnes he hadde grett payne
> His subjectes and people wolde not hym obey
> Off hym and his people thay had grett disfayne.
> There shewid hym unkyndnes and answered him playne.

It is interesting to consider the revisions that Edward made to the royal household in 1471 in the light of this notion, as if the exile served as a timely wake-up call for a self-indulgent king. The poet continues that Edward found his reward in returning to his family, who turned his sorrow to bliss:

> The kyng comfortid the queen, and other ladyes eke
> His swete babis full tenderly he did kys;
> The yonge priynce he beheld, and in his armys did bere.
> Thus his bale turnyd to blis.

On 26 June, Edward and Elizabeth's son Edward was created Prince of Wales. His life had overlapped only briefly with the Lancastrian Edward who had borne the same title; now that former prince's death at Tewkesbury meant there would not be the problem of two heirs bearing the same title. Edward established a council for the guidance of his son, which included the prince's mother, Queen Elizabeth; his uncles Anthony, Earl Rivers, George, Duke of Clarence and Richard, Duke of Gloucester; Thomas Bourchier, Archbishop of Canterbury; Robert Stillington, Bishop of Bath and Wells; and others. Yet the letters patent were very clear that this power was given to them as a result of Elizabeth's gift, and that this body was intended to oversee the boy's entire childhood: 'Giving unto them ... with the advice and express consent of the queen, large power to advise and counsel the said prince ... the said authority to continue until the prince should accomplish his age of fourteen years.'

At Westminster, the king and queen took part in a second coronation. There were two recrownings, which took place on Christmas Day and Twelfth Night in the abbey, although Elizabeth did not wear her crown on the second occasion as she was tired, being pregnant once again. It was more than a symbolic gesture: it was a celebration. Edward's second reign was beginning, won against seemingly terrible odds, signalling a new start, a step forward and a redefinition. Edward's first decade on the throne had been defined along chivalric lines, in an Arthurian court which employed a material magnificence to create majesty, but which was beset by conflicts between former friends. The band of close brothers who had conquered England in York's name in 1461 had been torn apart by personal and political disagreements. With the death of Warwick and the Lancastrian king and prince, Edward could put such tensions behind him and take his court forward into the rising tide of the Renaissance.

9

A COURT IN THE BURGUNDIAN STYLE
1471–1474

'Ordinate reverence.'

I

Edward returned from his exile in Burgundy invigorated by its culture and a desire to re-establish the Yorkist court. Loyal friends were returned to positions of power, with Robert Stillington as chancellor, Henry Bourchier, Earl of Essex, as Lord Treasurer and Richard of Gloucester, Anthony Woodville, Thomas Grey, William Hastings and John Dynham as prominent members of his council. This second reign, snatched out of the jaws of defeat, marked a new cultural phase, retaining the ritual and chivalry of an Arthurian-style court but moving into a more cosmopolitan redefinition of magnificence. The focus on conduct, self-discipline and patronage was in line with early Renaissance thinking on the Continent. It began with Edward's reforms of his household along Burgundian lines.

Edward's *Liber Niger* or *Black Book of the Household* of 1471, examined and redefined his court, to sharpen it up and fit it for purpose, make it more financially viable and clearly demarcate the roles of those within it. The new codes of conduct were intended to inspire harmony and reverence, which is hardly a surprise given the irreverence and overreaching of Warwick and the Nevilles. It began with the model of an ideal royal household based upon the visit made by the Queen of Sheba to the house of Solomon, when magnificence met wisdom. Observing the daily running of Solomon's court, the queen marvelled at the 'sad and studious directions' given to each estate: 'Every master officer in his sober demeaning, his honesty, his rich array, and of all their mannerly ceremonies done in that court, that each of them might be likened to a king in her country, also for the steadfast observance of the good rules, appointments and ordinances for the household.' The *Liber Niger* enshrined the complex rituals that indicated distinctions in status and created a harmonious whole through communal activity, making 'ordinate reverence after the distinctions of every high or low degree'. This drew on Edward's existing emphasis on majesty and the highly ritualised public performances that had been witnessed at Elizabeth's coronation and churching.

The most common occurrence of this was the king's regular dining in hall, which had been elevated almost to the status of a religious ceremony[1] or symbolic act in the Burgundian court. Burgundian ritual feasting began with a procession, the parading of the nef or salt cellar, testing the food for poison and washing of the hands, with specific amounts of plate and gold on display before any morsel was permitted to cross the diners' lips. Such small touches as the placing of the towel over the left shoulder so that it touched the skin were considered essential, in this case to demonstrate that the napery was uncontaminated. According to the *Liber Niger*'s introduction, the Queen of Sheba was impressed by the 'abundance, varieties and manner of disposition of suche metes' served to Solomon, and the text cites the households of historical precedents who elevated dining to an art: King Lud, for his solemn table kept through the day and night; Cassibellan, for his elaborate feasting of the ancient Britons; Hardeknoute, for being a father of cuisine and courtesy; Henry I, as an 'excellent mete gever'; and Edward III, as the 'house of policy and very flower of England', who lay down certain duties, customs, wages and liveries, greatly reforming his own court as the years passed. The connection between food and rank was inescapable. It mattered very much where people stood or sat, or what order of precedence they were given, as such external signs dictated how others would receive them. In 1464, a banquet was given in honour of the Lord Mayor of London by the Sergeants of the Coif, but when the mayor arrived to find that the Earl of Worcester was seated in his place beside the king, he turned around and went home again.

After this the work divides Edward's household in two: the *domus regis magnificencie*, which was more the public, upstairs court; and the *domus providencie*, which was responsible for provisioning it. It had been drawn up by Edward in conjunction with his brothers for the sake of efficiency and clarity:

> This is the new house of households, principall of Englond in tymes of peace, bylded upon kynges foundations, precedents and upon other more notable and husbandly households, by the great counsayll or lordes spirituall and temporall, the Cardinal of Canterbury, George, Duke of Clarence, Richard, Duke of Gloucester, the wise and discrete judges … many of them long tyme havyng knowlege of the expence and conduyte of the king's houses … poysed by wysedom and worship, profit and by reason, answering to every estate and degree, according to lyveres, competent wages, clothing, fees, rewardes and other duties, by which every officer shall mowe sufficiently be of power in all truth to do the kings service honourably. So the king wull have his goodes dispended but not wasted.

More than this though, the text gives glimpses into Edward and Elizabeth's daily regime and provisions, which bring a distant and archaic establishment to life in glorious detail. From the *Liber Niger* we know that Edward's allowance at breakfast time was two loaves made into four manchetts, or hand-sized rolls; two pandemayne, or white bread rolls; one large messe (portion) from the kitchen; and a gallon of ale. For solitary suppers, when Edward was not dining in state, he was brought eight loaves and several trenchers of bread, two pitchers of wine, two gallons of ale, wafers and fruit, in addition to the main kitchen dishes. The text acknowledged that predicting his needs could be difficult and set the precedent of Edward III being served with eight dishes at supper, so it was the job of the ushers of the chamber to record the king's consumption of bread and wine, especially between meals. We also learn that the lighting of the king's chamber, when it got dark and there was no press of strangers, required three torches, three prickets, six perchers and ten wax candles, with arrangement for litter and rushes overseen by the sergeant of the hall. Edward also made provision for his daily offerings of gold and a list of the occasions on which gifts were to be made to certain saints.

Only one specific shrine is mentioned in the *Liber Niger*: that of St Thomas of Canterbury, which received three gold florins a year from the king's coffers, 'in the name of chyvyage', which was an annual tax paid to a superior like to a lord. From this and his regular visits to Canterbury, it would seem that Edward felt a special affinity for the martyred twelfth-century archbishop. Perhaps this was because his reign witnessed the anniversaries of key events in the saint's life: his trial and exile in 1164 and his return and murder in 1170. There were also at least two plays about Becket's life in circulation during Edward's reign: one written in Ipswich in around 1400, which was in performance until 1530; and a second written in Ham in 1453. Towards the end of his reign, Edward would commission a full portrait in stained glass of all his family, to be set in a window above the spot where Becket was martyred. During the troubles of 1470, the city contributed £251 to the king, and after his return the following year Edward and Elizabeth went on pilgrimage to Canterbury to give thanks for the restoration of their regime. In addition to the usual preparations on this occasion, the city paid 6s for three tonnes of beer and 2s 2d for it to be carried to the Hall in the Blene, where Edward and Elizabeth stayed. Three men working two days each at the hall were paid 2s 7d and 10d went to the men who were responsible for guarding the gates.

The *Liber Niger* did not forget the queen. Arrangements made for Elizabeth, whose household was a separate entity, were designed to uphold her status: she must be fed along the same lines as the king, 'for the high estate of her proper person', with an allowance of 40s daily for the queen's diet and 12d for her servants. The queen's council, or counting house, were to keep a daily list of all those fed at her table to ensure that correct amounts had been consumed by people entitled to eat there. The concept of open house hospitality, when Warwick used to feast thousands at breakfast in the Erber, was becoming more closely and carefully defined. Edward and Elizabeth were both visible and conspicuous in their magnificence, but also distanced and elevated by such distinctions.

The *Liber Niger* also lays out the proceedings for feeding Prince Edward, who already had his own household even though his older sisters did not. There were provisions made that delineated between the ranks of duke, marquis, count, bishop, chancellor, chamberlain, judge, knights bachelor, Children of the Chapel, Master of the Chapel and Master of the Grammar. The annual expenses of a viscount's household was £1,000, while a baron's was £500 and a knight's was £100.[2] There was the secretary, chaplain, squires of the body, sewers or servers, surveyor, wardrobe, usher, yeomen and pages, all with their own food entitlements, livery, candles, servants and rushes. The men of the king's chamber were to feed two people to a messe, while the squires, chaplain, physicians, surgeon, confessor and secretary received a single messe each, overseen by ushers to record the expenses. The details of individual roles were also set out, like the sewers or servers, who 'owght to be full cunning, diligent and attendaunt; he receveth the metes [and] conveyeth it to the kings bourde with sauces accordingly and all that cometh to that bourde he setteth and directeth except the office of pantrie and buttrie; he seweth at one mele, and dyneth and soupeth at another mele, and to sitt in a hall with a person of like service'. Certain amounts of food and drink were specified for the king's minstrels and musicians, and the *Liber Niger* also extends to the provisions of food for servants who were sick.

It was most important to distinguish between those whose professions were similar, or whose duties involved some degree of overlap. The role of the doctor of physic was to stand in the king's presence during his meals, counselling the king 'which diet is the best according' and to describe 'the nature and operation of the meats', meaning their effects upon the body and their properties of heat or cold, dryness or moisture, according to the Galenic theory of the four humours. He was to discuss with the steward and master cook what the best meals were for the king and devise the king's medicine. No one who was sick was to be allowed to remain at court, but was to be sent away for three days and lodged at least a mile off, and the doctor had to keep an eye open for those who might be suffering from leprosy or pestilence. This role differed from that of the master surgeon, whose provision was accordingly attributed, along with the additional scraps of meat, broken towels and clothes, from which he was to make plasters. Further down the chain of command was the king's apothecary, who was permitted to share a bed with a groom at court and had his expenses and the remains of his medicinal supplies overseen by the physician. Then there was the barber, who received a pitcher of wine and two loaves for shaving the king on Saturdays.

The second half of the text, the *domus providencie*, reflected the below-stairs aspects of the court, including those offices which had less contact with the king, such as the steward, treasurer, controller, cofferer, the counting house, bakehouse, pantry, waferer, butler, cellarer, purveyors of wine, pitcher and cup house, spicer, confectioner, chandler, office of napery and the lavendry, or wash house. Although royal households had included a distinction between these two realms, it was not really until the fifteenth century that they were labelled and defined as dependent but separate. It emphasised Edward's focus on the split between his public and private selves, the face or mask which was shown to the world and the activity taking place behind the scenes. Such a division became increasingly marked within the architecture of Edward's palaces, keeping the locations for cooking and eating separate, marking a divide between the ceremonial and private apartments, which was increasingly the focus of his building works at palaces like Eltham and Dover, where new apartments or kitchens were created. This was more than just the former *camera regis* where the king slept: it marked a significant move away from the notion of a household based upon the king's retinue, towards a specific fixed establishment with specialist professions. The court was still peripatetic, but it was now a moveable institution with a clearer sense of self and the purpose of the individuals it employed. The *Liber Niger* is conscious of defining itself against previous practises, using the phrase 'thes esquires of household of old be accustomed to ...' suggesting changes within recent memory, perhaps from the first half of the Yorkist regime, or even those who had served in Henry VI's disorderly, cost-inefficient court. Edward's reforms created a 'complex of ideas and attitudes, as well as social habits and institutional forms, which had given the court a new, or at least an acutely intensified self-awareness'.[3]

A snapshot of the court surviving from 1472, shows a partial glimpse into the lives of Edward's family at play. When Louis de Gruuthuyse visited England in order to be created Earl of Winchester, he stayed at Windsor Castle as an honoured guest and friend. Although the royals were aware that they were being observed and this does not reflect the inner sanctuary of their private lives, it is a more familiar view than the formalised ritual witnessed by Tetzel six years earlier. The castle Gruuthuyse describes is richly hung with cloths of arras; bedrooms and chambers of relaxation were hung with white silk and linen, and beds were draped with fine French sheets, canopies and counterpanes of cloth of gold and ermine. The visitor was treated to a bath, which he shared with Lord Hastings, followed by a banquet of syrups, green ginger, sweetmeats and spiced wine. He was entertained in Elizabeth's apartments, where she was playing a version of bowls with her ladies, and Edward danced with Princess Elizabeth, who was then aged six. Gruuthuyse heard Mass with the king, which was 'melodiously sung', before they went hunting in the park and dined in the hunting lodge. He was given gifts of a hunting steed, a crossbow with a velvet cover and a gold cup decorated with a large sapphire and other jewels, which reputedly contained the horn of a unicorn. No doubt the royal family looked the part, with Edward's wardrobe spending in 1471 including almost £18 on five yards of cloth of gilt for one jacket and £13 6s 8d on another made from cloth of gold trimmed with satin, damask and linen. There were also yards of crimson velvet, satin and black damask for his gowns and a robe of gilt, tawny satin lined with velvet, which cost a not inconsiderable £32 6s 8d.

Edward's focus on self-definition and conduct was part of a wider phenomenon of the time. A proliferation of manuals and educational tracts catered to a more socially mobile middle class, whose sons might find themselves working in the household of a rising lord if they were shrewd enough and followed the rules. Poems such as *The Babees' Book* or *How the Goodwife Taught her Daughter* outline the basics of good behaviour, such as when in church, or how to treat neighbours, how to keep up appearances and good table manners. The education of the young as respectful servants who knew their place was nothing new, but setting it down in such careful guidelines created a helping hand for those wishing to transcend social class. Here, now, were behavioural rules that were something like a modern 'how to' book, spilling the secrets of access to the higher echelons of society. Edward had undeniably sent mixed messages on social mobility: he might have tightened the sumptuary laws and fixed the amount of loaves and livery allowed to his servants, but he had also promoted men like Anthony Woodville on merit, rather than birthright, showing that those who were prepared to play the game might receive the rewards.

Dating from the 1460, the poem 'Urbanitatis' in the Cotton Caligula manuscript is one of the best examples of a conduct manual. It describes the correct forms of behaviour for a youth appearing before a lord, perhaps for the first time. A young man should remove his hat or hood, keep it off until told to replace it and remain upon bended on knee, keeping his hands and feet still. He was to hold up his chin and look his lord in the face, without being shamefaced or 'pressing up too high' or spitting, because 'nurtur and manners maketh man'. At table, a youth must let his betters eat before him and not take the best pieces of food, but keep his knife sharp and his hands clean without wiping them on the cloth. He should not have food in his mouth as he speaks and should stop talking when his neighbour was drinking. More general advice included the instruction to look but not talk when among ladies, to not spread gossip but be austere in speech and to interrupt no one, in the knowledge that 'words make or mar you'.

Another manual of the era entitled *Instructions to his Son* was written by Peter Idley, who died in around 1473. It contained similar advice to 'Urbanitatis' to listen and speak wisely, not letting the tongue wag loose and avoid unnecessary conflict, so that a youth would keep his friends. Caution was strongly advised, as was meekness, honesty and discretion, while friendship was the greatest prize, more precious than silver or gold. This text may have had particular significance for the York family, as Idley's widow Anne was to be employed by Richard, Duke of Gloucester, as the governess of his nursery when his own son was born. Edward and Elizabeth may have had Idley's ideas in mind when they lay down ordinances for 'the virtuous guyding of the person of our deerest' eldest son Edward in 1473, who was being established in his own household under the watchful eye of his uncle Anthony Woodville. Elizabeth accompanied her son to Ludlow that September, staying a few weeks until he was settled into his father's boyhood home. With a careful balance of lessons and leisure, and rules to guide the manners and morals of those in his service, Prince Edward's education and the influence of one of the most cultured men of his age would have produced a future king on the cusp of the Renaissance, ready to take the Yorkist dynasty through the period of cultural transformation that was sweeping Europe. But circumstances dictated that this carefully nurtured heir would not have the chance to rule England.

II

It is difficult to define the vast and interdisciplinary nature of the Renaissance, let alone place Edward within its context. In a very general sense, its basis was the spread of humanism, a term that was applied to it retrospectively in recognition of a convergence of common themes across a certain period of time. Towards defining a general philosophy, Humanism looked back to the tenets of classical antiquity while seeking to escape the narrow doctrines of medieval thought. It was a widespread movement, not just confined to the upper classes, which focused on education and living a moral life. Most art historians agree that it originated in Italy, drawing attention to the fourteenth-century resurgence of classical culture, of Petrarch's sonnets and Brunelleschi's first use of visual perspective. Following this lead, the High Renaissance is often taken to have begun in 1490 with the painting of Leonardo's Last Supper in Milan, spreading through such centres as Venice, Genoa, Florence and Rome. In northern Europe, artistic developments may have been slower to take root, but the influence of particular advances, such as the new musical techniques of the Netherlands, led to an unprecedented flourishing that Edward himself would have appreciated in 1470–1.

It is often stated that, for various reasons, the Renaissance did not touch England in any significant way, or that its influence was not felt until the mid-sixteenth century. However, measures that rely upon a certain picture or a particular technique are artificial and exclusive rather than inclusive. Perhaps with its unique island status, England's cultural rebirth should not be measured on a scale established by Europe, but analysed as part of its own developing narrative, as the innovations and developments that led it to break from its former identity and forge another. In the fifteenth century, Edward's emphasis on self-fashioning magnificence, on conduct and culture, on literature and music, architecture and alchemy, straddle the medieval and modern. His shift from the Arthurian model to the consciously crafted decorum of the *Liber Niger* and his culturally rich court indicate that the first Yorkist king may have been more of a Renaissance man than has previously been suggested.

However we might define the Renaissance, its arrival was not uniform across the arts. It developed at different paces in architecture, art, politics, philosophy, literature, medicine, music, cartography and culture, with some areas advancing ahead of others depending on the particular climate and circumstances of the regions to which its ideas were spread. Certainly, in terms of fine art, England may have lagged behind the developments of the Italian artists, never producing a Donatello or Botticelli, a Uccello or Bellini, but maybe it would be wrong to expect it. Instead we might look towards a contemporary flowering of literature, with Chaucer, Langland, Malory and Lydgate as our artists. Direct comparisons between Yorkist England and the culture of southern Europe may be misleading. Perhaps the English Renaissance was a specific, national phenomenon – the product of the unique insular mood of an island, not connected to Europe in the same way as its interlocking neighbours. Perhaps it would be more accurate to look at a British Renaissance, although the only potential rival to Edward's court in the British Isles was that of the King of Scots. Instead of looking for comparisons with Italy, we might look instead at what was happening at the time in England specifically and identify points of rebirth along humanist lines, comparing this England with its former self: the reign of Henry VI against that of Edward and the second part of Edward's reign against the first. Thus, 1461 and 1471 emerge as years of transition. Yet, when the evolving narrative of Edward's cultural court is explored, it resonates with the preoccupations of the early humanist Renaissance in Europe.

Firstly, Edward's period of exile in 1470–1 was a formative period in his transmission of northern Renaissance culture to England. This was the Netherlands of Jan van Eyck and Rogier Van der Weyden, of arras woven in gold and silver, diptychs and triptychs, of elaborately carved sculptures and brassware that adorned the homes of the wealthy merchants of Bruges, Brussels and Ghent. At the house of Louis de Gruuthuyse, Edward was exposed to a rarefied culture of art and literature, perusing the extensive library of illuminated manuscripts which inspired him to commission his own. He witnessed the splendour of Charles's court with its elaborate ceremonies and feasting, saw the gorgeous clothing of the Burgundian nobles, their newly built homes and their extensive patronage based on the wealth generated by the textile industry. Edward would also have come into contact with the innovative music of the Netherlands school, which found its focus in the ducal court under such masters as Johannes Ockeghem and Guillaume Dufay. The latest musical style was typified by such works such as Antoine Busnois's 1467 motet in honour of Ockeghem, which was performed at the Burgundian court, and after Charles the Bold's marriage to Margaret, Busnois was appointed as one of the singers and *valets de chamber*. Charles was passionate about music and the work of his minstrels would have been heard by Edward in exile.

Humanism also focused on the question of moral conduct, with works such as Italian Matteo Palmieri's 1465 *La Citta di Vita* expounding how citizens might live according to the concept of the '*uomo universal*', or 'universal man', comfortable in any sphere and ready for any situation. This phrase was coined by Leon Battista Alberti, implying that a man could do anything he wanted, limitless in his capacities and constantly evolving. A Renaissance man was a polymath, proficient in many disciplines, excelling in several. The preparation for this was the training of the body and mind in the development of new education programmes, which expanded the mind and the ability to adapt socially and politically. The proliferation of conduct manuals and ordinances in Edward's reign must be placed in this context. Works such as *The Babees' Book* set out the rules for good manners and behaviour, for conduct and friendship but also delineated between what was useful and what was honest, seeking a sense of integrity in behaviour. Edward's emphasis on Arthurian chivalry and well-ordered reverence not only moved the culture of the court from the medieval into the Renaissance, but embraced a sense of social mobility, where education, merit and correct conduct could facilitate careers.

Additionally, it was Edward's exile that intensified his interest in literature and illuminated manuscripts. Although Bruges was an important centre of artistic production, Edward was fortunate in having the work of a number of significant and innovative authors, living and dead, at his command. England had witnessed a development of literature in the vernacular, from the writing of Chaucer through to Lydgate, Langland, Gower, Hoccleve and Malory, whose *Le Morte d'Arthur* was a vehicle for comment upon the conduct of great men. He also had copies of the recent chronicles by Capgrave, William Worcester and Hardyng, dedicated to himself, and the romances of Arthur, Alexander, Guy of Warwick and Charlemagne. Edward's library contained some didactic and moral works, in a similar vein to those conduct manuals for young people, but often embellished with narratives and the inclusion of legendary figures. There was Boccaccio's *Decameron* and his *Des Cas des Nobles Hommes et Femmes Malheureux*, along with Chartier's *Le Breuiaire des Nobles* and the religious texts *The Fortress of the Faith* and St Augustine's *City of God*. The collection also shows a particular interest in history books and historical romances, including works by Livy and Josephus, the anonymous *La Grant Hystoire Cesar*, Beauvais's *Speculum Historiale*, Mansel's *Fleur des Hystoires* and le Fevre's *Receuil des Histoires de Troyes*. More recent works were also included, such as a portion of Froissart's Chronicles, Tyre's *History of the Crusades* and Waurin's *Anchiennes et Nouvelles Croniques D'Angleterre*. The latter included an illustration of Edward seated on his throne being presented with the book by its author.

Edward and his circle patronised William Caxton, who was a member of the household of Margaret of York and lived in Bruges at the time of Edward's exile. It was there that he printed the first book in English in 1473, before coming to England and setting up his press in the precincts of Westminster Abbey in 1476. It may have been Anthony Woodville who was more closely connected with Caxton, as his patron and the translator of works that were then printed, but this would not have happened without the explicit support and permission of the king. In his prefaces, the printer three times includes the comment that he has 'enjoyed the umbre and shadow' of the king's protection. Along with Anthony's versions of Christine de Pisan's *Moral Proverbs* and *Dictes and Sayengis of the Philosophers*, Caxton printed a copy of Chaucer's *Canterbury Tales*, Ovid's *Metamorphoses*, Malory's *Le Morte d'Arthur*, the popular hagiographical collection *The Golden Legend* and Geoffroy de Tour Landry's *Book of the Knight in the Tower*. A *Life of Jason* was dedicated to the young Prince Edward, with the intention that it might help him learn to read.

After 1471, Edward began to commission manuscripts from Bruges. These were often large scale volumes, each of around 300–400 parchment folios, lavishly illustrated with symbols and motifs relevant to the York dynasty. More were written in French than Latin, reflecting fashion, but also the fact that Edward's early years meant he is likely to have been bilingual. One specific artist has been identified with the illustrations on these works. The anonymous man is often referred to as the 'Master of Edward IV', and was identified by historian Friedrich Winkler based on five miniatures in his 1479 work for Edward, *Bible Historiale* and other works commissioned by the king unp to 1482. His images employ a palette of salmon, grey-blue, azure and green, with touches of black, gold and white, and include posed figures with red lips and cheeks, receding hairlines and well-defined faces. This may well have been the Philip Maisertuell or Phillipe de Mazerolles to whom payments were made in 1479 'for certaine boks by the said Philipe to be provided to the king's use in the partees beyond the see'. One 1475 copy of Waurin's chronicle depicts Edward in this salmon-blue-green palette, wearing a blue gown embroidered with golden lions and fleur-de-lys, his hair dark and curly under his crown.

Like others of his era, Edward also had an interest in alchemy. In 1471, the cleric and chemist George Ripley dedicated *The Compound of Alchymy* to king, a verse treatise on the 'right and perfectest means to make the philosopher's stone', building on the research of his predecessors Ramon Lull and Guido de Montanor. Ripley had spent years in Europe, finding favour with the Pope, funding the Knights Templar and studying the methods of alchemists there before he returned to England to compose his book. Its discovery was something of a holy grail: the ultimate quest for philosophers of the era, of turning base metals into gold. Often associated more with those working in the sixteenth century and a favourite analogy among dramatists, this dedication shows its importance during Edward's reign, possibly under his patronage. It belonged in a tradition that included such controversial figures as Roger Bacon, John Dee and Simon Forman, overlapping astrology, medicine, divination and witchcraft; Ripley's work was also studied by scientists Robert Boyle and Isaac Newton. The Ripley scrolls, now in the Bodleian library and based on a lost fifteenth-century original, contain some wonderful illustrations of the process, with mythical beasts, suns beaming down from clouds, serpents bleeding onto the earth, toads, babies being boiled over stoves and hearts stabbed with knives. The quest is outlined in terms of the influence of the planets, each of which is associated with different metals. Ripley later became an anchorite, rather like a hermit who had taken a religious vow and lived as if they were dead to the world.[4]

A pupil of Ripley, Thomas Norton rose to even greater prominence in alchemy during Edward's reign. In his own account of his life, *Ordinall of Alkimie*, written in around 1474, Norton claimed to have discovered the 'Elixir of Gold', adding that he must not commit the recipe to paper, but transmit it 'from mouth to mouth … with sacred and most dreadful oath'. Norton relates the story of Thomas Dalton, a monk from Gloucestershire, who had succeeded in creating a 'red medicine' which transmuted base metals into gold. Upon hearing this, Edward sent Thomas Herbert, brother of the Earl of Pembroke, to remove Dalton from the abbey against his will and bring him to court. There, according to Norton, Edward instructed him to make more of his red medicine, but here accounts differed, either stating that Dalton poured away his mixture or that he was kidnapped by Herbert, who stole the £1,000 Edward had trusted Dalton with.[5] The truth of the story is unknown, but Edward certainly took an interest in alchemy, licensing David Beaupee and John Merchaunt in 1476 to study 'the natural science of the generation of gold and silver from mercury' for a four-year period. In many ways, Edward's symbol of the sun in splendour was representative of alchemical gold: a prize at the end of a process of quest and refinement.

Men like Edward, Anthony Woodville and Hastings straddled the medieval and modern worlds: part Renaissance men, part chivalric knights. They were products of the feudal system: Arthurian knights in the service to their lord, devout and pious crusaders who were also obedient to the laws of courtly love, but modern in their breadth and multiplicity, as politicians, diplomats, patrons of the arts, humanists. This is why Malory's work is such a fitting symbol of the age, rewriting an epic as a modern romance and capturing a culture in transition, as the medieval values of the Arthurian court met the early humanist principles and the concept of the universal man. For Malory, the central concept of the world is personified in the figure of Arthur himself, who defines his court and gives it cohesion through his powerful personality. In the same way, Edward was the stabilising heart of his world, keeping the various factions in check and leading through strong personality. In an opposite way to the example set by Henry VI, Edward proved that medieval sovereignty was essentially shaped by a king's character.

What role amid this cultural flourishing did Elizabeth take? The reforms of the court also saw her household reduced and made more efficient, being limited to a staff of 100. Yet she followed Edward's lead and continued to perform as a function of his projected magnificence, spending over £1,000 on her wardrobe in a single year, with individual payments of £54 going to her goldsmith and £14 on sable furs, £10 on minstrels and £18 on medicines from her apothecary. As a queen, she was the natural patroness of those arts encouraged by her husband. Caxton's *The Knight of the Tower* was dedicated to Elizabeth, and she commissioned or owned several books, including a history of Troy, Walter Map's *De Nugis Curialium* and the illuminated prayer book *The Hours of the Angel*. Elizabeth also bore two more children during this period. She was at Windsor on 10 April 1472 to bear a daughter she named Margaret, although the child did not survive long, dying that December. The queen was already pregnant again while she mourned this loss, and was in Shrewsbury the following August when she gave birth to a son, Richard. It was also in 1472 that Elizabeth's mother, Jacquetta, died at the age of fifty-six, having come through the recent political and personal turbulence, cleared her name and seen her daughter restored to her position.

It was as an Arthurian queen that Elizabeth took centre stage in Edward's Camelot, but she was a greater queen than Guinevere, whose implications of faithlessness damaged her reputation. Elizabeth was something of a female Arthur: the personification of the ideal qualities of her gender. She was a symbol of the feminine side of the performance of majesty, the pinnacle of fashion, beauty and compassion, a presence and focus for the half of the court that complimented Edward's martial, cultured circle. Her family connection with the house of Luxembourg and her innate qualities were championed by Edward as worthy of queenship, although she may not have been directly of royal blood. She typified the Arthurian ideal of femininity. Malory's character of Nymue, Lady of the Lake, who is not just a temptress but a powerful and positive figure – compassionate and strong and able to assist the men around her, combined well with the image of Melusina, the alluring half-woman, half-serpent creature of Luxembourgian mythology. Most of all though, Elizabeth was a mother, producing a line of children to continue the Yorkist tradition, in the same way that Cecily Neville and Edward III's wife, Philippa of Hainault, had done. During this time, Elizabeth founded a chapel in Westminster dedicated to St Erasmus, the protector of women in childbirth, perhaps suggesting that she had appealed to him for help during her confinement in sanctuary in 1470. Such shrines were common across the country, where women might go on pilgrimage to pray for the intercession of the saints in their reproductive lives. While Edward visited the tomb of Thomas Becket in Canterbury, Elizabeth may have gone into the crypt, where the altar of the Virgin Mary acted as a focus for women's hopes. Two decades earlier, Margaret of Anjou had prayed there for the conception of the son she bore in 1453. As Edward's wife, Elizabeth was not just responsible for bearing the children that would continue his dynastic line, she was also a figurehead for English women: the female face of majesty. Yet she was humanised and accessible by the universal experience of childbirth. The pain, fear and aspirations women felt during pregnancy and labour cut across the class divide and provided a direct link between Elizabeth and her female subjects, which is only analogous, in medieval terms, to the experience of men fighting alongside their king in battle.

Around the time that Elizabeth was delivering Margaret, her fifth child by Edward, the family welcomed another new member. In 1472, Edward's younger brother Richard, Duke of Gloucester, was married to Anne Neville, Warwick's daughter who was the widow of Prince Edward of Westminster. Yet, this was a complicated match for legal reasons, and the new bride was not welcomed with open arms by all. George was still married to Warwick's elder daughter, Isabel Neville, and had inherited the entirety of her father's estates in the absence of a male heir – estates that represented the most significant power and presence in the country outside that of the royal family. Whoever held the late earl's inheritance was guaranteed authority and the ability to command men, land and wealth. All three York brothers knew this. Edward was keen to divide the spoils between his brothers, whereas George hoped to keep them all for himself.

A dispute arose between George and Richard, over whether Anne should be entitled to her half of her father's legacy. Legally, this should never have been an issue, as the earl's widow, the Countess of Warwick, was alive and well in sanctuary in Beaulieu Abbey, and should have been in receipt of his properties and lands, or at least a say in their disposal. In 1472, Anne was still only sixteen, yet the last two years had been busy ones for her. Little is known of her marriage to the Lancastrian heir, but she had been captured after the Battle of Tewkesbury and entrusted to the care of her sister, living under Clarence's roof. According to Croyland, George had attempted to keep her and Richard apart, concealing her identity in the disguise of a kitchen maid. This smacks of romantic legend and is mentioned by no other sources, but it indicates a level of hostility towards the match on the part of George, and perhaps Isabel. Anne may have been just as keen to marry Richard as he was to wed her. He was an old friend, since they had spent childhood days together at Middleham Castle; he was perhaps someone for whom she even felt genuine affection, although he was certainly the only husband who could match Clarence and help her reclaim what she was owed. Romantic novelists have been keen to claim this as a love match, yet in reality it is likely to have been a mutually beneficial financial arrangement, which may also have inspired mutual respect and warmth. Such was the way of marital arrangements among medieval aristocrats. It was 16 February when the question of the disputed inheritance became widely known, along with the conflict it was causing. The following day, John Paston wrote,

> yesterday the Kynge, Qween, my Lordes of Clarance and Glowcester went to Scheen to pardon, men sey, nott alle in cheryte; what wyll falle, men can nott seye. The Kynge entretyth my Lorde off Clarance ffor my Lords of Glowcesterl and, as itt is seyde, he answerythe, that he may well have my Lady hys suster in lawe, butt they schall parte no lyvelod, as he seythe, so what wyll falle can I notte seye.

The wedding took place in secret, probably between February and April 1472. Clarence was not satisfied and the breach continued to rumble on as Gloucester attempted, with Edward's support, to claim back those lands his brother held in his keeping. The following year, Anne and Isabel's mother, the widowed countess, went to live with Anne and Richard at Middleham Castle and around that time Anne bore a son, whom she named Edward. It may well have suited the king for Richard to divide the Warwick inheritance because it was a dangerous amount of power to remain in the hands of a brother who had previously proved himself to be disloyal. According to Paston, Edward was acting as a 'stifler' between the two, especially as Clarence had said he 'woulde but dele with the Duke of Glowcester'. The matter was not settled until 1474, when Parliament recognised both the dukes as heirs of Warwick. Croyland describes the process and the way in which Edward acted as mediator:

> so much dissension arose between the brothers, and so many acute arguments were put forward on either side in the presence of the king, sitting in judgement in the council chamber that all present, even lawyers, marvelled at the profusion of arguments marshalled by the princes in their respective cases. Indeed, these three brothers, the king and the dukes, possessed such outstanding talents that, if

they had been able to avoid discord, such a triple bond could only have been broken with the utmost difficulty.

Croyland makes an important point here. Having striven for years against the Lancastrian threat, the triumvirate of Edward, George and Richard, the three suns in the sky, the three sons of York, should have been unstoppable. With these three highly competent and charismatic men in charge – Edward in London and the south, Richard in the north and George in the west – England should have been prosperous and secure. Threats from the outside could be successful in uniting the three, but the coming years would prove that the York dynasty could also be its own worst enemy. In addition, this highlights just how important Edward's personal rule was: that he had the presence and strength of character to embody justice, to ensure harmony and the resolution of a potentially damaging dispute. So long as the charismatic figure of Edward remained on the throne as the lawgiver, the disputes of his court would remain in perspective.

The final flourish of the Lancastrian sympathisers came in 1473. John de Vere, Earl of Oxford, had been pardoned after his father and elder brother were executed for treason in 1462; he had been brought into the Arthurian circle and created a Knight of the Bath at Elizabeth's coronation. In Warwick's absence, he had even officiated at the ceremony as Lord Great Chamberlain, and seemed to be reconciled to, even friendly with, the new regime. Yet at the end of 1468, he was arrested amid the wave of widespread Lancastrian sympathy in the wake of the Thomas Cook affair, suspected of conspiring to aid Queen Margaret. He was released early the following year only to join Warwick and Clarence against Edward at Edgecote, and again during the readeption of Henry VI, bearing the sword of state before the Lancastrian king at his recrowning in Westminster. His presence in Norfolk had prevented Edward from landing in 1471, and he successfully commanded a third of Warwick's army at Barnet, although ultimately that battle fell to the Yorkists. Oxford fled first to Scotland, and then to France, from where he attempted to land in St Osyth, Essex, in May 1473. When this failed, he launched an attack upon St Michael's Mount in Cornwall and occupied the island. Edward sent Sir John Fortescue to lay siege to it, until Oxford finally surrendered the following February. He was attainted and imprisoned in Hammes Castle in Calais, remaining in custody there for nine years until after the death of Edward, when he escaped and went to join the Lancastrians in exile, under the young hopeful, Henry Tudor.

10

ENEMIES, NEAR AND FAR
1475–1478

'To conspire new treasons.'

I

By 1475, Edward was determined to reopen the Hundred Years War and revive the English claim to the throne of France. Fresh from the amazing victories of Barnet and Tewkesbury, having survived a dangerous exile, he had risen from nadir of the wheel of fortune to decimate his Lancastrian enemies and begin an unprecedented second reign, so his confidence must have been high. It was time to make his mark as a European force to be reckoned with. Edward was still relatively young and determined to live up to his Arthurian ideals – determined to prove his worth in a long line of kings who had acquitted themselves on the battlefield. The voices of St George, Cadwallader, Brutus and his Mortimer descendants, painted into his genealogy, were calling over his shoulder. The glorious mantle of Edward III and Henry V had been passed to him by the ceremonial ointment in Westminster Abbey, and it was time to write the next chapter in England's domination of northern France and to teach the errant Louis a lesson; time for Edward to fulfil his promise to make the grand gesture that future generations would remember him for and become the second Arthur. In the event, these ideals gave way to a generous financial settlement. It was a chivalric embarrassment, but a shrewd political move for the king.

The Hundred Years War was older than its name suggests. It had actually begun a century and a half earlier, when the line of succession of the house of Capet was disputed and Edward III emerged as the closest male relative of the recently deceased Charles IV. He was keen to claim the kingdom as his own, and he had good reason. Edward's mother Isabella was Charles's sister, but, as predicted, the French nobility rejected the idea of the two countries becoming joined under English rule, along with the indignity of submitting to a foreign king. They offered the throne to Charles's cousin Philip instead, who readily accepted, marking the beginning of the reign of the Valois family. Edward challenged this decision, but the Pope in Avignon declared in favour of Salic Law, meaning that inheritance could not be transmitted through the female line. Yet, having had the whiff of potential ownership of their old enemy, the Plantagenet family was not likely to forget this chance. Since then, the struggle for ownership had continued, with England keeping a foothold in the north, including the pale of Calais, Normandy and a number of other locations. There had been notable English victories, such as the battles of Crecy, Poitiers and Agincourt, and marriage treaties including those of Richard II to Isabelle of Valois and Henry V to her sister Catherine, whose son, Henry VI, had coronations in both Westminster and Rheims. As a young man, Edward's father, the Duke of York, had been present in the French cathedral when the boy-king was anointed in 1429.

By 1475, relations between Edward IV and Louis XI had been frosty for a number of years. If nothing else, the English king was not prepared to forgive Louis for supporting the Earl of Warwick or harbouring the exiled Margaret of Anjou and her son. Edward knew it was Louis who had masterminded the reconciliation between the earl and the former queen, perhaps even suggesting the marriage alliance between Prince Edward and Anne Neville, or at least supporting and facilitating it. Edward had clearly been considering this move for a while, with much time in the long parliament of October 1472 to March 1475 being given over to speeches on the matter. His motives appear to have been glory and revenge. Later, Polydore Vergil would argue that Edward was drawn into the war in order to please Charles of Burgundy, but Edward had previously levied war taxes in 1463 and 1468 and was ready to press Parliament again to support his venture. Perhaps He was so keen to engage in battle because Warwick had criticised him for appropriating these funds, but it was certainly within his character to fight and reassert his Arthurian aims. Edward had enough excuses of his own to do so; he did not need to be talked into it by Charles.

Another key text completed during Edward's reign raised some of the same questions as Malory's *Le Morte d'Arthur*, particularly as to the conduct of the nobility and the relations between war and manhood. William of Worcester had been secretary to Sir John Fastolf, himself the Grand Master of the Household of Jacquetta's first husband, John, Duke of Bedford. Worcester had been tinkering with his *Boke of Noblesse* since the 1450s, but he rededicated it to Edward in 1475 as a call to arms – a challenge to reclaim English territories lost in France, a reminder of the inherited obligations of the aristocracy and a definition of medieval masculinity as essentially chivalric and warlike. Worcester argued for strong personal leadership to recapture the glories of the past for the benefit of the common weal, or common good, and for those 'burning for military fame'. Worcester's dedication named Edward as the 'undisputed king of England, and, like his predecessors, the titular king of France',[1] as if Edward needed much more of a prompt. In many ways it was Malory's message with a persuasive intent, and the king embraced it.

Edward's preparations started with diplomacy, arranging treaties with Louis's neighbours and enemies prior to announcing war. In July 1474, the Treaty of London had bound Edward and Charles of Burgundy in a formal alliance to invade France and divide the conquered territories between them. Agreements followed with Naples, Denmark, Brittany and the combined kingdoms of Castile and Aragon. Peace was also made with the Scots, to ensure they did not invade England in Edward's absence, and a betrothal was arranged between the five-year-old princess Cecily of York and James, the infant son of James III. Edward had hoped to land his forces in Normandy, following in the footsteps of Henry V, with the intention of emulating something of the past king's success.

To this end, he issued summons in February for his armies to assemble at Portsmouth that May. However, the Burgundian armies were engaged in fighting elsewhere, so Edward prepared to cross over to Calais, further to the east and closer to the border with Charles's territories. With so much European support, along with his past military victories, it seemed that Edward was heading for a new military show-down that would rival the fame of Crécy or Agincourt. But the king had learned from some of his former mistakes, and he was not naïve enough to anticipate striding into glory unscathed.

Launching an invasion was always a risky business. Before he left home, Edward made provision for the event of his death, which helps provide some answers to the questions that arose when he actually died, eight years later. Elizabeth was left in charge with £2,200 annual income for Prince Edward, who was brought from Ludlow to London on 12 May, aged four and a half. He was officially appointed Keeper of the Realm during his father's absence, and government was placed in the hands of Archbishop Bourchier. The documents Edward had prepared upon the inauguration of his son as Prince of Wales also contribute to the picture of who he imagined would form the boy's council: along with Elizabeth, the prince would be guided by Anthony Woodville; George, Duke of Clarence; Richard, Duke of Gloucester; Archbishop Bourchier; and Bishop Stillington. In the event of his death, Edward left instructions for his funeral, requesting that he be buried in his new chapel at Windsor, below ground, with an effigy of death placed on top of his tomb, probably carved in the shape of a rotting corpse. This sounds like one of the popular *memento mori* tombs of the era, combining a statement of magnificent living and status with the recognition that all men are equal in death – a sign of religious humility that equally spoke of the wealth of the person able to commission it. Edward may have witnessed a similar cadaver tomb in Canterbury Cathedral, where Archbishop Henry Chichele was laid to rest in 1443 in a sort of 'bunk-bed' style, his gorgeously attired effigy atop a box containing a carving of his skeletal remains. The legend on the tomb proclaims the ubiquity of the wheel of fortune to the fifteenth-century mind: 'I was pauper-born then to primate raised. Now I am cut down and served up for worms. Behold my grave.'

1475 must have been a testing year for Elizabeth. As a measure of his confidence in her loyalty and abilities, Edward named his 'derrest and moost entirely beloved wiff' as his main executor, allowing her the choice of how to distribute his goods, so that she might keep those that 'she shall thinke to bee moost necessarie and convenient for her' and divide what remained between their two sons 'by her discrecion'. What Elizabeth thought of her husband's intention to go to war is not recorded. Publically, she would have given him her complete support, yet privately, in the bedroom, where the medieval wife's influence was most felt, she may have expressed doubts. In recent years, she had lost both her parents and her elder brother John, so Elizabeth might understandably have been unwilling for Edward to put himself into a position of danger again when it was not strictly necessary. Although he was handing her the reins of political power, it does not mean that she was keen to wield it in the event of his loss. On a personal level, she would have been unwilling to lose her status as a wife and queen, especially given the genuine affection she seems to have felt for Edward; nor would she have wished her son and his siblings to lose such a powerful protector before they had come of age and marriages for them had been arranged. However, her feelings must not be judged in the hindsight of the events of 1483, when the political situation was different. History tells us how Richard of Gloucester declared Elizabeth's marriage invalid and her children illegitimate, setting aside their claim and becoming Richard III. Elizabeth could not have anticipated this in 1483, let alone in 1475, especially given the record of loyalty her youngest brother-in-law had hitherto shown. Had she feared Edward's death abroad in 1475, it may have been for other reasons than the likelihood that her children would be usurped. Perhaps she tried to influence her husband not to engage in warfare; perhaps she encouraged him, revelling in the potential glory and acquisitions. It's even possible that he shared with her his intention to make terms with Louis before blood had been shed.

Edward's army were ordered to assemble on Barham Downs, outside Canterbury. It was the 'finest, largest and best appointed force that has ever left England' according to a contemporary, and the most 'noble and impressive array' in the words of the Croyland chronicler. This was an impressive claim, given that

Agincourt was still within living memory. With these procedures in place, Edward left London on 30 May, and ten days later he left Canterbury for Sandwich. From there, he sailed for Calais, arriving on 4 July. However, the invasion immediately met with obstacles. Duke Francis of Brittany had promised 8,000 troops which failed to appear, and the Burgundian army was engaged elsewhere. Charles the Bold suggested that Edward marched eastward through Burgundy to join him at Peronne, from where they would launch a joint attack, ending in Rheims, where Edward would be crowned King of France. Yet to Edward's frustration, Charles refused the English army admittance to any of his towns, leaving them languishing outside the walls, uncertain of their next move. The glorious military conquest suddenly shifted gear into a tedious process of negotiation and diplomacy. Louis was unwilling to engage in combat and potentially lose territories, so he accepted Edward's suggestion to negotiate and they met at Picquigny on the Somme, near Amiens. Commines described the arrival of the English:

> The King of England came along the causeway ... very well attended, and appeared a regal figure. With him was the Duke of Clarence, his brother, the earl of Northumberland and certain other lords, his chamberlain called Lord Hastings, his chancellor and others; and there were not more than three or four dressed in cloth of gold similar to the king. The king had a bonnet of black velvet on his head, and had in it a great fleur de lys set with precious stones ... when he had come within four or five feet of the barrier he drew his bonnet and bowed to within half a foot of the ground.

This was the chronicler's formal portrait of the king, but he also recorded a conversation Edward had with King Louis, which sheds light on their interpretations of Edward the man. According to Commines, Louis expressed the view that Edward was 'very handsome and more than keen on the women', and suggested that if the English king were to visit Paris, he 'might quite easily meet some cunning female ... who would know just what to say to make him want to come back.' Commines replied that Edward was well known for his pleasures, 'especially in ladies, feasting, banqueting and hunting'. This glimpse of a king who was now in his prime captures a sense of the Edward of popular legend – the handsome, debauched lover who cared more for pleasure than politics – but taken on its own, this view underestimates the man. The Treaty of Picquigny alone shows Edward's intelligence and astuteness. Whilst reviving his chivalric image, he had concluded a treaty that was beneficial to England on a number of levels.

On 29 August, a treaty was signed by which the two monarchs agreed to a seven-year truce, free trade between the two countries and a marriage between the Dauphin and Princess Elizabeth. Better still, it guaranteed an initial payment of 75,000 crowns and an income for Edward of 50,000 crowns annually if the English relinquished their claim and left France at once. This was a wise move on Edward's part, which brought him financial security for the remainder of his life and allowed him to bring his troops home without a drop of blood having been shed. The deal meant that he had financial independence from Parliament and allowed for free Anglo-French trade. A solution to the awkward continuing presence of Margaret of Anjou in England was also reached, with Louis agreeing to ransom the captive and accommodate her in France. This transfer was completed the following January. Edward sailed for home on 19 September. He had pulled off an amazing coup. There is little reason to suspect, as the Milanese ambassador wrote, that he had done so 'to the great disgust of his kingdom'.

The Treaty of Picquigny had important cultural side-effects. With his generous allowance from Louis XI, Edward could afford to undertake an extensive building programme to modernise and improve certain royal palaces. In some cases, these architectural changes emphasised the split between the public and private, through the creation of new kitchens and the separation of private apartments from public rooms, where most elements of traditional living had long taken place. Although little of Edward's work survives today, his mark can literally be seen in the presence of his motifs of suns in splendour, white roses and others that can still be found in buildings associated with him. At Eltham Palace in Kent, Edward demolished the original fourteenth-century hall built by Anthony Bek, Bishop of Durham, and replaced it with a great hall for entertaining, with a hammerbeam oak ceiling, featuring his rose-en-soleil badge and the falcon and fetterlock of the house of

York. Traces of yellow undercoating found in the 1930s suggest that parts of the roof may have been gilded, in what would have been an awe-inspiring marriage of wealth, art and power. The hall was designed by Edward's master mason Thomas Jurdan, with the roof created by his master carpenter Edmund Graveley.[2] It still stands today, as a formidable piece of architecture, at 101 feet by 36 feet, rising 55 feet to its apex. A dais at the end was lit by bay windows, in the light of which Edward and Elizabeth would have dined. It also gave access to the private apartments of the king, to the left, and the queen, to the right, allowing them to manage their public entrances and retreats whenever they chose. An account for the construction of the roof survives from 1479, suggesting its completion soon afterwards. Edward undertook more domestic construction at Hertford, Dover and Fotheringhay, although none of this now survives, and at Nottingham in 1476–80 he restructured the royal apartments so that the king's suite was above that of the queen.[3]

The architectural project for which Edward is most famous, though, stands within the lower ward of Windsor Castle. If Edward held Canterbury and Thomas Becket in high esteem, it was no more than that which he felt for the home of the Order of the Garter. In 1473, Richard Beauchamp, Bishop of Salisbury, was appointed Master of the Works, responsible for hiring the masons and craftsmen required and acquiring supplies. Existing buildings were demolished and work began on St George's Chapel, partly to provide a separate mausoleum for the York family and to 'daily serve Almighty God', but also to rival Henry VI's chapel at Chertsey. It was undertaken by master mason Henry Janyns, who worked at Eton College, and overseen by Beauchamp. From 1478, a horseshoe cloister was added to the side of the church, and three years later the relics of a famous healer, John Schorn, were brought to Windsor and displayed alongside the fragment of the true cross owned by Edward III. Accounts show that the choir stalls and canopies were being carved in 1478–9 and work was beginning on Edward's tomb in the north of the choir, as outlined in his 1475 will. The cadaver tomb was to feature an image of Death dressed in armour and the figure of Edward as he looked in life, made of 'silver and gilt or at the least copper and gilt'.[4] In 1482–3, casks of black marble were shipped from the Netherlands for the completion of the tomb, but Edward's death meant his design was never completed. Instead of the grand *memento mori*, Edward is perhaps better remembered in terms of his architectural legacy, celebrated by John Skelton's elegy of 1483:

> I made the Tower strong, I wist not why
> I knew not to whom I purchased Tattershall
> I amended Dover on the mountain high
> And London I provoked to fortify the wall
> I made Nottingham a place full royall
> Windsor, Eltham, and many others mo
> Yet, at last, I went from them all.

Elizabeth would have been relieved to see Edward return from France safely, especially as she was only months away from giving birth again. On Prince Edward's fifth birthday, she gave birth to a daughter at Westminster, whom they named Anne. The contrast in circumstances must have struck the queen. Her previous delivery had taken place amid the chaos and uncertainty of Edward's exile, with the very real chance that he would never get to meet his infant son, whose very existence, as the king's heir, would have been under threat. Now, the wheel of fortune had turned again, placing the queen and her family in luxury at Westminster, their enemies defeated and their financial situation a cause for celebration.

In 1476, Edward also sought to honour his family roots and acknowledge the role played by his father in the rise of the Yorkist dynasty. Until this point, the bodies of Richard, Duke of York, and Edmund, Duke of Rutland, had been buried at Pontefract Priory, but now Edward brought them home to the chapel of the family church at Fotheringhay. The bodies were exhumed in July and brought east on ceremonial hearses decorated with the heraldic and dynastic symbols of York and draped with cloth of gold. An effigy of the Duke of York, dressed in the deep-blue velvet of royal mourning with an ermine trim, his hands clasped in prayer, lay on top of his coffin. Above his carved wax head was the figure of an angel holding a crown, to symbolise his rightful position as an uncrowned king. Richard of Gloucester headed the procession as it travelled through the countryside, stopping at Doncaster, Blyth, Newark, Grantham and Stamford, before reaching Fotheringhay on 29 July. The following day, the service of reinternment took place. York's black warhorse was ridden into the church, pennies were offered by the mourners and both coffins were lowered into the ground. York was buried in the choir, where his wife, Cecily, would later join him, and Edmund was laid to rest in the Lady Chapel. Apparently up to 20,000 people were feasted in makeshift tents following the service. Edward stayed in Northamptonshire until August, then travelled south on a slow progress, arriving at Windsor on 8 October.

II

The sixteen months after, the signing of the Treaty of Picquigny marked a period of peace for England and her allies, old and new. Then, in January 1477, news came of the death of Charles the Bold at the Battle of Nancy in horrific circumstances. Having led his forces against the Swiss in the dead of winter, losing many men to the extreme cold, Charles was killed attempting to besiege the city. His naked body was found in the frozen river, days later, the head cleft in two by a halberd, lances penetrating his stomach and loins, his face so badly mutilated by wild animals that his physician had to identify him by old battle scars and his long fingernails. Margaret of York was now a widow, and Charles's inheritance passed to his daughter, Mary of Burgundy, who was now a very eligible marital prospect on the international stage. Soon afterwards, Elizabeth was at Windsor, where she gave birth to a son whom they named George. For the little boy's namesake, though, the opportunity offered by Burgundy was to become a point of conflict with his family.

On 6 October 1476, Isabel Neville, Duchess of Clarence, had given birth to her fourth child in the new chamber of the infirmary at Tewkesbury Abbey, according to the chronicle kept by that establishment. She had completed the period of lying in, and had been allowed to return home to Warwick Castle on 12 November, where she had died on 21 December. Her newborn son, Richard, had died on 1 January, four days before Charles the Bold at Nancy. Isabel's body was returned to the abbey, where she lay in state before being buried in a vault behind the high altar. George took her death badly. He had always been a volatile character and this triggered his descent into what appears to have been a breakdown, affected by grief, anxiety and paranoia.

Blaming witchcraft, George sought a scapegoat among his wife's waiting women. He seized upon Ankarette Twynho, one of the ladies who had served Isabel, and took a troop of eighty men to drag her from her home in Somerset and carried her off to Bath, then Cirencester, then Warwick. There, she was deprived of her jewels, money and goods, and brought before a jury of Justices of the Peace at the Guildhall, who charged her with giving Isabel 'a venomous drink of ale mixed with poison, of which the latter sickened until the Sunday before Christmas, on which day she died'. Ankarette was condemned to death, and within three hours she had been hanged, even though a number of jury members visited the woman to beg her forgiveness. George was clutching at straws, or else his mind was unhinged; he was seeing conspiracies everywhere. The Parliament Rolls show that Twynho was not his only target: a John Thursby of Warwick was convicted of poisoning Isabel's baby and hanged alongside Ankarette, while a third man, Sir Roger Turcotes, was also condemned, but was lucky enough to escape. The real cause of Isabel's death, at the age of just twenty-five, might have been an injury or infection that was the result of her delivery, or possibly some wasting illness like consumption; her sister, Anne, would die at the age of twenty-eight. When Ankarette's grandson appealed to Edward for her name to be cleared, the king granted the woman a full pardon. This was probably in the light of what George did next.

As Croyland relates, 'The duke now seemed more and more to be withdrawing from the king's presence, hardly uttering a word in council, not eating and drinking in the king's residence. Many believed the duke had been angered because … he had lost the noble lordship of Tutbury.' Yet Clarence had bigger dreams. Shortly after Isabel's death, Margaret, Duchess of Burgundy, revived the plan for her brother to marry her stepdaughter, Mary, the daughter of Charles the Bold's first marriage. Mary was then aged twenty and heiress to the vast Burgundian empire. Just as before, Edward did not think that Clarence was a suitable husband for Mary, or else feared the power that such a position would give his unpredictable younger brother: 'So exalted a destiny for an ungrateful brother displeased the king who, therefore threw all possible obstacles in the way of such a marriage.' Edward tried to persuade Margaret that Maximilian, son of the Holy Roman Emperor, would be a far better match. George was not pleased by his brother's intervention. Through 1477, he spiralled into confusion, treason and indignation. Worse still, the old matter of witchcraft, which had followed Elizabeth since her marriage, reared its head again.

Rumours reached court of certain activities taking place under George's roof. His squire, Thomas Burdett, was arrested, along with John Stacey, an astronomer, who Croyland states was 'in reality a great necromancer'. They were examined and accused 'of having made lead figures and other things to procure the death of Richard, Lord Beauchamp, at the request of his adulterous wife', but the pair also confessed to other activities before being put to death, including plotting the death of the king. Mancini later described George's crime as having 'plotted the king's death by means of spells and magicians', while Thomas More could not decide if he was guilty of anything but pride. The following day, Clarence interrupted a session of the royal council at Westminster to read the confession and declaration of innocence made by Stacey and Burdett before their deaths. Edward was not present to witness this, but the news reached him at Windsor and his summoned his brother to explain himself. Not only this, but George also made accusations against the king and queen. Edward was angry: 'From his own lips [he] began to inveigh forcefully against the duke's conduct, as if he were in contempt of the law of the land and a great threat to the judges and jurors of the kingdom.'[5] It may also have triggered memories of George's past betrayals, with the king 'recalling to mind the information formerly laid against his brother, which he had long kept stored up in his breast'.

Clarence was summoned to appear before the council at Windsor, where Edward presented the evidence against him in person: 'No one uttered a word against the duke except the king: no one made answer to the king except the duke.' George denied all the charges brought against him and offered to submit to the medieval concept of trial by combat, to 'maintain his cause with his body'.[6] It did him little good. Having already given his brother a number of chances, Edward was resolved. An Act of Attainder was passed against George, beginning with the ominous reminder, 'The Kyng, our Soverreign Lord, hath called to his Remembraunce the manifold grete Conspiracies, malicious and heinous Tresons that ... have been made here within this his Royaulme for entent and purpose to have destroyed his moost Roiall person.'[7] The king had forgiven his brother in the past and had shown great love towards him in spite of his behaviour: 'Despite the king's professed love for Clarence, the large grants he has given him and his forgiving of past offenses the duke for all this, no love increasing but rather growing daily more malicious, has not been slow to conspire new treasons.' Edward continued that it had recently come to his attention that George had plotted against him and his family, conspiring

a moch higher, moch more malicious, more unaturall and lothely Treason, than ate eny tyme heretofirn hath been compassed, purposed and conspired from the Kings first Reigne ... for that not oonly hath it proceded of the moost extreme malice ... but also for that it hath been contrived, imagined and conspired by the persone that of all erthely creatures, beside the dutie of liegaunce, by nature, by benefite, by gratitude and by geftes and grants of Goodes and Possessions, hath been moost bounden and beholden to have dradde, loved, honoured and evere thanked the Kyng ... all this had been entendeth by his Brother, George, Duke of Clarence.

Specifically, Clarence had 'falsely and untruly noised, published and said that the king our sovereign lord was a bastard and not born to reign over us ... he obtained and got an exemplification under the great seal of Henry VI ... that, if Harry and Edward, his first born son, died without male issue, then the duke and his heirs should be kings of this land and the duke had kept this document secret.' These crimes were so serious that it left Edward little choice as to his:

The king, by the advice and assent of his Lords spiritual and temporal, and the Commons, in this present Parliament assembled, and by the authority of the same, ordains, enacts and establishes that the said George, Duke of Clarence, be convicted and attained of high treason.

While George was incarcerated in the Tower, the rest of his family gathered to celebrate the marriage of Edward and Elizabeth's second son, Richard of York, to Anne de Mowbray on 15 January 1478. It was little more than a nominal match, with the bride and groom being only four and six respectively, but it was a good union for a younger son, Anne being the sole heiress to the extensive estates of the Duke of Norfolk. The ceremony took place in St Stephen's Chapel in the Palace of Westminster, and was followed by pageants, disguisings and tournaments in the Burgundian style. A narrative of the occasion, written by an eyewitness, allows another insight into the ceremonial of the Edwardian court:

> The excellent princess [Anne] came to the place of estate, in the King's great chamber at Westminster, and there, according to her high and excellent estate, had a void [repast] after the forme and estate of this famous realme of England ... this princess before rehearsed came out of the queene's chamber at Westminster and so proceeded through the King's great chamber and into the White Hall, and so proceeded into Saint Stephens Chappell ... which was richly garnished with tappets [carpets] of azure culler, enramplished with flower de luces of gould curiously wrought ... Then was there grete number of gould and silver cast amongst the comone people, brought in basons of gold by the high and mighty Prince the Duke of Gloucester and after were accomplished the appurtenaunces of the said marriage and after, spices and wyne, as appertayneth to matrimoniall feastes ... And after the second course, Minstrells ... and then kings of armes and herauldes, thankeing her highness for her largesse ... And after the surnapp made, and wash, then the avoid [repast] marvellously reverently, with famous estates. The presse was soe great that I might not see to write the names of them that served, the abundance of the noble people were so innumerable.[8]

This marriage raised the question of who might be chosen as a bride for the Prince of Wales. The young Edward was then seven years old and his future marriage was still several years off. However, as his parents had already considered the futures of his siblings, it is likely they were already carefully considering the potential candidates for the future Queen of England. In 1480, a treaty would be concluded with Francis of Brittany, agreeing that Edward would marry the duke's four-year-old daughter, Anne, when they reached their majority. The eldest son of this marriage would inherit the English throne, and the second eldest would claim Brittany. The treaty gives a haunting glimpse of an alternative future in northern European history, which never came to fruition.

George, Duke of Clarence, was put to death on 18 February 1478. The chronicles are in agreement that it took place secretly within the Tower, with Commines and Fabyan asserting that he was drowned in a butt of Malmsey wine, and Mancini concuring that he was 'plunged into a jar of sweet wine'. Mancini also claimed that Richard, Duke of Gloucester, was grief stricken by his brother's death; this may well have been the case, even though Richard had played a part in the process by attending all the council meetings in the lead up to his brother's conviction, including the one that sentenced George to death. Mancini was keen to blame the event upon Elizabeth, saying that she recalled 'the insults to her family ... that according to established usage she was not the legitimate wife of the king', meaning that 'her offspring by the king would never come to the throne unless the Duke of Clarence was removed; and of this she persuaded the king'. According to the Italian's account, Elizabeth feared George because he was so 'comely', which would 'make him appear worthy of the crown', and also because of his 'mastery of popular eloquence'. Mancini does not give his sources, but as he was writing in the summer of 1483, he may well have ascribed these feelings to the key players in the knowledge of Richard's denunciation of Elizabeth's marriage and offspring. Shakespeare's later fabrication that Richard tricked Edward into signing their brother's death warrant has little basis in fact: Edward's actions made it clear that he was the prime mover in the case, and that he was souly responsibile for bringing his brother to trial, accusing him, passing sentence and ordering that sentence to be enacted. It would appear that both brothers had recognised the inevitability of the outcome. George had proved his disloyalty too often, and been forgiven too many times. This time he had pushed his luck too far. He was buried with Isabel in Tewkesbury Abbey.

11

A KING'S DECLINE
1478–1483

'A novel and remarkable spectacle.'

I

In April 1478, Edward turned thirty-five. Several later writers identified this as a turning point in his reign and character: the onset of physical and moral decline, the slippery slope towards death, the beginning of the end. It seems remarkably young to a twenty-first-century reader, when measured against modern lifespans, and even given the uncertainties of the times, so far as Edward knew he might still have had twenty or thirty years ahead of him, aches and pains aside. So what exactly has drawn such comments about this period in Edward's life? Are later historians simply casting the net backwards, looking for clues that might foreshadow his premature death? Was Edward ill at all, suffering from some undiagnosed ailment, or did his end come about by accident?

A good case in point is Polydore Vergil, who never saw Edward in person, arriving in England in 1502. Yet his influential account asserts a change in Edward's mood in the years following Clarence's death. Vergil hints at the darkening of the king's character, with a vengeful, miserly cast, as he 'began to mark more severely the offences of noblemen and to be more covetous in gathering of money, whereof many were persuaded in their opinions that he would from henceforth prove a hard and severe prince ... after the death of his brother ... he perceived that every man feared him, so now he feared nobody.' Ironically though, such characteristics have also been ascribed by historians, rightly or wrongly, to Vergil's master, Henry VII, who allegedly changed in character after the death of his wife. Mancini, who would not arrive in England for another four years, identified 1478 as a breach between Edward and Richard, as a result of the king's fratricide. Mancini states that Gloucester increasingly 'kept himself within his own lands', although this is part of a narrative which builds to Richard's 'usurpation' of the crown. He also states that as a result of Edward's downturn, the grasping Elizabeth seized the opportunity to ennoble her family members and introduced strangers to court to 'manage the public and private business of the crown'. Thus the stereotypes of Shakespearean drama make their early debuts. However, such comments cannot so easily be dismissed. Even the contemporary Croyland chronicler stated that following George's death, 'many people deserted King Edward who was fully persuaded that he could rule as he pleased throughout the whole kingdom now that all those idols had been destroyed to whom the eyes of common folk ... used to turn in times past'. Perhaps it might not be so surprising to expect to find some change in the king after he had undertaken the momentous decision of executing his own brother for treason.

Mancini, though, did offer a fuller pen portrait of Edward's character, which is worth quoting in full to balance the other comments about the king's reputedly debauched lifestyle, and to re-enforce the king's sense of public performance. What really emerges from this is the way Edward employed his powerful persona and the ease with which he was able to connect with people. He appears to have been in possession of considerable charisma, and the personal nature of his rule meant he was willing to extend this across the divide of class, inspiring true loyalty. He was a dazzling, larger-than-life figure of authority and justice:

Edward was of a gentle and cheerful aspect; nevertheless, should he assume an angry countenance he could appear very terrible to beholders. He was easy of access to his friends and to others, even the least notable. Frequently he called to his side complete strangers, when he thought that they had come with the intention of addressing or beholding him more closely. He was wont to show himself to those who wished to watch him, and he seized any opportunity that the occasion offered of revealing his fine stature … to onlookers. He was so genial in his greeting that if he saw a newcomer bewildered at his appearance and royal magnificence he would give him courage to speak up by laying a kindly hand upon his shoulder. To plaintiffs and to those who complained of injustice he lent a willing ear: charges against himself he contented with an excuse if he did not remove the cause. He was more favourable than other princes to foreigners who visited his realm for trade or any other reason. He very seldom showed munificence and then only in moderation, still, he was very grateful to those from whom he had received a favour.

These final years of Edward's reign have also been taken as a period of his rapid physical decline. Here, there appears to be more grounds on which to base some sort of diagnosis. In April 1477, Louis XI heard rumours that the king was ill, which were quickly squashed by Lord Hastings, but the whispers arose again in the early 1480s. Mancini's account is the source which is most damning when it comes to his health, and although he admits his description is based on rumour, this does not necessarily invalidate it. If nothing else, it explains what Edward's contemporaries were inclined to believe about him. He continues,

> In food and drink he was most immoderate: it was his habit, so I have learned, to take an emetic for the delight of gorging his stomach once more. For this reason, and for the ease, which was especially dear to him after the recovery of the crown, he had fat in the loins whereas, previously, he had been not only tall but rather lean and very active. He was licentious in the extreme.

Here, Mancini suggests that years of fine living meant Edward was no longer the fine figure of a man he had been in his youth, and that he was even in the habit of taking 'an emetic' to empty his stomach, so that he could continuously gorge on fine food and drink. When Commines saw Edward in France in 1475, he commented that he was 'beginning to get fat and I had seen him on previous occasions looking more handsome'. Yet Edward was tall enough, at over six foot three, to carry some extra weight, and even in his later years he remained an attractive and well-presented figure. Commines was forced to admit that Edward was 'more handsome than any man then alive'. As Vergil wrote, he may have grown 'something corpulent' and 'burly' with an 'over liberal and wanton diet', but 'nevertheless not uncomely' and still 'of visage full faced and lovely, of body mighty, strong and clean made', as well as being 'very tall' and 'broad chested'. Edward would not have been the first monarch to live too well – it seems death by surfeit had become an almost common side effect of medieval kingship – but this still does not mean that feasting and whoring guaranteed Edward's demise.

More than one source suggests that the circle around the king, which had once been a pseudo-Arthurian court of chivalric values, had disintegrated into a hotbed of debauchery. Yet once again, Mancini paints the bleakest portrait: Edward had many 'promoters and companions of his vices', but the most important was Edward Woodville, Elizabeth's brother, and her two sons from her first marriage, Thomas and Richard Grey, who 'earned the hatred of the populace, on account of their morals', but largely because they were 'ignoble and newly made men [who] were advanced beyond those who far excelled them in breeding and wisdom'. The others in Edward's intimate circle at this time were Thomas Rotherham, who was Lord Chancellor and Archbishop of York; John Morton, Bishop of Ely; and William, Lord Hastings. Apparently, the latter had 'shared every peril with the king, but was also the accomplice and partner of his privy pleasures'. This had incited a 'deadly feud' between Hastings and Elizabeth's son Thomas Grey, 'as a result of the mistresses they had abducted or attempted to entice from each other'. Thomas More added that this friendship made Elizabeth dislike Hastings: 'The queen specially grudged for the great favour the king bore him and also because she thought him secretly familiar with the king in wanton company.' More was born in 1478, but spent part of his childhood in Morton's household, where he certainly had access to oral memories, if not the bishop's written memoirs.

Amid that wanton company, there is one particular name that
became associated with Edward's during the end of his reign;
a name which Elizabeth would have known and may possibly
have disliked. Elizabeth Shore, or Jane Shore as Shakespeare
rechristened her, became Edward's mistress around the time of
his French campaign. Jane had been born Elizabeth Lambert, the
daughter of a London mercer, in 1445, and had been married to
goldsmith William Shore in her middle or late teens. She emerges
in the mid-1470s in an unusual case of annulment, attempting to
dissolve her marriage on the grounds of her husband's impotence.
The papal mandate for her case was dated 1 March 1476, and
must have cost a considerable amount of money to pursue, even
for the wife of a goldsmith.

> The recent petition of Elizabeth Lambert alias Schore, of London states
> that she continued in her marriage to William Schore, layman of the
> diocese of London, and cohabited with him for the lawful time, but
> that he is so frigid and impotent that she, desirous of being a mother
> and having offspring, requested over and over again the official of
> London to cite the said William before him to answer her concerning
> the foregoing and the nullity of the said marriage and that, seeing the
> said official refused to do so, she appealed to the Apostolic See.

Although annulments were usually granted on the grounds of
affinity, there were precedents for such cases of impotence. A man
whose wife accused him of being unable to perform was summoned
before a panel of matrons, usually to a room in which a fire was
lit, and with food and drink provided, all of which were believed
to provide bodily warmth and kindle desire. In July 1433 in York,
Alice Russell wished to annul her marriage to John Skathelok. He
was brought before a panel of women who 'exposed their breasts
and genitalia encouraging his arousal with explicit language'. In
1441, the same court heard how Joan Gilbert complained that
her husband, John, was 'naturally frigid', whereupon the man was
brought to the Guildhall kitchens and at least two women kissed
and embraced him and attempted to arouse him by touching his
penis. Historians who have investigated the cases believe that
sometimes local prostitutes were employed for the job, while on
other occasions it was widows. No husband would have given

permission for his wife to participate in such an event, no matter how canonically 'worthy'. Sometimes the ruling went against the wife, such as in 1432, when thirteen women found the husband of the complainant Katherine Barlay to be 'potent' and 'sufficient to serve and to please any honest woman'.[1]

Yet there was another matter at stake than just sex. Jane's appeal to become a mother struck at the heart of one of the tenets of medieval society. Apart from a life of pious virginity, maternity was considered the highest aspiration for a woman, defining herself as a functioning part of, and contributor to, the patriarchal system. This process would have been deeply shaming for William Shore, and in cases of conflict between a husband and wife the man was usually victorious. A married woman was defined by the law as her husband's 'chattel' or property; he was her 'king' and to repudiate him, or cuckold him, was considered a minor act of treason, as it undermined the whole social structure. However, Jane's right to become a mother was recognised as sacrosanct and her request was upheld, although there are no records to suggest that she ever did bear a child, even though she did remarry. Given the cost of the proceedings involved in addressing the necessary courts, it is likely that Jane had powerful friends who were willing to lend their financial support. At the time of the mandate being drafted, she may have already become the mistress of the king.

Little is known about Jane, save for the well-known description by Thomas More that she was witty and that she never abused her position, but only worked to do good rather than harm. In More's words,

> Proper she was and fair ... yet delighted not men so much in her beauty, as in her pleasant behaviour. For a proper wit had she, and could both read well and write, merry of company, ready and quick of answer, neither mute nor full of babble, sometimes taunting without displeasure and not without disport ... The merriest [of Edward's mistresses] was this Shore's wife, in whom the king therefore took special pleasure. For many he had, but her he loved, whose favour to say truth ... she never abused to any man's hurt.

What the queen thought of this situation is unrecorded, but it may be too modern a response to assume she was not prepared to tolerate a rival, or even that Jane presented any threat to her position. If Edward had always been a womaniser, Elizabeth may have preferred one trusted mistress to a stream of fertile beauties. Edward had already acknowledged at least two bastards – Arthur and Grace Plantagenet – and too many additional children of the royal blood could cause complications for future inheritance, as the Beaufort and Tudor lines were to later prove. Equally, the queen may have been more comfortable with her husband's casual liaisons, and disliked the deeper connection he clearly had with Jane. However, it is more likely that Elizabeth did not consider Jane her business at all: Elizabeth was the queen and Jane had no aspirations to that role, nor was it any departure from the norm for a king to take a mistress. Modern romantic sensibilities may bristle at the concept, but it was simply what kings did. For Edward, being faithful to his wife meant being her ally, upholding the dignity and respect due to her position and protecting her. It did not exclude extramarital relationships. In fact, it was almost a convention that a man take a mistress while his wife was pregnant and sexually unavailable, so long as he was discreet. In return, Elizabeth provided him with children, fulfilled the duties of her position and provided a female foil for the vehicle of majesty. She had played the part of the beautiful, fertile and submissive queen to perfection. Ultimately, though, the sexual double-standard dictated that she had to be faithful, if only to ensure the purity of the royal line. Elizabeth may even have welcomed the presence of Jane, especially during these later years, when this other woman became a trusted member of the palace's intimate circle, and perhaps also the lover of William Hastings and Elizabeth's own son Thomas. There is no indication that Jane or any other mistress exerted any influence over Edward's policies or reign – yet another clear division he made between his public and private selves.

For Elizabeth, the overlap of public and private was inescapable. Her record of pregnancies had certainly been a demanding one, and the progress and success of each was very much in the national interest. In the space of fourteen years, she had borne Edward ten children, and including the sons of her first marriage to Sir John Grey, this made a total of twelve pregnancies. On average, there was a nine-month interval between Elizabeth giving birth and conceiving her next child, even accounting for Edward's absences and exiles and Elizabeth's periods of recuperation, which would have lasted at least a month spent lying in. When it came to Elizabeth's first four children, Elizabeth, Mary, Cecily and Edward, this was a reliable pattern, with nine or ten months elapsing before the queen fell pregnant again. Of course, Edward was born while his father was in exile, when there was little certainty regarding the couple's future, and no chance of conceiving another child. Yet after the king's return, Elizabeth fell pregnant again after just four months, and after the birth of her subsequent child, Margaret, only seven months elapsed before she conceived again. After the birth of Richard of York in the summer of 1473, Elizabeth experienced her longest conception interval yet, which lasted eighteen months. She wasn't preganant for the entirety of 1474, which must have come as something of a relief and provided an opportunity for her body to rest and recover. Having provided Edward with two sons and a number of daughters, there was no longer the dynastic imperative to reproduce, but Edward and Elizabeth were clearly still intimate on a regular basis. Baby Anne arrived in November 1475, and seven months later the queen was pregnant again with George, who was born in March 1477. An entire twenty months elapsed before the start of her next pregnancy. Catherine was born in August 1479, and six months later Elizabeth conceived her final child, Bridget, who arrived in November 1480.

This conception pattern is entirely typical of women of the upper classes, who bore large families and did not use any form of contraception or experience the contraceptive benefits of breastfeeding. It was an established convention that royal babies were supplied with wet nurses so that queens could return to their public and private duties, and their menstrual cycles resumed more quickly as a result. Conception can be an unpredictable thing, but from comparisons with the family trees of similar women, it is possible to state that Edward and Elizabeth experienced good levels of fertility and regularly shared a bed. It is also typical for a conception pattern to be regular at the beginning of a woman's reproductive life, but to include increasingly long periods between pregnancies as she gets older. Bearing in mind that Elizabeth had already been married once, she was forty-three when she bore her final child, which was fairly late according to the standards of her day. There were two and a half years remaining of her marriage, but she did not conceive during this time: it may have been that Mancini and Commines' reports of Edward's health made it less likely for him to father a child, but it is perhaps more plausible that Elizabeth had experienced the onset of her menopause. Recent NHS research suggests that the onset of the menopause is inherited. Interestingly, Jacquetta was forty-three in 1458 when she bore her final child, suggesting this was genetic predisposition for women of the family, transmitted from mother to daughter. Jacquetta's mother, Margaret of Baux, bore nine children, but their birthdates are unclear, as are those of her grandmother, Sueva Orsini. However, out of Elizabeth's sisters who married and survived until the same age, Anne Woodville was married twice and bore her last son at the age of forty-three, and Catherine Woodville bore a final daughter in 1483, at the age of forty-one, although her husband was executed in the same year, so there is no way of knowing if she was approaching her menopause or simply had not further opportunity to conceive.

Edward's family were also known for their high levels of fertility. Cecily Neville bore thirteen children with an average of seven months between delivery and the next conception. Two of her children, Edmund and George, were conceived just two months after the birth of their older sibling, yet after the birth of her sixth child Cecily experienced a wait of sixteen months before her next conception. She fell pregnant with her final baby, Ursula, after two years, which is consistent with the idea of fertility tailing off towards the end of a woman's reproductive years, and delivered her in 1455, at the age of forty. Likewise, Cecily's mother, Joan Beaufort, bore sixteen children, with the last arriving when she was thirty-six. Her paternal grandmother, Philippa of Hainault, gave Edward III fourteen children over a period of twenty-five years, bearing the last when she was forty-one. To the modern eye, the late thirties and early forties seem comparatively young for the onset of the menopause when the average age for women in the UK today is fifty-one. A modern woman whose menstrual cycle ceases for this reason before the age of forty is classed as experiencing a premature menopause. However, in Elizabeth's day, it must have been fairly common. The rigours of frequent childbearing, which often began in the mid-teens, made it more likely for fertility to dwindle earlier in life; the menopause also left women vulnerable to certain cancers, contributing to the numbers of mothers who died within a decade of their final delivery. In 1480, Elizabeth had completed her family, although she may not have realised it at the time.

By the standards of the day, Edward and Elizabeth were now a middle-aged couple. Several chroniclers suggest that the king was less mobile in his final years, that he was living at a slower pace and travelling less. This may not be strictly true; it may simply be that he suffered from the comparison with his former, athletic self, for whom distance had proved little obstacle. Edward certainly did not stay tied to London, as in August 1478 he visited Nottingham, and spent September in Pontefract and York before heading back to Greenwich in October. The following September he was at Woodstock and Oxford, then spent three weeks in his new apartments at Nottingham Castle. In May and June 1482, he stayed for the last time at Fotheringhay in Northamptonshire, although it was urgent business that took him there. Increasingly, though, he seemed to prefer being in the southern counties and left the running of the north to his brother Richard. If Mancini's comments about Edward's 'fat loins' are to be taken seriously, he may have been suffering from impaired mobility. There is a chance that he was already suffering from a malady that would soon kill him, although the cause of his death is unknown, or else his immobility may have contributed to the development of the said mysterious illness. At Easter 1479, Edward had applied to the Pope for a dispensation to eat eggs, meat and milk products, which were usually prohibited at Lent, except for invalids. He would have needed a good reason for this, but it appears to have been a one-off rather than a regular request, which implies he was suffering from a temporary illness. Or else that he feared one.

Earlier in 1479, there had been a terrible outbreak of the plague in the south. This was a fairly regular occurrence, with the most famous occurrences of 1348 and 1381 being enshrined in cultural memory because of the extent of their devastation. It had returned in 1438–9, 1456–7 and 1464–6, making it a recognisable horror in the lives of Edward's subjects, who would have been very familiar with the warning signs: the fever, headaches and muscle aches, followed by the appearance of swellings or buboes in the groin and armpit, after which death could swiftly follow. On such occasions, the court would close up or retreat to the countryside. Edward's *Liber Niger* made allowances for the sick to be provided for and kept away from the healthy. However, not every malady could be legislated against. That March, the two-year-old Prince George died at Windsor. His loss is usually attributed to the plague, although the rest of the family appear to have emerged unscathed, so there is a chance it was caused by some other infantile disease. Little George was not the first child Elizabeth and Edward had lost, with Margaret dying in 1472, but he was the first to be buried in the new family mausoleum at Windsor which bore his name.

In September 1481, Edward and Elizabeth travelled together from Woodstock to Oxford, where the founder of Eton and Magdalen College, William Waynflete, had invited them to 'come to see his college and lodge therein'. The royal party included Edward's sister Elizabeth, Duchess of Suffolk, 'with a considerable retinue', and arrived after sunset, lit by a procession of people carrying torches. The newly elected chancellor, Lionel Woodville, gave a speech of welcome in the college, which offered the guests gifts of wine and gloves. They were then given a tour of the cloister and estates and attended public debates and divine service, before departing in 'great content'.

Edward's final years were still magnificent, especially as he could now afford to finance his taste for finery, thanks to the generous income provided by Louis of France. His building works at Windsor and Eltham continued apace, with the latter palace becoming a firm royal favourite and a regular venue for the Christmas season, as well as the venue Elizabeth chose to deliver her last two daughters. Certainly, approaching forty, Edward may not have been the same eighteen-year-old who fought for hours at Tewkesbury: such comparisons might be inevitable, but they are hardly realistic. More than ever, Edward used the royal wardrobe as a means of asserting his majesty. He may have grown corpulent, but his large frame sparkled with gold and jewels. In many ways, he had even more presence than before, when abundance of food and drink were equatable to wealth and status. As the royal wardrobe accounts show, his clothes and trinkets proclaimed his power. A bill presented in 1478 by Cornelius, the royal jeweller, included gold rings, gold flowers and a gold toothpick decorated with diamonds, sapphires and rubies. Edward paid £4 for a cross of gold garnished with a diamond, four rubies and seven pearls, and £6 for a flower of gold garnished with a fleur-de-lys diamond. He also bought a jewel costing £160 from the Duke of Suffolk, which had an image of 'Our Lady of gold with Our Lord in her arms and the images of St John the Baptist and St Katherine on either side of Our Lady and two other images with seven angels thereto pertaining', which was adorned with precious stones. Edward's household accounts of 1480 include twenty-six gowns, doublets and jackets made from cloth-of-gold, furred with ermine and sable, hats, bonnets, forty-eight handkerchiefs and several dozen pairs of boots, shoes and slippers.[2] Slippers aside, the king clearly had no intention of embracing a quiet old age.

II

In 1480, the widowed Margaret of Burgundy paid a visit to England. Then aged thirty-three, it was the first time she had returned since her wedding in 1468, and she was now one of the richest and most influential women in Europe. In recent years she had overseen the marriage of her stepdaughter, Mary, to Maximilian, future Holy Roman Emperor, and the birth of their son Philip, the first of three children. By a nice act of symmetry, one of the boy's godfathers was Pierre of St Pol, Count of Luxembourg and Elizabeth's cousin. Since Edward had signed the Treaty of Picquigny which agreed his French income, his relations with Burgundy had cooled a little; Margaret's mission was a diplomatic one, to attempt to forge a new friendship between England and the Netherlands, secure military help against Maximilian's enemies and possibly arrange a betrothal for the baby Philip with the four-year-old Anne of York. Now, the Burgundian magnificence that had inspired the English king for the past decade was arriving on his shores.

Margaret left Bruges on 24 June, travelling with a suitably large retinue. Edward dispatched his brother-in-law Sir Edward Woodville to collect her in a ship named the *Falcon*, sailing back from Calais to Gravesend and going from there by barge to London. King Edward had put his French money to good use, sparing no expense to impress his sister, with the twenty-four oarsmen dressed in livery of murrey and blue embroidered with white roses, and attendant knights in black, velvet jackets that featured a pattern of purple and silver. Two properties had been prepared to receive her. On 24 July, sheets, blankets and other bedding were sent from the royal wardrobe to Greenwich Palace and Coldharbour House, 'against the coming thither of my Lady of Bourgoigne; green sarsanet, hooks and stuff for hanging tapestries were also sent to Coldharbour and a black camlet gown was given to the Master of the King's Barge'. They were both properties she had called home during her youth. Edward chose gifts for his sister of ten hobbies and palfreys, which were dressed up in green and crimson velvet hung with silver aglets and spangles, along with a saddle of blue and violet cloth of gold fringed with Venetian gold thread. Yards of cloth of silver, scarlet, violet and black velvet were set aside for the use of her retinue.[3]

The occasion proved something of a reunion for the house of York: Margaret was welcomed by her brother the king, her sister-in-law Elizabeth and their children; along with her mother Cecily Neville; her sister Elizabeth, Duchess of Suffolk; and her brother, Richard of Gloucester. She stayed until the end of September 1480, with the London Chronicle stating that Edward 'shewed to her great pleasure'. Margaret's ambassadors were lodged at the Erber, the house which had first belonged to the Earl of Warwick, and then to George, Duke of Clarence, who was something of a spectre at the feast. Items from the wardrobe were delivered to Rauff Dowell at the Erber, to provide for the guests, including lengths of traditional red worsted for the beds and curtains. Edward hosted a banquet at Greenwich in his mother's name, during which Margaret admired the wine being drunk, and later received a pipe of wine worth 36s 8d from Edward. On 5 August, the hoped-for marriage treaty was signed, binding Philip of Burgundy to Anne of York, with the promise that no other alliances would be sought for either child in the coming three years. During her visit, Margaret also persuaded Edward to introduce the Order of the Observant Friars to England, to which intent he founded a monastic site in the grounds of Greenwich Palace in 1482. Just as she had in 1468, Margaret visited the shrine of Thomas Becket in Canterbury Cathedral before she returned home again. She would die in 1503.

Edward's wardrobe accounts from 8 April to 29 September 1480 survive in glorious detail, as recorded by Piers Courteys,

Keeper of the Great Wardrobe. They provide a wonderful insight into the kind of lifestyle the king and his family enjoyed towards the end of his reign, allowing us a glimpse behind the scenes of the formal court. There is an almost tactile quality to the palette of fabrics, textures and colours, including French black cloth; russet cloth; Montpelier crimson velvet; white lamb skins; black velvet speckled with white; blue velvet figured with tawny; white velvet with black spots; chequered velvet; green, changeable velvet; white tissue cloth of gold; and cloth of gold 'broched' upon a satin background at 24s a yard. In comparison, William Misterton, Clerk of the Wardrobe, received 12d a day in wages.[4]

The accounts also give a rare glimpse into the behind-the-scenes working of the department of the wardrobe. Payments were given to those who had transformed the yards of fabric into clothing: to George Lufkyn, for making doublets, gowns and jackets; to Robert Boilet, for washing and drying sheets; and to Martin Jumbard, for sewing 426 ounces of silver spangles onto horses' bridles. Alice Shapster was paid for making and washing twenty-four shirts, twenty-four stomachers, five dozen handkerchiefs and dozens of pairs of sheets, and John Coppersmith received 3d for mending a broken chair with small, gilt nails. Rauff Underwood was paid for his work hanging verdours against the bay window in the queen's old chamber, while Richard Gardyner was indeed a gardener, and tallowchandler William Whyte supplied the department with the finest candles for whenever the king visited. A Richard Carter was paid 3s and 4d for making three pairs of lined hose from black French cloth, and one Piers Herton was paid 20d for lining a pair of blue, leather boots with black velvet.[5]

An inventory of spare items left in the wardrobe includes sheets of cloth from Flanders and Brussels, cushions with silk embroidery, Arras tapestries, feather beds, pillows, blankets, canvas and thread. There were gloves, hose and bonnets, four pairs of fustian socks and three pairs of slippers, and for the table, napkins, towels and tablecloths. They also had escutcheons or coats of arms made from coloured paper, featuring the arms of 'Lorde George', which would have been made to celebrate the birth or christening of Edward's short-lived son George, who had died the previous year of the plague. Expenses for the christening of Princess Catherine of York, born on 14 August 1479 at Eltham Palace, included a fabric called latisnaille used to cover the font.[6] Just two weeks after her birth, Edward opened negotiations for the girl to marry John, Prince of Asturias, the elder brother of Catherine of Aragon.

Edward was generous when it came to his family. The Prince of Wales, approaching his tenth birthday, was allotted five yards of white cloth of gold tissue from which the tailors would make him a gown. A list of gifts given to Richard, Duke of York, who turned seven in August 1480, included a harness and saddle, green, purple and crimson velvet, silks, satin and cloth of gold. He also had five yards of white cloth of gold, two yards of tawny sarsenet and a blue-velvet mantle lined with white damask and garnished with blue silk lace and gold buttons. Elizabeth's son Thomas and her brother Earl Rivers were each the recipients of three yards of white cloth of gold tissue in order to make a short gown and two yards of purple cloth of gold upon satin ground. Elizabeth's brother Edward, who was to be responsible for escorting Margaret of Burgundy across the Channel, was granted a yard of purple velvet and a yard of blue, to make a jacket from. Young Edward, Earl of Warwick, the son of George, Duke of Clarence, received four pairs of shoes, double soled, and one pair made of Spanish leather, single soled, while other royal wards, such as George Grey, were given velvet gowns and satin, and Edward's cupbearer Edward Stanley was gifted several yards of sarsenet and chamelet from which his clothes were to be made.[7]

The wardrobe accounts coincide with a surge in Edward's spending on manuscripts, and give a good reflection of his preferences at the time. Piers Bauduyn, a stationer, was paid 20s for binding, gilding and dressing a book entitled *Titus Livius*, which was probably Livy's *The History of Rome* in six volumes, and also received 16s a piece for performing the same process on a copy of the Holy Trinity, a copy of Froissart's Chronicles and another Bible. In addition, Bauduyn was employed in binding, dressing and gilding a copy of *The Governance of Kings and Princes*, by Cornishman John Trevisa – a contemporary of Chaucer. He bound three French books for a cost of 6s 8d, dressed a copy of *The Book of Joseph* and bound and guilded a Historical Bible.

Bauduyn was also responsible for dressing a copy of *La Forteresse de Foy*, which is a series of arguments made against the enemies of Catholicism by the Spanish Catholic Alphonsus de

Spina. A copy of the text now in the British Library has illuminated pages that originate from France and the Netherlands, so Edward probably acquired the text as a sheaf of loose manuscript pages, or else as bound pages whch he ordered his stationer to make a suitable cover for. The British Library's copy has been bound again since Edward's reign, certainly in a post-1600 style, so Bauduyn's work is no longer visible, but the draftsmanship inside, which Edward would have known, is exquisite. Created by the scribe Jean Duchesne or Du Quesne, its central images are surrounded by full foliate borders, with initial letters in gold with gold, red and blue flourishes. It is likely to have been commissioned by Edward himself, or perhaps by his sister Margaret as a gift for her brother, especially as the order was given to Bauduyn in the same year as the duchess's visit to England. By 1480, Caxton had already set up his printing press in the Westminster precincts, and had produced copies of Chaucer's *Canterbury Tales* and Anthony Woodville's translation of the *Dictes or Sayeings of the Philosophers*. Yet the process by which the manuscripts were beautified and bound was clearly important to Edward, as a symbol of status. That year 76s 8d was spent upon parchment paper, ink, red wax, thread, needles, counters, leather bags and other 'small necessaries' for the Department of the Wardrobe. 2s and 8d was paid to Alice Chaver for making 16 laces and 16 tassels for the king's books, which were conveyed from the wardrobe in London to Eltham Palace in a box lined with fur at a cost of 5d.[8] Edward clearly loved his luxuries as symbols of his kingship, but soon his mind would be occupied by a far larger concern.

Since 1471, Edward's international policies had largely been focused to the south and east of England, in France, Brittany and Burgundy. Now, his relationship with Scotland came to the fore. Although James III had formerly sheltered the Lancastrian family in exile, warmer relations had developed once Henry VI, Queen Margaret and their son, Edward, had left the country, and the Scots realised it was advantageous to ally themselves with the triumphant Yorkists. In October 1474, a peace treaty had been signed so that 'their subjects might be encouraged to live in peace, love and tenderness' and that considering 'the long continued troubles, dissensions and debates between the two realms, with great and mortal war ... a nearer and more special way it to be found than merely the assurance of the present truce'. The 'special way' that the two countries would be bound was by marriage. One union was suggested between Margaret, the King of Scots' sister, and the widowed Anthony Woodville, but this never came to fruition. More hopes were placed on the betrothal of James to Cecily of York, after which Edward paid the Scots a dowry and his daughter was referred to as the Queen of Scots.

Then, in 1480, a number of skirmishes took place on the Scottish border. Richard of Gloucester responded, repelling the invaders where he could find them and making counter raids of his own. Croyland blames this upon the influence of Louis of France, James's old ally, who had encouraged him to 'shamelessly [break] the ... truce we had with them, in spite of the fact that King Edward had long paid a yearly sum of 1000 marks by way of dowry'. This was also the opinion of the Milanese ambassador in Tours, who believed that 'the Scots have attacked the English and I think it is the handiwork of the king here', after having 'seen a letter of the King of Scotland to the king here, in which he advises him that the English made an incursion into his country, but his people had forthwith cast them out'. Vergil also places the blame firmly on the French, with whom James sided to 'molest the borders with sudden incursions'. When Edward demanded an explanation, the Scottish king 'excused the fact as done by the arrogance of some of his subjects without his knowledge'. This might have been an end to it, except Edward was approached by James's own brother, Alexander, Duke of Albany, who was then an exile in France and promised to support an English invasion.

Albany landed at Southampton in April 1482, and travelled to meet Edward and Richard at Fotheringhay. The treaty they signed proposed an English invasion which would place Albany on the throne, who would rapidly divorce the French wife he had wed that January in order to marry Cecily of York, and repay Edward with a number of Scottish lands. Edward fully intended to lead the army himself, and when the Pope attempted to involve him in a crusade, the English king excused himself with the line that he would have preferred to fight the infidels, but instead had to repel the Scots. However, by the early summer of 1482, ill-health forced him to acknowledge this was impossible, and on 12 June he appointed Gloucester as head of the army:

James, King of Scotland ... decided to wage war ... against us and invade our realm by sudden and armed attack. We therefore ... trusting with full powers our illustrious brother Richard, Duke of Gloucester, in whom not only for his nearness and fidelity of relationship but for his proved skill in military matters and others virtues, we name, depute and ordain him our lieutenant general ... to fight, overcome and expel the said king of Scotland, our chief enemy, and his subjects, adherents and allies, however great the fight may be.[9]

It must have been a difficult admission for the man who had won Towton, that he was no longer capable of military campaign. Edward returned to London, while Albany and Gloucester travelled north, arriving at York on 17 June. The English advanced to Edinburgh, leaving a trail of burning and destruction behind them, and entered the city. James was waiting in the castle, but in an unexpected move, Albany then made peace with his brother and the invasion collapsed. On 4 August, the city of Edinburgh begged the English for mercy and promised to reinstate the treaty of 1474, so Richard returned home having taken Berwick. It was a strange sort of campaign, with Croyland referring to it as a 'trifling' which he knew not whether to refer to as a gain or loss amid the money Gloucester 'foolishly squandered away'.

1482 brought sad news on two fronts. On 27 March, Margaret's stepdaughter, Mary of Burgundy, died after a fall from her horse. Then, on 23 May, Edward and Elizabeth's second daughter, Mary of York, died at the age of 14 at Greenwich, and was buried in St George's. The cause of her death is unknown. According to Mancini, Edward attempted to divert himself by ordering 'many performances of actors amidst great splendour, so as to mitigate or disguise his sorrow ... yet he was never able altogether to hide it'. To make matters worse, France and Burgundy signed a peace treaty that December, overriding the marriage between the Dauphin and Elizabeth of York that had been arranged in 1475. Edward might have been down, but he was not out. Not just yet. The family's last Christmas together was spent at Eltham, where 2,000 guests were fed in the newly finished great hall. One eyewitness described the how king strode into court 'clad in a great variety of most costly garments, of quite a different cut to those which had usually been seen hitherto in our kingdom. The sleeves of his cloak hung in ample folds like that of a monk's frock, lined inside with the richest furs and rolled out on the shoulders. Thus the prince, who was of imposing build, presented a novel and remarkable spectacle.' His court presented 'no other appearance than such as fully befits a most mighty kingdom, filled with riches and with people of almost all nations, and boasting of those the most sweet and beautiful children'. It was to be Edward's last performance of magnificence.

When it came, Edward's death was comparatively swift. He fell ill after taking a fishing trip on the Thames on 30 March, but improved a little before experiencing a rapid decline. It took the court by surprise, given that he was just a few weeks short of his forty-first birthday and no other symptoms had marred the robust physical health he had previously enjoyed. Croyland states that Edward was 'neither worn out with old age nor yet seized with any known kind of malady and blames an apoplexy', although he also added that the king had lived a life of overindulgence, 'vanities, debauchery, extravagance and sensual enjoyments'. Commines believed the king had suffered an apoplexy – a 'quaterre' brought on by a bout of excess – which is what killed Louis of France a few weeks later. He also entertains the notion that the king was heartbroken by the Franco-Burgundian treaty. French chronicler Thomas Basin suggested that Edward had eaten too rich a dinner, while Mancini had heard 'that he being a tall man and very fat although not to the point of deformity, allowed the cold damp to strike his vitals, when one day he was taken in a small boat, with those whom he had bidden go fishing'. Commines thought he had been killed by a stroke, Vergil later hinted at poison, without foundation, and Edward Hall believed he had caught fever in France in 1475, which developed into something deadly eight years later.

An interesting possibility was put forward by a Dr John Rae in 1913, who drew attention to the description of Edward lying on his left side in bed, which is the usual position in which the symptoms of pneumonia find the most relief. This would accord with the fishing trip and the progress of the illness, as the effects of the illness may either come on quickly or else develop over several days. Edward may have experienced fever, headaches, a cough, sweating and shivering, nausea and vomiting, or a combination of a couple of these and fatigue, which may have been considered non-life threatening for several days before they intensified. This would account for the surprise at court when the king's condition may initially have appeared to have simply been a cold, as Mancini wrote. If Edward had another underlying medical condition, such as type two diabetes, he may have developed complications such as blood poisoning or pleurisy. No signs were visible on his body after death, nor upon his skeleton when it was exhumed. It is likely that Edward was an undiagnosed diabetic who died of pneumonia, but this can only be a theory based on what was recorded at the time. Ultimately, unless further tests are conducted upon his remains, the cause of his death cannot be known. The results of his death, however, would prove dramatic.

12

ANXIOUS MOTHER
1483–1485

'Her bloody adherents and affinity.'

I

In Westminster Abbey, Edward's broad-shouldered, six-foot-three-and-a-half-inch body was out laid naked save for a loincloth. Stripped of his cloth of gold, his violet velvet and miniver, his golden rings and chains, he must still have been an imposing figure. The mayor and aldermen, the lords and bishops came to see him, less as a macabre spectacle than as confirmation that he was truly dead and to appreciate the very medieval lesson of the mortality beneath the magnificence. Then he was embalmed, wrapped in strips of wax linen and dressed, from his red leather shoes to his cap of estate. In this condition, his body remained in Westminster's St Stephen's Chapel for eight days, watched over by members of his court while requiem masses were sung. There must have been an element of shock to the proceedings, as men who sat with his corpse remembered the tall, handsome nineteen-year-old at his coronation, or else thought of his father, the Duke of York, as Lord Protector of England during the illness of Henry VI. A number of Edward's Garter knights were still alive to mourn the loss of their Arthur, including Lord Hastings, Sir John Astley, Baron Scrope, the Earl of Arundel, Lord Ferrers, the Duke of Norfolk, Lord Maltravers, the Earl of Northumberland and the Duke of Buckingham, as well as Edward's close family of Richard of Gloucester; his brother-in-law John de la Pole, Duke of Suffolk; Thomas Bourchier; and four of the Woodville brothers – Anthony, Richard, Edward and Lionel. Edward's ageing mother, Cecily, is also likely to have come to London from Berkhamsted Castle to pay her respects.

On 17 April, Edward was lifted onto a bier and covered in cloth of gold. Above him was carried a canopy of imperial cloth fringed with gold and blue silk, with banners at each corner depicting St George, St Edward, the Trinity and the Virgin Mary. Archbishop Rotherham, Edward's chancellor, led the procession into the abbey, followed by the Duke of Norfolk, who carried the king's own banner before the bier and after them came a number of lords and knights. A life-sized effigy of Edward wearing a crown and dressed in royal robes, holding orb and sceptre, stood before the bier as offerings were made. The next day, Edward's body was taken from Westminster to Charing Cross and on to Sion Abbey for the night. Then it travelled to Eton, where the bishops of Lincoln and Ely censed him as he was brought into the chapel of St George. Nine knights and other loyal servants kept an overnight vigil at the king's side, and in the morning the final masses were read and Edward's shield, sword and helmet were placed upon his tomb. The members of his household ceremoniously broke their white staves of office and cast the pieces into the grave. The king was dead, and his twelve-year-old son was now Edward V.

The anonymous poem 'The Death of Edward IV' was written at the time of the king's death or soon after; two copies remain, although it is likely to have been widely distributed. Its poet extols Edward as a paragon of a man: 'the lanterne and light' of his people, 'the worthiest, without comparison,' the 'well of knyghthode', the 'lode-star' of all princes – 'in gesits, in romansis, in Chronicles, nygh and ferre, well knowen it is, ther no man it deferre, perelees he was'. According to the poem, Edward had conquered 'his right' in England, made Scotland yield and won France by 'very force and might, without stroke'. Just as Edward had planned a *memento mori* tomb, the poem built to a predictable moral about the transience and vanities of the mortal world:

Ye wofull men that shall this writing rede,
Remembre well here is no dwelling place.
Se howe this prince is from us goon and dede
And we shall aftir hym sue the trace,
There is no choise, there is noon other grace;
This knowe ye well – he was here yestirday.

A similar poem, 'The Lament for the Soul of Edward IV', possibly by Skelton, contains a similar message around the chorus line: 'Behold now I sleep in dust.' Related by the king himself, he laments his love of the riches now lost and asks for prayers for his soul: 'And ye commyners, with your hert unbrace benyngly to pray for me also.'

I stored hucches, cofers and chyst
With tresore taking off my commynalte
Ffore there tresore that I toke there prayers I myst ...
I had inogthe, I hyld nott me content
With-outt remembraunce that I schuld dy
More to encresse was myne entent ...
Where is my gret conquest and victory?
Where is my Rentis and my Rally array?

Elizabeth had little time to mourn her husband of nineteen years or their reputed lost coffers. With her younger children and her siblings, she waited in Westminster for the arrival of her eldest son, who was being conducted from Ludlow to London by Anthony Woodville. Parliament had rejected Elizabeth's request that a larger escort should be sent to accompany him, fearing that this might send the wrong message about the Woodvilles' power, so the guard was limited to 2,000 men. Croyland wrote that the queen had 'most beneficently tried to extinguish every spark of murmuring and disturbance', placing her firmly in the role of peacemaker rather than agitator. A coronation day of 4 May was set. The nobility were summoned to the capital. There were robes to embroider, streets to clean and feasts to plan in advance. In the meantime, there were Edward's last wishes to be considered, and the question of who would run the country during the remaining years of his son's minority. Prince Edward was then twelve and a half and barely eighteen months might elapse before he could take the reins of power into his own hands. However, Elizabeth quickly realised that her husband's power had died with him; whatever his final requests had been, they were not to be respected by the living.

One question arising for historians is that of Edward IV's will. The king had clearly experienced periods of lucidity in his final days, so it is unlikely that he would not have left fresh instructions for his executors, if not dictated a full new will. His deathbed attempt to reconcile Hastings and Dorset shows that his thoughts had already turned to the future stability of his son's court and those likely to form his council. Many of the wishes Edward recorded in 1475 were still relevant in 1483, but the general consensus among chroniclers and historians is that he attempted to make some codicils, which were recorded and passed on to his main executor, Bishop Morton. Croyland relates that he was able to repent his sins and acknowledge that he revered the sacraments of the church. 'To those who were present at the time of his death,' Croyland wrote, especially 'those whom he left as executors of his last will, he declared, in a distinct and Christian form, that it was his desire that' his debts were paid and that 'long before his illness he had made a lengthy testament ... and had, after mature deliberation, appointed many executors to carry out his wishes'. If Edward made a second will, or added to the first, it did not survive. The question remains, though, of just how long it did last. Was it lost or destroyed? By whom, and why?

Three decades later, Vergil cited Edward's second will as a source, claiming the king had appointed Richard of Gloucester as the guardian of his boys: 'He made his will wherein he constituted his sons as his heirs and committed them to the tuition of his brother.' This, said Vergil, was the reason why Lord Hastings sent a message to Richard, informing him that 'the king at his death had entrusted to him alone his wife, children, wealth and everything else', and inviting him to London to 'undertake the government'. Where Vergil found this information is unclear; he may have had a document in front of him or else was paraphrasing others' memories, but Edward's nomination of Richard as protector seems highly likely in this case, especially as he had been the king's choice to lead the army against the Scots. The Privy Council's confirmation of Richard as Lord Protector on 10 May appears to endorse the theory that this was one of Edward's last requests. Lord Hastings emerges as one of the body's leading figures, which would have accorded with Edward's wishes, but his suspicion of the Woodvilles had not diminished, despite the king's deathbed attempts at reconciliation. Hastings wrote to Richard, who was still in the north, urging him to come south and exert his control to prevent the queen's family dominating the court. Edward would also have made provision for his other children. His 1475 will left 10,000 marks to each of his daughters, drawn from the revenues of the duchy of Lancaster, along with the instruction that they and his sons be 'governed and ruled in their marriage by our dearest wife the queen and by our son the Prince of Wales if God fortune him to come to age of direction'. Edward clearly intended Elizabeth to play a significant part in her children's futures; her brother-in-law did not.

Edward V set out from Ludlow on 24 April, accompanied by his uncle Anthony Woodville, his half-brother Richard Grey and his chamberlain Thomas Vaughan. Richard of Gloucester had left York three days earlier, meeting with Henry Stafford, Duke of Buckingham, who was married to the queen's sister Katherine. What followed was either the result of Richard's distrust of the Woodville faction, or a cynical move on his part to step closer to the throne. Perhaps he used the former to justify the latter, or maybe he took exception to something that was communicated to him by Buckingham. Ultimately, it is not possible to know what his motivation was. Likely suggestions can be posed, but these must be done so with caution, given the paucity of material surviving from the period. Richard and Anthony arranged to meet in Northampton, in order to enter London together. On 29 April, the king's party reached Stony Stratford, where Woodville left Edward and rode the fourteen miles alone to meet Richard and Buckingham. Did Gloucester see this as an attempt to keep him from his nephew? Was it merely an opportunity for the child to rest after five days on the road? According to Polydore Vergil, this was the moment when Richard divulged his intent to claim the throne to Buckingham. That night the three men dined together in apparent friendliness, but early the next morning Richard arrived at the Stony Stratford inn, confiscated the keys and arrested Rivers and Grey. Edward V defended his kinsmen, but was told that they had been plotting to take control by force and their baggage contained weapons 'privily conveyed' from Ludlow. The news of the arrests reached London at midnight. Perceiving the danger to herself and her children, Elizabeth immediately took flight into sanctuary at Westminster. In a highly romanticised account, Thomas More pictures her sitting 'on the rushes in dismay, her long fair hair, so renowned for its beauty, escaped from its confinement, and streaming over her person, swept on the ground'.

Shut away in sanctuary, Elizabeth could not witness events that took place over the coming weeks. Yet she had one friend. Thomas Rotherham, Archbishop of York, had also been the late King Edward's chancellor, and now handed the dowager queen the great seal of his office. This was an act of defiance against the Lord Protector, showing his belief that political power should reside in the hands of the queen. It got Rotherham in serious trouble. The council met to discuss his actions, and although Rotherham took the seal back, Richard ordered that he be stripped of the role of chancellor. He awarded the seal instead to Thomas Bourchier, Archbishop of Canterbury.

The mood was one of uncertainty as Edward V arrived on 4 May, which was supposed to have been the day of his coronation. He was welcomed in Hornsey Park by the mayor and aldermen and 500 citizens dressed in velvet, who swore an oath of loyalty to the king, 'with the greatest pleasure and delight'.[1] The boy was lodged in the Bishop of London's palace beside St Paul's, and a new date of 22 June was nominated for his coronation, with his first parliament set to meet three days later. In mid-May, Edward was moved to the Tower on the wishes of the council, but this was the normal procedure for kings ahead of their crowning and caused no alarm. On the same day, the order was given for coins to be minted in the name of the new king. The executors of Edward IV's will – presumably his will of 1483 – then met at Baynard's Castle, the home of the late king's mother, and declared that his bequests to his children could not be honoured while they were in sanctuary. However, the council at this point was still not entirely dominated by Richard, and criticised him for not showing proper concern for the safety and dignity of Elizabeth in sanctuary.

Over the coming month, something changed. If she had not been already, Elizabeth became an enemy in her brother-in-law's eyes. It is to be expected that Thomas More's interpretation of these events would be hostile towards Gloucester, who he saw as having been provoked by the 'execrable desire for sovereignty', but the protector's motivation cannot be so easily summed up or dismissed. It may have been that during these weeks Richard was approached by Bishop Stillington, who claimed to have conducted a secret wedding ceremony between Edward IV and Eleanor Butler: Commines dates this event to 8 June. On 9 June, Richard held a meeting of the council, after which he wrote letters to the mayor and dignitaries of York, asking for their assistance against the queen:

> The Duke of Gloucester, brother and uncle of kings, Protector, Defender etc of England. Right trusty and well-beloved, we greet you well. And as you love the weal of us and the weal and surety of your own self, we heartily pray you come unto us to London in all the diligence ye can possible, after the sight hereof, with as many as ye can make defensibly arrayed, there to aid and assist us against the queen, her bloody adherents and affinity, which have intended and daily doth intend to murder and destroy us and our cousin the Duke of Buckingham and the old royal blood of this realm and [as is now openly known] by their subtle and damnable ways forecasted the same.

Again, did Richard genuinely believe that Elizabeth was plotting against him from sanctuary? Was she actually doing so? She would have needed allies on the council if she had intended to bring about the death or removal of Richard from office, and her resources in sanctuary were limited. Perhaps Richard's displeasure arose from her refusal to hand over her younger son – his namesake – to join his brother in the Tower. A letter written by a Simon Stallworthe, servant to the Bishop of Lincoln, stated that the council had been negotiating with Elizabeth in sanctuary, but that these talks had broken down and the members were now refusing to visit her there. There was certainly a mood of distrust in the city, which may have infected the protector: a surviving fragment from the common place book of a London merchant indicated that 'divers imagined the death of the Duke of Gloucester', and that Hastings' name was reputed to be among them. The account of Welshman

Humphrey Lluyd reflected this, claiming that 'Hastings would not freely have this man crowned'. The mood was shifting, with uncertainty and fear feeding itself, leading to the sense that those involved may need to take pre-emptive action and strike before their enemies could act.

On 13 June, the council met as planned, but Richard left early and returned distressed, claiming he had been bewitched and holding out his 'withered' arm as proof. Although examinations of his skeletal remains in 2013 showed there was no deformation of the bones in his arm, Richard may well have experienced a temporary condition like muscle spasms, puckering of the skin or an allergic reaction, which made him fear witchcraft. Equally, he may have deliberately employed the idea to associate the Woodvilles once again with sorcery. Richard embarked upon a speech about treason and ordered the arrest of six members of the council. This was followed by the immediate execution of Lord Hastings, who within minutes was dragged outside and beheaded on the spot. Such a process was shocking and irregular. There was no formal trial, nor was this the aftermath of battle, it was simply the sudden execution of a man who had served the York family for over two decades. The Great Chronicle commented that this was done 'without any process of law or lawful examination', while Croyland lamented the shedding of innocent blood and that 'the three strongest supporters of the new king were removed'. Elizabeth's ally, the Bishop of Rotherham, was among those arrested, along with Lancastrian sympathisers Bishop Morton and Sir Thomas Stanley. Vergil stated that these four had been meeting to discuss the possibility of deposing Richard and seizing the king by force for his own protection; they may have been in contact with Elizabeth and shared their concerns with her. Also accused was Jane Shore, making her only appearance in a political context, accused of carrying messages between Hastings and Elizabeth in sanctuary. She may well have done so. There might have been co-operation between Hastings and the dowager queen, facilitated by an old friend. Perhaps they feared the Protector's intentions and resolved to observe his moves. Perhaps Jane was kindly keeping Elizabeth informed about the arrangements being made for her sons. Equally, they might have been plotting against Richard, as Elizabeth was to do later in the year, although this only took place after Richard had become king and Edward V had forever disappeared within the confines of the Tower. Three days later, Elizabeth was persuaded to hand over her and Edward's second son, Richard, to Thomas Bourchier, Archbishop of Canterbury, probably in the belief that he was a man she might trust. Vergil believed that she did so because Richard surrounded sanctuary with troops and she feared violence.

The intended day of the coronation came and went. It must have been an anxious one for Elizabeth. A sermon was preached at the cross outside St Paul's Cathedral by Dr Ralph Shaa, brother of the Mayor of London. Entitled 'Bastard Slips Should Not Take Root', it was designed to destroy the claim of Edward V to the throne by invalidating the marriage of his parents and was echoed in church pulpits across the city. This was pre-arranged, clearly part of a widespread propaganda campaign, and signalled Richard's intention to take the throne for himself. He had put aside his mourning clothes for Edward IV and now dressed in regal purple. Mancini described how Gloucester 'so corrupted preachers of the divine word that in their sermons to the people they did not blush to say in the face of decency and all religion that the progeny of King Edward should be instantly eradicated, for neither had he been legitimate king, nor could his issue be so. Edward, they said, was conceived in adultery.' It was the same old rumours again, as had been employed by Warwick in the 1460s. What Cecily of York made of her son's claims went unrecorded, but the suggestion of her adultery was quietly dropped after this. When news of the sermons reached the Westminster sanctuary, it must have been devastating. Worse was still to come. Three days later, Richard ordered the executions of Anthony Woodville, Richard Grey and Thomas Vaughan. On 6 July, the man appointed as the protector of Elizabeth's son was crowned as Richard III.

Hidden away in sanctuary with her daughters, Elizabeth must have felt helpless regarding the fate of her sons. As a widow without friends, whose relatives and allies had been brutally removed, there was little she could now do except pray. Richard had confiscated her lands and she had no income. The last of Edward V's attendants were paid and dismissed from the Tower on 13 July. The young king's doctor, John Argentine, recorded that Edward 'like a victim prepared for his sacrifice made daily confession because he thought that death was facing him'. The boys were then moved into the inner sanctum of the Tower and seen less and less. The last occurrence of Edward V's signature as king was on 17 June. This was around the point that Mancini left England, writing that their lives were already despaired of: 'I have seen many men burst forth into tears and lamentations when mention was made of him [Edward V] after his removal from men's sight and already there was a suspicion that he had been done away with. Whether, however, he had been done away with and by what manner of death, so far I have not at all discovered.'

Yet there was a possible plot being hatched to free the boys, along the same lines that Hastings may have proposed. The Croyland chronicler writes that at the end of July, the princes were 'under special guard' and in the south and west of the country people began to 'murmur greatly and to form assemblies and confederacies, many of which worked in secret, others openly', with the intention of releasing them 'from such captivity'. John Stow wrote in 1580 of a plan to divert the boys' gaolers by setting a fire in the grounds of the Tower, and there were rumours of a plot to smuggle Elizabeth's daughters out of sanctuary to safety overseas. Ironically, it may have been these plans that guaranteed the boys' fate. Thomas More claims it was on 29 July, when Richard road to Gloucester, that the new king decided to order the princes' deaths, and that two days later he dispatched Sir James Tyrrell to London on 'king's business'. After this point, neither Edward V nor Richard of York were seen again. Alison Weir speculates that the deed took place on 3 September, when Tyrrell returned to the capital with wall hangings and robes for the investiture of Richard's son as Prince of Wales.

Different rumours must have reached Elizabeth through the summer about the fates of her sons; some conspirators may even have attempted to confide their plans in her. However, as autumn arrived, her hopes must have been fading. If she did not already suspect as much, she then had to face the very real possibility that they had been killed. The fate of the Princes in the Tower is still debated by historians today. Some believe that they were smuggled out of the country and survived, or that they were killed by a servant trying to please Richard, if not on his direct command. A box of mixed bones discovered under a staircase in the White

Tower in 1674 were examined in 1933, but the tests proved inconclusive. Currently these remains are sealed within an urn inside Westminster Abbey.

II

Then, seemingly inexplicably, Richard's closest ally turned against him. That September, while the king, his wife and son were on a tour of the north, the Duke of Buckingham launched a plot to oust him from the throne. It is likely that Buckingham influenced Richard at Stony Stratford regarding the seizure of the king and the arrests of his protectors. It was certainly the duke who declaimed the illegitimacy of Edward's marriage and children, and then chaired the council meeting which offered Richard the throne. In the space of only a few weeks, something had shaken this close conspiracy to the core. One theory is that Buckingham's ambition was as powerful as Richard's. He was also, after all, a great-great-grandson of Edward III, with an impressive three out of four grandparents being directly descended from the past king, and he was cousin to Richard by virtue of their mothers being sisters. Did Buckingham have his own sights set on the throne? If so, he may have seen Richard as a stepping stone to his own power, or else he had reflected on how rapidly the transition from one king to another had been made and felt he might bring about a similar coup on his own behalf. It may have been that he felt Richard was ungrateful and had failed to reward his friend and facilitator. Given his role, the duke may have perceived himself as something of a kingmaker. He may have hoped that another king would heap him with rewards, or that he could harness support in order to facilitate his own path to the throne. Then there may be the question of conscience: if Buckingham learned something that turned him completely against Richard between July and September that year, it can only really have been to do with the fate of the Princes in the Tower. Either Buckingham learned that Richard had ordered the deaths of the princes and could not stomach this, or else Buckingham was implicit in the boys' deaths on the king's orders, and understood that Richard needed to remove him. If Buckingham had been responsible for their murders, he might have hoped to blame this on Richard and then replace him on the throne, although he appears not to have made any formal accusation. Alternatively, the purpose of the rebellion was to restore Edward V to the throne, in the event that he was still alive. The truth may never be known. What is clear, though, is that Buckingham's allegiance changed.

The duke turned to the last hope of the Lancastrian line: Henry Tudor, Earl of Richmond, the son of Edmund Tudor – who had been a half-brother of Henry VI – and Lady Margaret Beaufort, who was then the wife of Thomas, Lord Stanley. Henry's claim to the throne was not a strong one, but after the death of Prince Edward he appeared as an attractive candidate for those who loathed the Yorkist regime, or who disagreed with Richard becoming king. Tudor had fled the country as a boy of fourteen in the aftermath of the Battle of Tewkesbury, and had grown up in exile in France, then Brittany. In the autumn of 1483, he was twenty-six years old and had built up a degree of support for his cause abroad. According to the Parliament Rolls, Buckingham wrote to Tudor on 24 September, urging him to invade England. The planned date for this was 18 October. Henry responded eagerly. He secured a loan of 10,000 crowns from Francis, Duke of Brittany, a fleet of ships and 5,000 mercenaries, and attempted to set sail on 3 October. However, a terrible storm in the Channel beat his boats back to port. The bad weather was to prove Buckingham's undoing.

On 2 August, Buckingham had left Richard's progress at Gloucester and headed to his castle at Brecon. There, he was responsible for the custody of John Morton, Bishop of Ely, who had been incarcerated since his arrest at the council meeting where Hastings was killed. Morton was a close friend of Margaret Beaufort, whose husband Lord Stanley was also arrested. In communication with Margaret, Morton was probably responsible for turning the duke's opinion of Richard and suggesting Margaret's son as a viable alternative candidate for king. Instead of initiating what is now known as 'Buckingham's Rebellion', it may have been that the duke was drawn into an established plan in which the Woodvilles were deeply involved. It was around this time that Elizabeth's son Thomas Grey, Marquis of Dorset, fled from sanctuary into the west, while her brother Edward, whom the council had recently appointed Admiral of the Fleet, took his ships to Brittany. The final crucial player in the drama was Elizabeth herself. Margaret sent her own physician, a Welshman named Lewis, to attend upon Elizabeth in sanctuary, gambling that his presence would go unnoticed. Lewis proposed to the dowager that Henry Tudor should oust Richard and be married to her eldest daughter, Elizabeth of York, who was then approaching her eighteenth birthday. In the account of Edward Hall, the dowager queen

> bade him tell his lady that all King Edward's friends and dependants should join with her for the Earl of Richmond, on condition he took his corporal oath to marry Lady Elizabeth, her eldest daughter, or, in case she were not living, her second daughter. Dr Lewis carried this pleasing answer to his mistress, from whom he went frequently to the queen as physician, and from her to the countess, till matters were fully concluded between them.

Although the weather had temporarily beaten Tudor back, the sense of anger against Richard in the south was still strong and did not deter the rebels, many of whom had been loyal servants of Edward IV. Buckingham gathered troops in Brecon, Dorset did the same in Exeter, and Lionel Woodville followed suit in Salisbury. However, premature timing meant the plans were revealed, when the men of Kent, focused on the Woodville property of the Mote, Maidstone, rose too early, on 10 October. They were suppressed by the Duke of Norfolk, who then communicated Buckingham's treachery to Richard a week before the revolt had been scheduled to start. The king publically proclaimed his former friend a traitor, and put the price of £1,000 on his head. Hearing this, Buckingham tried to escape south, to catch a boat and join Tudor in exile. However, another terrible storm hit the country, leaving the River Severn impassable and halting Buckingham in his tracks. He sought sanctuary at Beaulieu Abbey, perhaps in the hope of navigating a ship down the River Beaulieu to the sea as Henry Tudor had made a second attempt to sail and was approaching the south coast. It was too late. Buckingham was arrested and convicted of treason. He was beheaded in the marketplace at Salisbury on 2 November. Tudor heard the news when he reached Plymouth, and turned his ships around.

This was a terrible outcome for Elizabeth. Potentially, the uprising could have been the answer to her problems, giving her back her freedom, vindicating her concerns, restoring her position and opening a bright future for her daughters. Instead, the plot's failure exposed her as guilty of treasonous activity, which carried with it the penalty of death. Sanctuary was the best place for her now, but it was still not completely inviolable. She had little to lose now except her life, so there was little to do but pray and wait to see what action Richard would take. Fortunately, he did very little. The rebel leaders were caught, and although some were executed, a good number, including Thomas Grey, managed to flee to Brittany, or else were pardoned. Margaret Beaufort had all of her lands confiscated for the role she had played, but these were simply put into the hands of her husband, so there was little real material loss. However, the idea of a Tudor–Woodville marriage had been firmly established. Elizabeth could not hope to have any influence over future events and was forced to resign herself to failure, although the continuing existence of Henry Tudor overseas was a glimmer of light in a dark winter. On Christmas Day 1483, Henry swore an oath in Rennes Cathedral that he would return to England, defeat Richard and make Elizabeth of York his wife.

In January 1484, Parliament passed the Act of Titulus Regis, which retrospectively made legal Richard's reasons for claiming the throne. It also formally deprived the ex-queen of her dower payments. Unsurprisingly, given the sermon preached by Dr Ralph Shaa, Edward and Elizabeth's marriage and Edward's lifestyle was a target for attack. When Elizabeth was informed of its content, she can hardly have recognised her former husband from it; the deliberate recasting of such a strong but affable king must have filled her with horror.

This land was ruled by silf will and pleasur, fere and dread, al maner of equite and lawes leid apart and dispised, whereof ensued many inconvenientes and myschefes, extorisions and oppressions, namely of poore and impotent people, soo that no man was sure of his lif, land ne lyvelode, ne his wyf, doughter ne servaunt, every goode maiden and woman standing in drede to be ravysshed and defouled. And besides this, what discordes, inward batailles, effusion of Cristen mens blode, and namely, by the destruccion of the noble blode of this londe, who has and committed within the same, it is evident and notarie throughout this reame, unto the grete sorowe and heyness of all true Englisshmen.

Why did Richard describe his brother in this way? Firstly, it was politically urgent for him to justify taking the throne from Edward's designated heir, so he needed a villain. Just as Cecily had once threatened to swear to her son's illegitimacy to undermine his marriage, Richard was prepared to blacken his brother's character in order to justify his own actions. It was essential that Edward serve as a foil for Richard's 'prudence, justice [and] princely courage'. Because Richard was already king, he could leave no shadow of doubt when it came to Edward's foulness and moral degeneracy. What really mattered, though, was whether or not Richard believed what was said of Edward in Titulus Regis; whether he was exaggerating in order to secure his reign, or if he accepted this as an accurate portrait of his elder brother. Right up until the summer of 1482, Richard had demonstrated loyalty to Edward, accompanying him in exile, fighting beside him in battle, leading armies to France and Scotland in his name. Perhaps he kept his intense personal dislike and disapproval of Edward concealed, or else he simply felt no such thing. Did Richard genuinely change his mind about Edward after his death? If he did, it can only be because he learned certain things he had not previously known, such as the suggestions made by Bishop Stillington that Edward had been precontracted to Eleanor Butler. If not, it implies the exploitation of rumours for sinister purposes.

The question of the Butler marriage has still not been satisfactorily answered and may well never be, due to the secret nature of it. With both Eleanor and Edward dead, there was only Bishop Stillington's word that a precontract had taken place, and, back in the early 1460s, Edward would have had to sufficiently trust the man to hold his tongue. Perhaps Stillington was afraid of reprisals and so did keep quiet until 1483, or perhaps he confided in another member of the royal family. The bishop had been closely associated with George, Duke of Clarence, and both were imprisoned during 1478, although the cause of Stillington's incarceration is unclear. Had he imparted information to George which made the duke believe that Edward's children were illegitimate and that he was, in fact, the next rightful heir to the throne? If the bishop had spoken up in 1478, Clarence's revolt can be seen as a rehearsal of Richard's actions in 1483: different brother, same reasons. Yet, if this was the case, it seems strange that Stillington was released and not punished by Edward. It may be that the king no longer saw the information as a threat, now that George was dead, never believing that the previously loyal Richard would take the same line, nor anticipating his own early death. It could also be that Stillington cynically embroidered the story for the benefit of Richard III. The bishop was imprisoned under Henry VII and only briefly released before he became involved in the Lambert Simnel plot of 1487 and was returned to jail, where he spent the rest of his life. The real questions of motive concerning Clarence and Richard, as well as the truth of Edward's connection with Eleanor, may never be unravelled.

On 1 March, Elizabeth made a pact with Richard that has attracted controversy ever since. She agreed to leave sanctuary so long as the king swore a public oath to protect her daughters and arrange suitable matches for them. It was an unprecedented move on her part, but Richard agreed, reciting the following promise in the presence of the mayor and aldermen of London and the lords and bishops of the King's council and swearing upon holy relics:

> I promitte and swere that if the doughters of dam Elizabeth Grey, late calling herself Quene of England, that is to wit Elizabeth, Cecille, Anne, Kateryn and Brigitte, wolle come unto me out of the Saintwarie of Westminstre and be guyded, Ruled and demeaned after me, that I shalle see that they shalbe in suertie of their lyffes and also not suffer any maner hurt by any maner persone or persones to theim or any of theim in their bodies and persones to be done by Ravisshment or defouling contrarie their willes, not theim or any of theim emprisone within the Toure of London or other prisone, but that I shalle put theim in honest places of good name and fame and theim honestly and curtesly shalle see to be foundene and entreated and to have alle things requisite and necessarye for their exibicione and findinges as my kynneswomen. As that I shalle do marie suche of theim as now bene mariable to gentilmen borne, and everiche of theim geve in marriage lands and tenements to the yerely valewe of CC (200) marks for terme of their lyves, and in

like wise to the other doughters when they come to lawfulle age of marriage if they lyff, and suche gentilmen as shalle happe to marie with them I shalle straitly charge from tyme to tyme lovingly to love and entreate theim as their wiffes and my kynneswomen, As they wolle advoid and ecschue my displeasure.[2]

Elizabeth had bought freedom for her daughter, but she was exchanging one form of imprisonment for another, as well as accepting that she was merely Elizabeth Grey, and that her marriage to Edward had been invalid. She was to be trusted to the keeping of Sir John Nesfield, Constable of Hertford Castle, and Richard promised,

I shalle yerely from hensfurthe content and pay or cause to be contented and paied for thexibicione and finding of the said dame Elizabeth Grey during her naturelle liff at iiii termes of the yere, that is to wit at pasche, Midsomer, Michilmesse and Christenmesse to John Nesfelde one of the Squires for my body for his finding to attende upon her the summe of DCC [700] marks of lawfulle money of England by even porcions. And moreover I promitte to theim that if any surmise or evylle report be made to me of theim or any of theim by any persone or persones that than I shalle not geve thereunto faithe ne credence nor therefore put theim to any maner ponysshement before that they or any of theim so accused may be at their lawfulle defence and answere.[3]

Some historians have responded to Elizabeth's action with unjustified savagery. Realistically, what choice did she have but to submit to a regime that could conceivably last another three decades? Given that Richard was fifteen years her junior, Elizabeth must have concluded in 1484 that she was unlikely to live to see another monarch on the throne. She had been in sanctuary for ten months, and she must have realised that while her sons were now beyond her help, she could act to improve the lives of her surviving children. Tudor's uprising had failed and her allies had fled or been punished. Necessity and pragmatism dictated her actions, rather than any desire for reconciliation; it was an unpleasant but necessary truce with the enemy. It may be difficult for modern readers to sympathise with an action that placed Elizabeth's daughters in the hands of the man whom she probably believed had killed her sons, but she had no real alternative. They could not stay in sanctuary forever, with the girls approaching a marriagable age. Elizabeth was forced to do a deal, but she managed to arrange it in such a way that Richard publicly swore to protect and aid his nieces. For this piece of realpolitik, Elizabeth was branded weak and corrupt by Tudor historians. Thomas More had her dissolving 'alone on the rushes all desolate and dismayed', while Vergil says she 'fell into a swoon and lay lifeless a good while ... struck her breast, tore and cut her hair ... prayed also [for] her own death'. Holinshed stated that all her maternal scruples were won over by 'glorious promises and flattering words', which led her to 'blot out the old committed injurie and late executed tyrannie', as she was only a 'weake woman of timorous spirit'. Elizabeth's motivation and actions get caught up in Holinshed's late Elizabethan dialogue of gender stereotypes:

> Suerlie the inconstancie of this woman were much to be marvelled at, if all women had been found constant, but let men speake, yet women of the very bonde of nature will follow their own sex. But it was no small allurement that king Richard used to overcome her for we know by experience that women are of a proud disposition and that the waie to win them is by promises of preferment and therefore it is the lesse marvell that he by his wilie wit had made conquest of her wavering will.

In the following months, Richard made peace with some of the other remaining members of the Woodville family, including Richard Woodville, Elizabeth's brother, who was pardoned in exchange for a surety payment and pledge of allegiance. Elizabeth even wrote to her son Thomas Grey in exile to persuade him that he would be forgiven if he came home.

Elizabeth's whereabouts over the ensuing year are unknown. She may have retired to Hertford Castle under the watchful eye of Sir John Nesfield, and taken her daughters with her. Equally, Elizabeth of York and her sisters might have entered the household of Queen Anne Neville, as some of them were present at court that Christmas, when comparisons were drawn between the eldest princess and the queen. The Croyland chronicler describes the controversial rumours which were flying that season about Elizabeth and her uncle:

> During this Christmas feast too much attention was paid to singing and dancing and vain exchanges of clothes between Queen Anne and Lady Elizabeth … who were alike in complexion and figure. The people spoke against this and the magnates and prelates were greatly astonished; it was said by many that the king was applying his mind in every way to contracting a marriage with Elizabeth either after the death of the queen, or by means of a divorce for which he believed he had sufficient grounds.

Whether or not this was ever a serious concern cannot now be established. If Richard ever had any intention of making his niece his wife, it could have been achieved with a papal dispensation, and would have allowed the king to hopefully father more children. His only son by Anne had died in the spring of 1484, and Anne herself conveniently followed him on 16 March 1485, during an eclipse of the sun. Two weeks later, Richard issued a public denial of any such intentions towards his niece, and a damaged letter written by Elizabeth, which antiquarian George Buck believed proved she was in love with the king, is likely to refer instead to a double marriage planned for herself and Richard with members of Portuguese royalty. It is not impossible that rumours about the king and his niece were deliberately used to dampen the hopes of Henry Tudor, waiting in exile. Nor can it be ruled out entirely that the pair did fall in love, and that the king was warned by his council that the loyalty of his northern subjects had been bound up with their allegiance to the daughter of the Earl of Warwick, and that a new queen would need to be acceptable to them. Would Elizabeth Woodville have supported such a match? It is impossible to guess. When Richard heard that Tudor was preparing for a second invasion attempt that summer, he sent Elizabeth north to his castle of Sheriff Hutton. Her mother's whereabouts at the time are unknown, but it would have made sense for her to accompany the girl. They would not see Richard again.

Henry Tudor's army landed at Milford Haven on 7 August. With him were Jasper Tudor; Edward de Vere, Earl of Oxford; Edward and possibly Richard Woodville. Lionel had died the previous year, and Sir Thomas Grey was kept behind in Brittany as surety for Francis's loans. Henry had an initial 2,000 men, but more joined him as he marched east, reaching the Leicestershire town of Market Bosworth on 21 August. The following day, his army met that of Richard III, advancing from the city of Leicester with his banner and cross held high. In theory, it should have been an easy victory for the seasoned campaigner, who had the advantage of experience, numbers and the law. At the crucial moment, however, as Richard launched a charge against Tudor, Henry's stepfather, Thomas Stanley, finally committed his troops to the battle in defence of the invader. Richard was cut down as he fought his way towards his enemy. His helmet was lost and the ceremonial crown atop it rolled away, traditionally coming to rest under a hawthorn bush. When it was recovered, it was placed upon Tudor's head, making him King of England by right of conquest.

13

RETIREMENT
1486–1492

'A broken heart is here at rest.'

I

If Elizabeth had hoped to live out her final years in retirement, she still had a few obstacles to overcome. The next couple of years were to mark a significant improvement in her condition, a restoration of her rightful status and the fulfilment of her maternal aspirations, but there were also to be shadows. Firstly, everything had to be made official. One of Henry's initial acts as king was to send Sir Robert Willoughby north to collect Princess Elizabeth from Sheriff Hutton and bring her to London. Apartments were prepared for her in Coldharbour House, which was then in the possession of Margaret Beaufort. Elizabeth, her mother and her sisters would have attended Henry's splendid coronation in Westminster Abbey on 30 October, when the new king wore purple cloth of gold tissue and crimson cloth of gold, and walked beneath almost 500 yards of fine scarlet cloth which draped the abbey and the palace hall. The bill submitted by the Steward of Henry's household for clothing, boots, ribbons, leathers, furs, harnesses and banners totalled over £1,506, even before the expenses of the Great Wardrobe were added. Seven new Knights of the Bath were created, and the pageantry and decorations featured crimson-velvet dragons, falcons, red roses and the figures of St Edward and Cadwallader. Perhaps it reminded the Dowager Queen Elizabeth of the celebrations for her own coronation twenty-two years before. The resurrection of St Edward and Cadwallader no doubt stirred memories of her husband.

When Henry's first parliament met that December, Titulus Regis was repealed and the king ordered all copies to be 'cancelled, destroyed ... burnt and utterly destroyed' by the following Easter, on penalty of fine or imprisonment. Elizabeth Woodville was restored to her former position as queen dowager, and her children were again considered legitimate. Elizabeth must have been relieved and even more delighted when Henry sent for her only surviving son, Thomas Grey, to return home. Henry was also planning to fulfil the oath he had made in Rennes Cathedral two years previously, ordering wedding rings before Christmas and requesting a papal dispensation, which arrived on 16 January. The wedding ceremony for the marriage of Henry VII to Elizabeth of York took place two days later, officiated by Archbishop Thomas Bourchier, and very soon Elizabeth had fallen pregnant. On 4 March, Henry granted his mother-in-law the lordships of Waltham, Badowe, Magna, Masshebury, Dunmore, Lieghes and Farnham in Essex, as part of the dower due to her after the death of Edward IV, followed by an annual £102 from the fee farm of Bristol.[1]

With her eldest daughter now Queen of England, her status restored and her financial future provided for, Elizabeth's mind turned towards a quieter life. On 10 July, she obtained the lease of Cheneygates, the house of Abbot Millyng within the Westminster precincts that she had taken refuge in during Edward's exile in 1470-1. This also suggests that the time she spent there had not been too uncomfortable, although the circumstances had been those of extreme duress. It was there that she had given birth to Edward V and nursed him for five months before the return of her husband, and there that they had been reunited. This also indicates Elizabeth's desire to step aside, out of the limelight, in her final years. In comparison, Henry VII's mother, Margaret Beaufort, would continue to play an active role in his administration until her death, but this only highlights the different characters of the two women. Elizabeth had never involved herself directly in politics. She may have influenced Edward regarding the appointments of her friends and family, but she had opted for the typical medieval role of the passive queen: submissive, beautiful and fertile. Now that role was behind her, she sought a life of quiet contemplation, away from the business of the Tudor court. She spent much of the summer months with the pregnant queen in Winchester, and was present at the birth of her grandson, Arthur, to whom she stood as godmother. Her daughters Cecily and Anne, her brother Edward and her daughter-in-law, the Marchioness of Dorset, were also present.

It may have been difficult for Elizabeth to witness the establishment of a new reign under a young king. Like Edward, Henry deliberately employed the imagery of the Arthurian legends, compounding his Welsh birth and the claim of his grandfather Owen Tudor's descent from Arthur, and marching under the banner of the red dragon at Bosworth. When the coronation of her daughter took place, one of the barges featured a huge, red, fire-breathing dragon, the symbol of Cadwallader, while the horse of her champion, Jasper Tudor, featured the same creature in its decoration, although the dowager queen did not attend this event. It must have been difficult for her to avoid drawing comparisons between herself and Edward, and Elizabeth and Henry; perhaps these were less than favourable comparisons, given that Henry's claim to the throne was less strong than Edward's, and even his resounding victory at Bosworth paled beside the memories of Towton and Tewkesbury. Edward had been a giant of a man: tall, golden, beautiful, athletic and seductive. He had dressed the part in cloth of gold and jewels, was cultured, chivalric and easy of manner. Standing perhaps a head shorter than Edward, Henry VII with a cast in his eye and poor teeth, cannot have shone in comparison in Elizabeth Woodville's eyes. In dynastic terms, however, marriage to the victor of Bosworth had been a coup, and on a personal level the dowager may have considered her daughter to be 'depressed not advanced'.

Then, the newly established Tudor regime experienced its first real threat. On 2 February, Henry was informed that a ten-year-old boy, by the name of John or Lambert Simnel, had emerged in Ireland under the tutelage of a priest named Richard or William Simons, and was claiming to be first, Richard, Duke of York, and then Clarence's son, Edward, Earl of Warwick. Later the same month, the council deprived Elizabeth Woodville of all her possessions, for the reason that she had, three years earlier, 'made her peace with king Richard, had placed her daughters at his disposal and had, by leaving sanctuary, broken her promise to those ... who had, at her most urgent entreaty, forsaken their own English property and fled to Henry in Brittany'. On 20 February, she was granted an annuity of 400 marks and registered as a resident of Bermondsey Abbey, which was obliged to house her as a descendant of its founder. Was this just a question of timing, or was there a connection between these two events? The strange excuse of Elizabeth's pact with Richard can hardly have gone unnoticed in the first eighteen months of his reign; was this being used as an excuse for something else? Had Elizabeth somehow been drawn into, or corresponded with, those supporting Simnel? If so, it seems unlikely that she planned to join an invasion that threatened the future of her daughter and grandson. With so many losses in her life, it would be human and excusable if she had been tempted to investigate the possibility that one of her sons was still alive. There is also the question of the King of Scots. James III was widowed in 1486 and Henry considered a match between him and Elizabeth, which he would not have done if he did not trust her, although this may have been mooted before the Simnel revolt. As James died in 1488, it cannot be used as a reliable measure of the king's faith in his mother-in-law. Equally, Elizabeth's retirement may have been her decision, perhaps even her own suggestion, as the final stage of her withdrawal from public life. It may even have been news of the threat that triggered her actions. Having lived through so much turmoil and uncertainty, she may have felt that this was the final straw, and no longer wanted to experience the terrors associated with holding on to a volatile crown. Then again, maybe she was ill. Approaching the age of fifty, she could have been experiencing symptoms of ageing, or the illnes that would kill her five years later.

Standing on the site of the present Bermondsey Square in Southwark, Bermondsey Abbey is thought to have been founded in the eighth century. It is first mentioned as a monastery in the

Domesday Book, being refounded in 1082 and dedicated to St Saviour, surrounded by woodlands filled with hogs and twenty acres of meadow. It was home to a number of Clunaic monks who had emigrated after the conquest from their base at the Monastery of La Charité on the Loire. In the fourteenth century, the monastery became an abbey, and it was there, in 1437, that Catherine of Valois had died. A survey commissioned in 1679 was used to draw a floorplan of the abbey in the nineteenth century, featuring gardens, orchard, apartments, base court, long walk and church, stable yard, pond and gateways. The dowager queen was shut away behind the abbey's bucolic walls when Lambert Simnel was crowned Edward VI in Dublin Cathedral in May that year, and when he was defeated at the Battle of Stoke on 16 June, along with Richard III's designated heir, John de la Pole, Earl of Lincoln. To add to the heartbreak for Elizabeth, Lincoln was her nephew, as the son of her husband's sister, and the army was funded by Burgundian troops supplied by Margaret of York. Lincoln had appeared to adjust well to the new regime, being present at the council meeting where Elizabeth's lands and properties were taken from her, before sailing to Ireland in March. The ten-year-old Simnel, only a figurehead in the scheme, was forgiven and placed in Henry's kitchens.

Many widows did choose a life of retirement and contemplation in their declining years, scaling down their households and expenses and devoting themselves to prayer and charity. Although Elizabeth may have differed from Margaret Beaufort's energetic and consistent activity during Henry's reign, her chosen path bore much resemblance to that of Cecily Neville, Edward's mother. Having lost her husband and all her four sons, plus her grandson Lincoln in 1487, Cecily retreated to Berkhamsted Castle and became a vowess. This meant she lived according to a strict religious regime, apparent in the ordinances she drew up for the running of her household. Cecily rose at seven, said prayers as she dressed, then attended Mass followed by divine service and more masses. At dinner she was read to from religious texts, and then concluded an hour of business, giving 'audyence to all such as hath any manner to shewe unto her'. She then slept for a quarter of an hour, prayed until evensong, after which she drank a glass of wine. At supper, she recited to her household the text of the sermon she had heard at dinner, after which she pursued 'honest mirth' with her gentlewomen before retiring to bed.² Elizabeth's life probably followed a similar model. The difference may have been that Cecily and Elizabeth had both lost their sons, while Margaret's was still very much alive and invested as King of England.

Elizabeth emerged from Bermondsey on one known occasion after her retirement. Her daughter went into confinement again towards the end of the year and Elizabeth joined her at Westminster for the birth of her daughter Margaret on 28 November. During the period of waiting, they were visited by the French ambassadors, led by the dowager's cousin Francis de Luxembourg. She received sad news too: Sir Edward Woodville was killed in July 1488 when leading an attack in support of the Duke of Brittany at the Battle of St Aubin du Cormier. Then, in February 1490, Elizabeth learned of the death of her other brother Richard Woodville, who had taken the title of Earl Rivers after Anthony's execution seven years earlier. He left all his cattle to the church at Grafton, so that an annual obit could be said for his soul, and named Elizabeth's son Thomas Grey as his heir, leaving him his lands and requesting that enough wood be cut down around Grafton to pay for a bell for the church tower 'for a remembrance of the last of my blood'.³

Henry was still paying the allowance to Elizabeth that had been arranged in 1487, but not always promptly. On 31 May 1491, her signature appears on a receipt for £30, in part payment for the £200 she was owed by Henry that had been late arriving: 'due to me at ester last past as hyt aperyth be my annuete grauntyd be the kyng'. However, she was not being neglected, as that Christmas she received a gift of £50 from the king: 'unto oure right dere and right welbeloved quene Elizabeth moder unto our most dere wif the quene'. Elizabeth probably did not attend the delivery of the future Henry VIII at Greenwich Palace in June 1491. Perhaps she was too ill or immobile; only ten months later, on 10 April 1492, she was sufficiently unwell to give instructions for her will to be drawn up. As with other decisions she made, the simplicity of her requests has caused debate, but they do appear appropriate within the context of her chosen pious retirement. If Elizabeth had any axe to grind with Henry, her will was not a suitable vehicle for complaint. She would have believed it to be a document between her and God – a final chance to make amends for earthly sins and express the piety and dignity of her rank. It must also be remembered that Edward had expressed his desire for a cadaver tomb; Elizabeth chose a different method to demonstrate her humility. If nothing else, her life had re-enforced the concept of the wheel of fortune, and few were better placed than she to comment that the world was a transitory place:

I, Elizabeth, by the grace of God Queen of England, late wife to the most victorious Prince of blessed memory Edward the Fourth, being of hole mynde, seying the worlde so transitory, and no creature certayne whanne they shall departe from hence, havying Almyghty Gode fresh in mynd, in whome is all mercy and grace, bequeath my sowle into his hands, beseeching him, of the same mercy, to accept it graciously, and oure blessed Lady Quene of comforte, and all the holy company of hevyn, to be good meanes for me. Item, I bequeath my body to be buried with the bodie of my Lord at Windsor, according to the will of my said Lord and myne without pompe entreing or costlie expensis done thereabought. Item, where I have no wordlie goods to do the Queene's grace, my dearest daughter, a pleasure with, neither to reward any of my children according to my heart and mind, I beseech Almighty God to bless her Grace, with all her noble issue; and as good heart and mind as is to me possible, I gave her Grace my blessing and all the aforesaid my children. Item, I will that suche smale stufe and goodes that I have to be disposed truly in the contentac'on of my dettes, and for the helthe of my sowle, as farre as they will extende. Item, if any of my bloode will of my saide stufe or goodes to me perteyning, I this my present testament I make and ordeyne myne Executors, that is to say, John Ingilby, Prior of the Charterhouse of Sheen, William Sutton and Thomas Brente, doctors. And I besech my derest doughter, the Quene's grace, and my sone Thomas, Marques Dorsett, to putte there good willes and help for the performans of this my testament. In witnesse whereof, to this my present testament I have sett my seale, these witnesses, John, Abbot of the Monastry of Sainte Saviour of Bermondsey, and Benedictus Can, Doctor of Fysyk [Physic].[4]

Elizabeth died two months after completing her will, on 8 June 1492. Two days later, her body was placed in a wooden coffin and taken by barge to Windsor, accompanied by a small retinue, including John Ingilby, the prior; her cousin Edward Haute; and Grace Plantagenet, the illegitimate daughter of Edward IV. Her own children Thomas Grey, Anne, Catherine and Bridget, along with her nephew Edmund de la Pole and other relatives, travelled to Windsor to meet her body. Elizabeth of York was absent due to her approaching confinement: she gave birth on 2 July to a daughter whom she named after her mother. Elizabeth's wishes for a humble funeral were granted. A herald commented that 'ther was nothing doon solemply for her saving a low herse suche as they use for the comyn peple with iiii wooden candilstikks abowte hit' and 'never a new torche, but old torches, nor poure man in blacke gowne nor hoods, but upon a dozeyn dyvers olde men holding old torches'.⁵ She was buried in St George's Chapel, beside Edward, on 12 June. Her only surviving son, the Marquis of Dorset, paid the 40s in alms out of his own pocket. Elizabeth's burial was consistent with her final years in retirement and suggests that her desire for poverty and piety was genuine. She had chosen a humble wooden coffin: a marked contrast between the regal magnificence lavished on her in life by her husband, wrapped in jewels, furs and cloth of gold as his entire court remained on bended knee before her.

II

Representations of Edward and Elizabeth have appeared in several works of literature since their deaths, each of which seem to have drawn out a different aspect of their story. Sometimes this has been integral to the narrative, unavoidable and dictated by subject matter. Their presence is to be expected in such medieval and Tudor chronicles as those written by Warkworth, Croyland, Mancini, More, Vergil, Hall, Holinshed and others, where the events of their lives are related with varying degrees of accuracy and sympathy. Of course, these have to be taken as historical sources with their inevitable biases and problematic interpretations. It is inevitable that non-fiction writers have looked at the facts of Edward IV's reign from a fixed perspective, depending upon their own place in time and political sympathies. Thus, Edward is often a sideline in the narratives of Richard III or Henry VI, or a bit player in the longer story of the Wars of the Roses. He might be simply the son of York, or the father of the Princes in the Tower. Equally, Elizabeth has often been presented in just the context of her family, the 'grasping' Woodvilles, or an anecdote in the history of witchcraft, or as a romantic figure who captured a king – whose secret marriage triggered a string of catastrophic events.

Yet it is when Edward and Elizabeth appear in poetry and drama that the legends are born – that their characters are elevated to the level of popular myth, with the ability to enter a wider cultural context and inspire the imagination. That is not to deny the very genuine inspiration that can be found in non-ficton, but rather to acknowledge the genre-specific differences: the artistic licence and flights of fancy, subtle and stirring, on which a text can embark when it is classified as 'art'. The BBC and STARZ's adaption of Philippa Gregory's 2009 novel *The White Queen* drew around 6 million viewers in the UK for its first episode on 16 June 2013, and went on to be nominated for three Golden Globe awards. Although it had its critics, the series spawned a new interest in Edward and Elizabeth, played by Max Irons and Rebecca Ferguson, and captured something of the sexual dynamic between them. Essentially, the series presented their lives as a love story – that of a magnificent, chivalric king and the most beautiful woman of the age – and the deeply human element of privacy behind the public front. This rings true in their case, with the king's attempts to divide the two when it came to his marriage, in spite of his reputation for 'wantonness'.

Equally, both Edward and Elizabeth deserve to be assessed in their own right, in terms of character and achievement, although this will typically yield an unbalanced response, given the more masculine public field of kingship, politics and military endeavour. Elizabeth's contribution as queen was of a personal nature, especially in comparison with the role taken by Margaret of Anjou, or even the one taken by the kings' mothers, Cecily Neville and Margaret Beaufort. Typically, the feminine contribution goes unrecorded, partly for the reason that it took place behind the scenes, in dialogue, domesticity, service and affection, but also because it was unquantifiable in a world accustomed to measuring worth differently depending on gender. While Edward's foreign and domestic policies can be established through Acts of Parliament, treaties, wars and commands, Elizabeth was aspiring to a more amorphous scale of beauty and piety. Her frequent confinements can be counted more easily than her influence upon Edward, even if one might appear to imply the other.

Edward and Elizabeth's romance was featured by the Elizabethan poet Philip Sidney in his sonnet cycle Astrophil and Stella, written in the 1580s. In a romantic take on their story, he lauds Edward's achievements and appearance before concluding that his motivation was love of Elizabeth, in sonnet 75. The couple were a archetypal set of star-crossed lovers for the era of their great-granddaughter's reign, as part of her illustrious inheritance, attracting attention from many writers, perhaps occasioned by the centenary of their deaths.

> Of all the kings that ever here did reign,
> Edward named Fourth, as first in praise I name;
> Not for his fair outside, nor well-lined brain,
> Although less gifts imp feathers oft on fame;
> Nor that he could, young-wise, wise-valiant, frame
> His sire's revenge, joined with a kingdom's gain;
> And, gained by Mars, could yet mad Mars so tame,
> That balance weighed what sword did late obtain;
> Nor that he made the Flower-de-luce so 'fraid,
> Though strongly hedged of bloody lion's paws,
> That witty Lewis to him a tribute paid;
> Nor this, nor that, nor any such small cause;
> But only for this worthy knight durst prove
> To lose his crown, rather than fail his love.

The first significant dramatic portrayal of them came in Shakespeare's *Henry VI, Part 2*, written in 1594 at the latest, in which Edward appeared as the Earl of March, still a child, who gives a testimony for his father in the wake of the Duke of York's attempt to influence Henry at Blackheath. The play also puts Edward and his brother Richard at the First Battle of St Albans, although Edward was only thirteen and Richard was just two at the time, but it is less the historical inaccuracy that matters than their symbolic presences during the struggle, as future kings of England. The final play in the trilogy, *Henry VI, Part 3*, depicts York's death, Edward's victory at Towton, his exile and return, culminating in the Battle of Tewkesbury and the death of Henry VI. From the start, Edward is ambitious, stating, 'But for a kingdom any oath may be broken: I would break a thousand oaths to reign one year.' Shakespeare places Edward incorrectly at Sandal Castle in December 1460, but this serves to make the point about his military prowess, as he appeared in battle 'painted to the hilt in blood of those that had encountered him'.

It is Edward who introduces 'Lady Grey':

> Brother of Gloucester, at Saint Alban's field
> This lady's husband, Sir Richard Grey, was slain,
> His lands then seized on by the conqueror:
> Her suit is now to repossess those lands;
> Which we in justice cannot well deny,
> Because in quarrel of the house of York
> The worthy gentleman did lose his life.

Gloucester anticipates their relationship in an aside, saying, 'I see the lady hath a thing to grant, before the king will grant her humble suit.' Clarence responds, saying, 'He knows the game,' which beginns a bawdy exchange that undermines the interaction between Edward and Elizabeth. Yet the brothers have accurately assessed the situation, as Edward finally admits, 'I aim to lie with thee,' and Elizabeth responds, 'I had rather lie in prison.' The story unfolds predictably enough, with Edward asserting his authority: 'I am Edward ... and must have my will.' He then defies France by marrying Elizabeth instead of Bona of Savoy. It is Richard and Clarence who are the voices of malcontent when it comes to the new queen and the marriages of her kin:

> And yet methinks your grace hath not done well,
> To give the heir and daughter of Lord Scales
> Unto the brother of your loving bride;
> She better would have fitted me or Clarence:
> But in your bride you bury brotherhood.

Yet Edward supports his new wife and their speeches may stand as the most likely representative of their attitudes towards their marriage. It is a presentation of their marriage as might be expected, with the handsome charismatic king elevating the beautiful lower-born widow to the status of queenship, rather like a fairytale, and, no doubt, Shakespeare's version contributed to today's image of the pair, which is visible in popular fiction. Yet, it also makes the crucial point about the nature of Edward's kingship. Elizabeth expresses concern about her status being recognised and he illustrates how, as her protector, her security is bound up in his person:

QUEEN ELIZABETH

My lords, before it pleased his majesty
To raise my state to title of a queen,
Do me but right, and you must all confess
That I was not ignoble of descent;
And meaner than myself have had like fortune.
But as this title honours me and mine,
So your dislike, to whom I would be pleasing,
Doth cloud my joys with danger and with sorrow.

KING EDWARD IV

My love, forbear to fawn upon their frowns:
What danger or what sorrow can befall thee,
So long as Edward is thy constant friend,
And their true sovereign, whom they must obey?
Nay, whom they shall obey, and love thee too,
Unless they seek for hatred at my hands;
Which if they do, yet will I keep thee safe,
And they shall feel the vengeance of my wrath.

In 1599, a play entitled *Edward IV* was first recorded, probably as the work of Elizabethan dramatist Thomas Heywood and his circle. Instead of focusing on the story of Edward and the Woodvilles, though, Heywood makes Jane Shore the main character, appearing to merge her story with that of Elizabeth, as he shows her struggling with the morality of entering a relationship with the king. Later, she repents, and is reconciled with her husband, before suffering an ignominious death in 'Shore's ditch'. In reality, Jane was forced to undertake public penance by Richard III, before being imprisoned in Ludgate Gaol. There, she attracted Thomas Lynam, the king's Solicitor General, who resisted Richard's warnings and made Jane his wife. She died in 1527. The play contains criticism of Edward's marriage by his family, with Cecily being especially enraged:

DUCHESS OF YORK

Here is a marriage that befits a King!
It is no marvel it was done in haste!
Here is a bridal, and with hell to boot:
You have made work!

...

But tell me, son, how will you answer this?
Is't possible your rash, unlawful act
Should not breed mortal hate betwixt the realms?

Edward responds with an unusual metaphor to defend Elizabeth, in blank verse rather than his mother's iambic pentameters:

Tush, mother, you are deceived: all true subjects shall have cause to thank God, to have their king born of a true English woman. I tell you, it was never well since we matched with strangers; so our children have been still like chickens of the half kind. But where the cock and hen be both of one breed, there is like to be birds of the game.

Heywood's play remained popular throughout the seventeenth century, being reprinted in 1605, 1613, 1619, 1626 and featuring on a register of 1661. Another play, performed in Germany, entitled *The King of England and the Goldsmith's Wife*, may well have been a variant of this text.

Over a century later, the Romantic poet Robert Southey wrote in recognition of Elizabeth's grief, inspired by seeing her final resting place: 'Fatal daughter, fatal mother, raised to that ill-omened station, father, uncle, sons and brother, mourn'd in blood her elevation … a broken heart is here at rest.' His epitaph emphasises the end of her grief and loss, seeing death as a bringer of peace and relief after the suffering of her life:

Thou, Elizabeth, art here;
Thou to whom all griefs were known;
Who wert placed upon the bier
In happier hour than on the throne
Fatal daughter, fatal mother
Raised to that ill-omen'd station
Father, uncle, sons and brother,
Mourn'd in blood her elevation!
Woodville, in the realms of bliss
To thine offspring thou may'st say
Early death is happiness:
And favour'd in their lot are they
Who are not left to learn below
Lightly let this ground be prest
A broken heart is here at rest.

At rest beside Elizabeth's 'broken heart' was Edward, who never received the cadaver tomb he desired. Instead, they were covered with a slab of touchstone. This was an interesting choice both literally and metaphorically: it had long been used by alchemists as a standard or measure, by which other rocks could be tested. Possibly slate or lydite, its surface had a fine grain, allowing it to be scratched by soft metals, which meant it was often used to identify the quality of gold. In a metaphorical sense, Edward's tomb stood as a symbol of his achievements: a standard by which other kings might be measured. Yet, it also came to emphasise the centrality of Edward to his era, his country and to English kingship. Above the touchstone slab were two gothic steel gates, each flanked by a tower. Initially, these were hung with pearls, rubies and gold, until the tomb was plundered in 1642.

A century and a half later, in 1789, when the Chapel of St George at Windsor underwent repairs, the tomb in the north aisle of the choir was opened. As previously mentioned, Edward's lead coffin revealed a skeleton that measured six foot three-and-a-half inches, and which had long, brown hair. On top of it lay another coffin of wood, 'only much decayed, which contained the skeleton of a woman; who, from the marks of age about the skull was supposed to be that of his queen'. Briefly, the public were allowed in to see them, with the result that several items from the tomb were reputedly plundered, including locks of hair, teeth and fingers. When the bodies were replaced, a slab of black marble was put over the top of the tomb, with Edward's arms and crown above, suspended by angels.

Two years later, the fifteen-year-old Jane Austen compiled a history of England, in which she wrote of Edward:

> This Monarch was famous only for his Beauty & his Courage, of which the Picture we have here given of him, & his undaunted Behaviour in marrying one Woman while he was engaged to another, are sufficient proofs. His Wife was Elizabeth Woodville, a Widow who, poor Woman! was afterwards confined in a Convent by that Monster of Iniquity & Avarice Henry the 7th. One of Edward's Mistresses was Jane Shore, who has had a play written about her, but it is a tragedy & therefore not worth reading. Having performed all these noble actions, his Majesty died, & was succeeded by his son.

More balanced versions of Edward's life have been written recently by Charles Ross (1974), Mary Clive (1975), Hannes Kleineke (2009) and David Santiuste (2011). Full-length biographies of Elizabeth have been written by David MacGibbon (1938, reissued 2012), David Baldwin (2002) and Arlene Okerlund (2005), and she has been portrayed in fiction by Marjorie Bowen (1929), Josephine Tey (1951), Maureen Peters (1972), Rosemary Hawley Jarman (1972), Jean Plaidy (1982), Sharon Kay Penman (1982), Sandra Worth (2008), Philippa Gregory (2009) and others.

Edward and Elizabeth's life together was paradoxically one of privilege and privation. Nowhere is this better illustrated than in the concept of the wheel of fortune, catapulting them both to unexpected heights of power and down again into exile and sanctuary, parted from each other and distanced from rule. Individually, they had to find extraordinary reserves of strength, and as a pair their success lay in their mutual respect and love for one another. No doubt their stories will continue to be told, their relationship analysed and their emotions guessed at in the coming years. As a king, Edward's contribution was one of strong personal rule, of chivalric ideals and military glory; as a man he was a more complex figure, likely as capable of great debauchery as he was of great love. Elizabeth was in many ways a model queen, against whom criticisms were levelled of nepotism and aloofness – charges which raise questions of gender and social mobility. Her posthumous reputation gives a fascinating insight into the processes by which historical reputations are created, rightly or wrongly, and a study in the patriarchal definition of women. In their prime, they were a late medieval golden couple, an ideal of beauty and culture, straddling the old and new, looking back to Edward's descent from Edward III and forward to the reign of their grandson Henry VIII and great-granddaughter Elizabeth I. Five centuries after their deaths, Edward and Elizabeth's lives continue to fascinate, separately and jointly, as an enduring love story set against the most turbulent of times.

NOTES

Introduction

1. Saul, Nigel *For Honour and Fame: Chivalry in England 1066–1500* Random House 2011

Preface

1. Pernoud, Regine *Joan of Arc: By Herself and her Witnesses* Scarborough House 1990
2. Ibid.
3. Ibid.
4. Ibid.
5. Warner, Maria *Joan of Arc: The Image of Female Heroism* University of California Press 1999

1 Elizabeth, 1435–1459

1. Johnes, Thomas, tran. *The Chronicles of Enguerrand de Monstrelet* William Smith, London 1840
2. Ibid.
3. Gairdner, James, ed. *Gregory's Chronicle 1461–9* London 1876
4. Hall, Edward *The Union of the Two Noble Families of Lancaster and York* 1550

5. Baldwin, David, et al. *The Women of the Cousin's War* Simon and Schuster 2011
6. The Menagier de Paris, see ed. Amt, Emilie *Women's Lives in Medieval Europe: A Sourcebook* Routledge 1993
7. CPR 27 May 1433
8. Amt
9. Gairdner, *Gregory's Chronicle*
10. CPR July 1433
11. MacGibbon, David *Elizabeth Woodville: A Life* 1938, Amberley 2013
12. CPR March/October 1437
13. MacGibbon
14. Ibid.
15. Baldwin, David *Elizabeth Woodville: Mother of the Princes in the Tower* Sutton 2002
16. Ibid.
17. Ross, Charles *Edward IV* Methuen 1974
18. Stevenson, Joseph *Letters and Papers Illustrative of the Wars of the English in France during the Reign of Henry VI* Longman 1864 Volume 2 Issue 2

2 Edward, 1442–1459

1. Griffiths, R. A. *Henry VI* Ernest Benn 1981
2. Clive, Mary *This Sun of York: A Biography of Edward IV* Sphere 1975
3. Johnson, P. A. *Duke Richard of York, 1411–1460* Oxford Historical Monographs 1988
4. Griffiths
5. Paston Letters
6. Markham, Clements R. *Richard III* 1906, Cambridge University Press 2014
7. Clive
8. Gairdner's Paston Letters
9. Scattergood, V. J. *Politics and Poetry in the Fifteenth Century* Blandford Press 1971
10. Paston Letters
11. Wright, *Political Songs and Poems Composed During the*

Period from the Accession of Edward III to the Accession of Richard III 1841 Forgotten Books 2015

3 The Making of a King, 1459–1461

1. Paston Letters
2. Ibid.
3. Gregory's Chronicle
4. Paston Letters
5. Ross
6. Seward, Desmond *A Brief History of the Wars of the Roses* Constable and Co. 1995
7. Ross
8. Scattergood
9. Ibid.
10. Bib Nat MS Fr 20136 Fo 6
11. Ibid.
12. James, Jeffrey *Edward IV* Amberley 2015
13. SLP Milan Jan 1461
14. Ibid.
15. Some sources give 2 February, some 3 February as the date of battle.
16. Hughes, Jonathan *Politics and the Occult at the Court of Edward IV* in eds Gosman, Martin, et al. *Princes and Princely Culture 1450–1650* Volume 2 Brill, Boston 2005
17. CSP Milan Feb 1461
18. Ibid.
19. Gregory's Chronicle
20. Paston Letters
21. CSP Milan Feb 1461 C Gigli to M Arnolfi
22. Baldwin, David, et al. *The Women of the Cousin's War* Simon and Schuster 2011
23. Ibid.
24. Baldwin
25. Corbet, Dr Anthony *Edward IV, England's Forgotten Warrior King: His Life, His People and His Legacy* iUniverse 2015
26. CSP Milan April 1461
27. MacGibbon

28. Coore, Henry *The Story of Queen Elizabeth Woodville* Pamphlet 1845
29. Gypsies, or Egyptians, arrived in England in the sixteenth century
30. Coore
31. Paston Letters

4 To Fulfil an Ideal, 1461–1464

1. Lewis, Katherine *Kingship and Masculinity in Late Medieval Europe* Routledge 2013
2. Ibid.
3. Paston Letters
4. Kleineke, Hannes *Edward IV* Routledge 2009
5. Clive
6. Ibid.
7. CPR
8. Ibid.
9. Rotuli Parliamentorum Volume 5 1439–1472
10. Gosman, M. et al. *Princes and Princely Culture 1450–1650* Volume 2 Brill 2005
11. Barber, Richard 'Malory's *Le Morte d'Arthur* and Court Culture' in *Arthurian Literature XII* ed. Carley, James P. and Riddy, Felicity, Boydell and Brewer 1993
12. Radulescu, Raluca *The Gentry Context for Malory's Morte D'Arthur* D. S. Brewer 2003
13. Astell, Anne *Political Allegory in Late Medieval England* Cornell University Press 1999
14. Barber
15. Ibid.
16. MS Cotton Caligula Aii Fol 88
17. Levitt, Emma *Scoring Masculinity: The English Tournament and the Jousting Cheques of the Early Sixteenth Century* University of Huddersfield 2014
18. Weightman, Christine *Margaret of York, Duchess of Burgundy 1446–1503* St Martin's Press, New York 1989
19. Myers A. R. *The Household of Edward IV, The Black Book and the Ordinance of 1478* Manchester University Press 1959
20. Ibid.

21. Tyerman, Christopher *England and the Crusades 1095–1588* University of Chicago Press 1996
22. Paston Letters
23. http://www.british-history.ac.uk/survey-kent/vol12/pp612-662
24. Bristow, W. *The History and Topographical Survey of the County of Kent* Volume 9 Canterbury 1800

5 The Secret Wife, 1464

1. Letter from Professor Richard Marks to Malvern Priory http://www.littlemalvernpriory.co.uk/Window.htm
2. Gregory's Chronicle
3. Lebrun, François *La Vie conjugale sous l'Ancien Régime* Armand Colin, Paris 1975

6 Queen, 1464–1468

1. CPR Oct, Nov, Dec 1464
2. Weir, Alison *Lancaster and York: The Wars of the Roses* Vintage 2009
3. MacGibbon
4. Ballard, William 'Account of the Coronation of Elizabeth Woodville' http://bodley30.bodley.ox.ac.uk:8180/luna/servlet/detail/ODLodl~1~1~50082~121812:Account-of-the-coronation-of-Elizabeth
5. Lehman
6. CPR 26 August 1465

7 Trouble Ahead, 1468–1469

1. CSP Milan Feb/Apr 1476
2. Weightman
3. Ibid.
4. Strong Roy *Feast: A History of Grand Eating* Jonathan Cape 2002
5. Croyland Chronicle

8 Rebellion in the Family, 1470–1471

1. Holinshed's Chronicle, London 1577, 1578
2. Warkworth, John *The Chronicles of the White Rose of York: A Series of Historical Fragments*. ed. Giles, John Allen
3. Fabyan, Robert *The New Chronicles of England and France* ed. Sir H Ellis, 1811
4. Ibid.

9 A Court in the Burgundian Style, 1471–1474

1. Strong
2. Ross
3. Vale, Malcolm *The Princely Court: Medieval Courts and Culture in North-West Europe 1270- 1380* Oxford University Press 2001
4. Thank you to Anne Marie Bouchard for alerting me to this.
5. Thompson, C. J. S. *Alchemy and Alchemists* Courier Corporation 2012

10 Enemies, Near and Far, 1475–1478

1. Allmand
2. Emery, Anthony *Greater Medieval Houses of England and Wales 1300–1500* Cambridge University Press 2006
3. Ibid.
4. Ross
5. Croyland
6. Ibid.
7. Rot Parl
8. Black, W. H. 'Narrative of the Marriage of Richard Duke of York with Anne of Norfolk: the Matrimonial Feast and the Grand Jousting' in *Illustrations of Ancient State and Chivalry from manuscripts preserved in the Ashmolean Museum* Roxburghe Club 1840

11 A King's Decline, 1478–1483

1. Kane, Bronach Christina *Impotence and Virginity in the Late Medieval Ecclesiastical Courts of York* Borthwick Publications 2008
2. Nicolas, N. H. *Privy Purse Expenses of Elizabeth of York; Wardrobe Accounts of Edward IV* 1830, 1972
3. Ibid.
4. Ibid.
5. Ibid.
6. Ibid.
7. Ibid.
8. Ibid.
9. Rot Parl

12 Anxious Mother, 1483–1485

1. Croyland
2. Baldwin
3. Ibid.

13 Retirement, 1486–1492

1. CPR March 1486
2. Various *A Collection of Ordinances and Regulations for the Governance of the Royal Household, made in divers reigns from King Edward III to King William and Queen Mary* Society of Antiquities, London 1790
3. Nicolas, N. H. *Testamenta Vetusta Vol 2* London 1892
4. MacGibbon
5. Ibid.

BIBLIOGRAPHY

Allmand, C. T. *War, Government and Power in Late Medieval France* Liverpool University Press 2000

Amt, Emilie, ed. *Women's Lives in Medieval Europe: A Sourcebook* Routledge 1993

Ashdown-Hill, John *Eleanor: The Secret Queen* The History Press 2009

Astell, Anne *Political Allegory in Late Medieval England* Cornell University Press 1999

Baldwin, David *Elizabeth Woodville: Mother of the Princes in the Tower* Sutton 2002

Baldwin, David, et al. *The Women of the Cousin's War* Simon and Schuster 2011

Ballard, William 'Account of the Coronation of Elizabeth Woodville' http://bodley30.bodley.ox.ac.uk:8180/luna/servlet/detail/ODLodl~1~1~50082~121812:Account-of-the-coronation-of-Elizabeth

Barber, Richard 'Malory's *Le Morte d'Arthur* and Court Culture' in *Arthurian Literature XII* ed. Carley, James P. and Riddy, Felicity, Boydell and Brewer 1993

Black, W. H. 'Narrative of the Marriage of Richard Duke of York with Anne of Norfolk: the Matrimonial Feast and the Grand Jousting' in *Illustrations of Ancient State and Chivalry from manuscripts preserved in the Ashmolean Museum* Roxburghe Club 1840

Bliss, Thomas *Some Account of Sir H Johnys, Deputy Knight Marshal of England* John Williams 1845

Bristow, W. *The History and Topographical Survey of the County of Kent* Volume 9 Canterbury 1800

Calendar of the Close Rolls, Edward IV, Edward V, Richard III, 1461 1954

Calendar of the Patent Rolls, Edward IV, (1898, 1900) Edward V, Richard III, (1901) Henry VII (1914)

Chrimes, Stanley Bertram *Henry VII* London 1972

Clark, Linda, ed. *Of Mice and Men: Image, Belief and Regulation in Late Medieval England* Boydell Press 2005

Clive, Mary *This Sun of York: A Biography of Edward IV* Sphere 1975

Coore, Henry *The Story of Queen Elizabeth Woodville* Pamphlet 1845

Corbet, Dr Anthony *Edward IV, England's Forgotten Warrior King: His Life, His People and His Legacy* iUniverse 2015

Crawford, Anne *The Yorkists: The History of a Dynasty* A and C Black 2008

Davies, J. S. ed. *An English Chronicle of The Reigns of Richard II, Henry IV, Henry V and Henry VI* Camden Society, London 1856

Dockray, Keith *Edward IV From Contemporary Letters and Records* Fonthill 2015

Emery, Anthony *Greater Medieval Houses of England and Wales 1300–1500* Cambridge University Press 2006

Fabyan, Robert *The New Chronicles of England and France* Sir H Ellis, ed. 1811

'The Chronicle of the Grey Friars: Henry VI', Chronicle of the Grey Friars of London: Camden Society old series, volume 53 (1852), pp. 15–21

Gairdner, James, ed. *Gregory's Chronicle 1461–9* London 1876

Gairdner, J. *History of the Life and Reign of Richard III* Cambridge 1898

Gairdner, J. *The Paston Letters* 6 vols 1904

Gosman, M. et al. *Princes and Princely Culture 1450–1650* Volume 2 Brill 2005

Griffiths, R A *Henry VI* Ernest Benn 1981

Gristwood, Sarah *Blood Sisters* Harper Press 2012

Grummitt, David *Henry VI* Routledge 2015

Hall, Edward *The Union of the Two Noble Families of Lancaster and York* 1550

Halsted, Caroline Amelia *Richard III as Duke of Gloucester and King of England* Longman, Brown, Green and Longmans, London 1844

Hammond, P. W. et al. *The Reburial of Richard, Duke of York, 21–30 July 1476* Richard III Society 1996

Hay, D. ed. *The Anglia Historia of Polydore Vergil* Camden Society 1950

Hicks, Michael *Warwick the Kingmaker* Oxford 1998

Higginbotham, Susan *The Woodvilles: The Wars of the Roses and England's Most Infamous Family* The History Press 2013

Hilton, Lisa *Queens Consort: England's Medieval Queens* Hachette 2010

Hinds, A. B. ed. *Calendar of State Letters and Papers and Manuscripts existing in the Archives and Collections of Milan 1385–1618* London 1913

Hughes, Jonathan *Politics and the Occult at the Court of Edward IV* in eds Gosman, Martin et al. *Princes and Princely Culture 1450–1650* Volume 2 Brill, Boston 2005

James, Jeffrey *Edward IV* Amberley 2015

Johnes, Thomas, tran. *The Chronicles of Enguerrand de Monstrelet* William Smith, London 1840

Johnson, P. A. *Duke Richard of York, 1411–1460* Oxford Historical Monographs 1988

Kane, Bronach Christina *Impotence and Virginity in the Late Medieval Ecclesiastical Courts of York* Borthwick Publications 2008

Kingsford, Charles Lethbridge *English History in Contemporary Poetry, Volume II, Lancaster and York,* G. Bell and Sons 1913

Kleineke, Hannes *Edward IV* Routledge 2009

Laynesmith, J. L. *The Last Medieval Queens: English Queenship 1445–1503* Oxford University Press 2004

Lebrun, François *La Vie conjugale sous l'Ancien Régime* Armand Colin, Paris 1975

Lehman, H. Eugene *Lives of England's Reigning and Consort Queens* Author House 2005

Levitt, Emma *Scoring Masculinity: The English Tournament and the Jousting Cheques of the Early Sixteenth Century* University of Huddersfield 2014

Lewis, Katherine *Kingship and Masculinity in Late Medieval Europe* Routledge 2013

Leyser, Henrietta *Medieval Women; A Social History of Women in England 450–1500* Weidenfeld and Nicolson 1995

MacGibbon, David *Elizabeth Woodville: A Life 1938*, Amberley 2013

Mancini, Dominic *The Usurpation of Richard III* ed. and tran. C. A. J. Armstrong, Oxford 1969 (2nd edition)

Markham, Clements R. *Richard III* 1906, Cambridge University Press 2014

Michelet, Jules *History of France: From the Earliest Period to the Present Time, Volume II* D. Appleton and Company, France 1847

Myers A. R. *The Household of Edward IV, The Black Book and the Ordinance of 1478* Manchester University Press 1959

Nicolas, N. H. *Privy Purse Expenses of Elizabeth of York; Wardrobe Accounts of Edward IV* 1830, 1972

Nicolas, N. H. *Testamenta Vetusta Vol 2* London 1892

Pernoud, Regine *Joan of Arc: By Herself and her Witnesses* Scarborough House 1990

Radulescu, Raluca *The Gentry Context for Malory's Morte D'Arthur* D. S. Brewer 2003

Rickert, Edith, ed. 'The Babees' Book or Medieval Manners for the Young' Chatto and Windus 1908

Riley, H. T. ed. *Ingulph's Chronicle of the Abbey of Croyland* 1854

Robbins, R. H. ed. *Historical Poems of the XIVth and XV th centuries* New York 1959

Ross, Charles *Edward IV* Methuen 1974

Santiuste, David *Edward IV* Pen and Sword 2011

Saul, Nigel *For Honour and Fame: Chivalry in England 1066–1500* Random House 2011

Scattergood, V. J. *Politics and Poetry in the Fifteenth Century* Blandford Press 1971

Seward, Desmond *A Brief History of the Wars of the Roses* Constable and Co. 1995

Shaw, William Arthur *The Knights of England: A Complete Record from the Earliest Time to the Present day of the Knights of all the Orders of Chivalry in England, Scotland and Ireland, and of Knights Bachelors* Clearfield 2002

Spedding, Alison J. *At the King's Pleasure: the Testament of Cecily*

Neville Midland History Volume 35 Number 2, Autumn 2010, pp. 256–72

Stevenson, Joseph *Letters and Papers Illustrative of the Wars of the English in France during the Reign of Henry VI* Longman 1864 Volume 2 Issue 2

Strachey, J. et al. eds *Rotuli Parliamentorum* 6 vols 1767–77

Strickland, A. *Lives of the Queens of England* 8 vols, revised 1857

Strong Roy *Feast: A History of Grand Eating* Jonathan Cape 2002

Thompson, C. J. S. *Alchemy and Alchemists* Courier Corporation 2012

Tyerman, Christopher *England and the Crusades 1095–1588* University of Chicago Press 1996

Vale, Malcolm *The Princely Court: Medieval Courts and Culture in North-West Europe 1270–1380* Oxford University Press 2001

Various *A Collection of Ordinances and Regulations for the Governance of the Royal Household, made in divers reigns from King Edward III to King William and Queen Mary* Society of Antiquities, London 1790

Wagner, John A *Encyclopaedia of the Hundred Years' War* Greenwood Publishing Group 2006

Warkworth, John *The Chronicles of the White Rose of York: A Series of Historical Fragments.* ed. Giles, John Allen 1839

Warner, Maria *Joan of Arc: The Image of Female Heroism* University of California Press 1999

Waurin, Jean de *Recueil des Chroniques et Anchiennes Istories de la Grant Bretagne, a present nomme Engleterre* Hardy, W. and Hardy, E. L. C. P. eds, London 1891

Weightman, Christine *Margaret of York, Duchess of Burgundy 1446–1503* St Martin's Press, New York 1989

Weir, Alison *Lancaster and York: The Wars of the Roses* Vintage 2009

Weir, Alison *The Princes in the Tower* Vintage 2008

Worcestre, William *Itineraries* ed J. H. Harvey OUP 1969

Wright, *Political Songs and Poems Composed During the Period from the Accession of Edward III to the Accession of Richard III* 1841 Forgotten Books 2015

ACKNOWLEDGEMENTS

Thanks go to Jonathan, Nicola, Annie and all the team at Amberley for their encouragement and support, but to Annie in particular for being flexible when I overran my deadline. I have been particularly blessed to have some wonderful friends: thank you to Jonathan Howell, Magdalen Pitt, Anne Marie Bouchard, Neville Brett, Tim Byard-Jones, Geanine Teramani-Cruz, Sharon Bennett Connolly, Kyra Kramer, Karen Stone and Harry and Sara Basnett, for keeping me sane during the writing of this book. There are others whose kind words and support have meant a great deal.

When I started a Facebook discussion group on Edward IV back in 2013, I had no idea how it would grow, so that there are now over 3,000 members worldwide: thank you to everyone who has been a part of it, for their interesting contributions, questions and discussion. A number of other friends have been very generous in regularly sharing their thoughts and research on Edward and related topics: thank you to Susan Higginbotham, Karen Clark, Alan Hurley and Erika Millen, and again to my sterling co-admins, Anne Marie, Sharon and Harry.

Many thanks go to my family: to my husband, Tom, for his love and support, to Paul Fairbrass and also the Hunts, for Sue's generosity and John's supply of interesting and unusual books. Thank you to my godmother Susan Priestley, 'Lady Susan', for her unfailing support. Most of all, thanks go to my mother for her invaluable proof-reading skills, and to my father for his enthusiasm and open mind: this is the result of the books they read me, the museums they took me to as a child and the love and imagination with which they encouraged me.

INDEX

Also available from Amberley Publishing

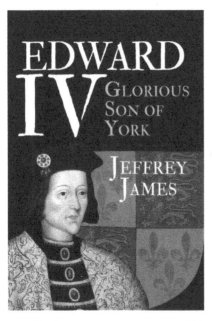

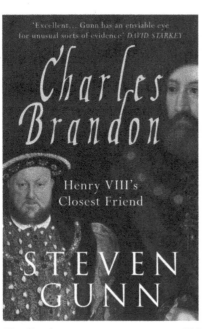
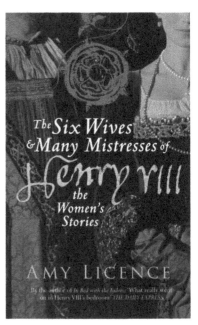